A brilliant, fast-paced narrative that does so much more than make an incomprehensible book comprehensible. It shows us how white evangelicals lost our theological grounding, becoming the very monster we were supposed to resist; it emboldens us to become dissident disciples, leaving team dragon and returning to the side of the Lamb; and it gives us hope that a world where justice rolls down like water will one day be more than a dream. This is the most powerful interpretation of Revelation I have ever read, reorienting us away from bizarre prophecies and fiction bestsellers back to the truth of the gospel. You do not want to miss it.

Beth Allison Barr, James Vardaman Professor of
History at Baylor University and bestselling author of
*The Making of Biblical Womanhood: How the Subjugation
of Women Became Gospel Truth*

Finally, someone makes sense of the confoundingly beautiful mystery that is the book of Revelation. McKnight and Matchett's *Revelation for the Rest of Us* not only debunks speculative, spectacular, and specious interpretations, it explains Revelation's prophetic message of God's justice and peace, the way of the Lamb. Reading Revelation is a trumpet call to "dissidents," God's people, to faithful public discipleship in today's "Babylon" built by arrogance, greed, exploitation, and militarism. McKnight and Matchett refocus attention on the true center of Revelation: worshiping God on the throne and the Lamb.

Lynn H. Cohick, provost/dean of academic affairs,
Northern Seminary

If Revelation is not a book for speculation about the antichrist and the millennium, what is it? Scot McKnight and Cody Matchett have gifted the church, especially (but not only) its evangelical wing, with a revelation about Revelation. It is a call for dissident discipleship. This challenging but also pastoral book is a must-read for anyone concerned about the new forces of Babylon confronting the church and the world today.

Michael J. Gorman, Raymond E. Brown Professor of
Biblical and Theological Studies, St. Mary's Seminary
& University, Baltimore

A fascinating and engrossing book about one of the most puzzling—and hopeful—books of the Christian Bible. Revelation is about how to live as dissidents in the Babylon of our time, how to hope actively for the New Jerusalem, the home of God and the goal of creation.

> **Miroslav Volf,** Henry B. Wright Professor of Systematic Theology, Yale Divinity School, founding director, Yale Center for Faith & Culture, and coauthor of *The Home of God*

Revelation

for the Rest of Us

———

Revelation
for the Rest of Us

A PROPHETIC CALL
TO FOLLOW JESUS
AS A DISSIDENT DISCIPLE

Scot McKnight

WITH CODY MATCHETT

ZONDERVAN
REFLECTIVE

ZONDERVAN REFLECTIVE

Revelation for the Rest of Us
Copyright © 2023 by Scot McKnight and Cody Matchett

Requests for information should be addressed to:
Zondervan, *3900 Sparks Dr. SE, Grand Rapids, Michigan 49546*

Zondervan titles may be purchased in bulk for educational, business, fundraising, or sales promotional use. For information, please email SpecialMarkets@Zondervan.com.

ISBN 978-0-310-13578-4 (hardcover)
ISBN 978-0-310-13580-7 (audio)
ISBN 978-0-310-13579-1 (ebook)

Cover design: Darren Welch
Cover art: © Tsuji; La_Puma / Getty Images
Interior design: Kait Lamphere

Printed in the United States of America

23 24 25 26 27 28 29 30 31 32 /LSC/ 15 14 13 12 11 10 9 8 7 6 5 4 3 2 1

for

Beth Allison Barr
Kristin Kobes Du Mez
Christian dissidents

Contents

Part 4:
Living in Babylon

Part 5:
Discipleship for Dissidents Today

Introduction

1972

Between my junior and senior years in high school I (Scot) had a conversion-type experience. I was at a church camp in Iowa, and the only way to describe the experience is that the direction of my life was completely changed. I went from being hometown jock to an on-fire-for-Jesus (and fundamentalism) high school teenager.

Which also meant by that winter, 1972, I turned to the book of Revelation. Dave, my youth pastor, recommended that I read *Guide to Survival* by Salem Kirban, so I bought a copy, devoured it, and made marks all over my Bible from Kirban. I gave it to my girlfriend, and she read it (and we've been married forty-eight years!). I gave it to a brilliant scientific friend named Kent, he read it, gave his heart and life to Jesus, and he's still following the Lord. What that book did, though, was turn me on to reading *Revelation as speculation*. One speculative book was not enough. Eventually I read the far more popular (than Kirban) book by Hal Lindsey called *The Late Great Planet Earth*. By the time I graduated from college in 1976, I had collected and read dozens of books about the book of Revelation, eschatology, and the rapture. I loved debating whether the rapture was before, in the middle, or after the so-called tribulation. The lingo, which I used as often as I could, was *pre*, *mid*, and *post*-trib. For some I was a radical because I was a post-tribber. We had maps and charts and timelines. One of my timelines was a book that must have been about two feet wide with huge timelines that mapped the future by putting together the prophecies of Daniel, Isaiah, Ezekiel, Jesus, and the book of Revelation. I kept it near my desk should I need to understand what was about to happen.

Back in 1972 our high school youth pastor rented the blockbuster movie called *A Thief in the Night*, and we watched it one evening in youth group. It brought Salem Kirban to life for me. Many of us were scared witless by the movie. For sure, we thought, the end of the world was nigh, that we needed to look up or we would be lost and left behind, and that this whole world was about to burn. Others, terrified, needed toilet paper in their shoes. Speculations about how the political events of the 70s fit into the Bible were a craze. It was no small comfort to my soul that we were on the right side of history, that we would be raptured, and we would escape the hellish nightmares of the tribulation as we were learning about it.

I heard in those high school days a traveling evangelist who made the stunning claim that Jesus was coming back—scratch that, the rapture was going to happen—before 1973 because one generation from the formation of the state of Israel was about twenty-five years. I was on the edge of my seat, pondering where to go to college, so I asked my youth pastor if I should even bother. He said, "Go, prepare yourself just in case the (visiting revivalist) preacher is wrong."

He was.

I did.

We're still here.

Being here means many preachers and authors were just plain wrong. And that for me grew into a very serious problem with how these preachers, pastors, and authors interpreted the book of Revelation.

Was Billy Graham wrong too? You answer. In 1949, two days after it had become public that the Soviet Union had successfully detonated a nuclear bomb, Billy Graham grabbed Los Angeles by the throat, called it to repent or else, and as described by Matthew Sutton, said, "Russia has now exploded an atomic bomb. An arms race . . . is driving us madly towards destruction! . . . I am persuaded that time is desperately short!" A year later he said, "I'm revising my figures. Last year in Los Angeles I thought we had at least five years, now it looks like just two years—and then the end." Graham fed the hysteria of post-World War II fear of the final war, a global holocaust called "Armageddon," and America has never been the same sense.

Many were also overcome by the books-become-movies like *A Thief in the Night.* There was an experience to be created, and not a little money to be made, so a few more movies were produced, like *The Rapture*, and then *Left Behind* with Nicolas Cage. They operate similarly: the rapture, the horrors of drivers disappearing from cars now careening into other cars, buildings, and humans, and then earth-scorching heat and famines in the tribulation, and the evil powers of the antichrist dominating the screen. They induce fear, and such movies were used by youth leaders to motivate young unbelievers to give themselves to Jesus before time runs out.

I can't take another step without admitting that this *speculation* stuff was what I believed for a long time. I believed it as a child, as a teen, as a young adult studying theology, and then into my early career as a professor. I believed it.

Until I didn't.

I changed my mind not only because *every one of the certain predictions I heard from preachers and youth pastors and read in books were wrong.* Not just slightly off but totally wrong. I wanted to learn how to read the book of Revelation better, and in so doing I became convinced that the *Left Behind approach* seriously misreads the book of Revelation and Christian eschatology. We'll say more about this in the chapters that follow, but I came to see that approach as dangerous for the church. The *speculation readings of Revelation* teach escapism and fail to disciple the church in the moral dissidence that shapes everything in the amazing book of Revelation. Escapism is as far from Revelation as Babylon is from new Jerusalem.

PART 1

—

Reading Revelation as if for the First Time

CHAPTER 1

Revelation for Too Many

Speculation is the biggest problem in reading Revelation today. Many treat it as a databank of predictive prophecy—what one Revelation scholar, Christopher Rowland, calls "a repository of prophecies concerning the future." Readers want to know if *now* is the time of fulfillment for that symbol, figure, or event. Speculations about who is doing what, sometimes standing on stilts, has ruined Revelation for many.

I (Scot) have taught about the book of Revelation for decades. While I've not experienced every nook and cranny of church people's reading of this book, at least one thing has been true (in my experience): most everyone reads the book as I first learned to read it. Every time I teach the book of Revelation, students come to me and say something like "I don't like this book" or "I'm turned off about this book" or "I gave up on Revelation years back, and I'm really hesitant even to read it."

I (Cody) taught my first *class* on the book of Revelation last summer to a group of eighty-five eager students through my church. We had students ranging in age from sixteen to eighty-six, coming from diverse cultural backgrounds and theological dispositions. Reactions were largely the same. *On the one end* we had those who were eager to discuss the book, those whose imaginations had largely been captured by *excitation* and *speculation*. While *on the other end*, there was an even larger portion of students (mostly younger) who were skeptical of the *speculators*, left only to conclude that the bizarro last book of the Bible should be ignored, removed, or simply 'left behind.' On a scale from *speculation* to *silence*, most simply wanted *silence*. In the end, they all came for the class (entitled "Revelation for the Rest of Us") because they knew something far more important than speculation *must* be going on in this strange book.

Times have certainly changed since the 70s when speculation was in vogue. Do you know how many pastors and preachers today refuse to open Revelation for sermons? *Most* either ignore Revelation or choose to preach from safer passages, like the messages, or so-called letters, to the seven churches in Revelation 2–3 or the passage about new Jerusalem at the back of Revelation. Indeed, readings from Revelation assigned for Sundays by the *Revised Common Lectionary* are the safe texts.

Why the shift from obsession to silence?

Four Basic Readings

Before getting to those speculative readings of Revelation, a quick sketch of four basic readings of Revelation:

Preterists read Revelation as written to first-century churches about first-century topics.

Historicists read Revelation as a sketch of the history of the church from the first century until the end.

Futurists think Revelation is totally, or nearly entirely, about the future. This approach is populated by the speculators.

Idealists read Revelation as timeless images and truths about God, the church, the state, and God's plan for this world.

For sketches of major interpretive approaches, see the various views of evangelicals in Kenneth L. Gentry, Sam Hamstra, C. Marvin Pate, and Robert L. Thomas, *Four Views on the Book* of Revelation (Grand Rapids: Zondervan, 1998); for a broader approach to studies, see Michael Thompson, "The Book of Revelation," in Scot McKnight and Nijay K. Gupta, *The State of New Testament Studies* (Grand Rapids: Baker Academic, 2019), 459–75.

Paradise for Fanatics

Why are preachers afraid of this book? An expert on the Bible's language and imagery, and especially on how to understand the language about prophecy, G. B. Caird, tells us why: Revelation has become a "paradise of fanatics and sectarians"! That's why. Add to the language and fanatics America's cultural history. Matthew Sutton, in his probing of that history, opens with a salvo that puts that cultural history into a tightly woven bundle:

> Perceiving the United States as besieged by satanic forces—communism and secularism, family break-down and government encroachment—Billy Sunday, Charles Fuller, Billy Graham, and many others took to the pulpit and airwaves to explain how biblical end-times prophecy made sense of a world ravaged by global wars, genocide, and the threat of nuclear extinction. Rather than withdraw from their communities to wait for Armageddon, they used what little time was left to warn of the coming Antichrist, save souls, and prepare the United States for God's final judgment.

Many Americans have experiences of Revelation inducing fear of a global holocaust, with the book providing a roadmap of *who* does *what* and *when*. Experts on the history of reading Revelation as speculation woven into culture have shown that in the middle of the nineteenth century the book of Revelation went populist—that is, it became, as Amy Johnson Frykholm put it, the "ordinary person's game." All one needed was a dispensationalist framework, the rapture on the horizon, and a Bible in one hand and news sources (or *Left Behind* books) in the other. Everything "fit": politics, international treaties, economic trends, moral decline, family breakdowns. East Coast elites and sophisticated biblical interpretation were easily swept out the church door when the experience of personally knowing the inside story became the norm. Such persons supernaturally knew what no one else knows.

> Revelation "is not prediction but perception."
> —Eugene Peterson, *Hallelujah Banquet*, 7

In the middle of it all was one's politics, and you don't have to be a cynic to track the correlation of Revelation's popularity with American political parties. For instance, the so-called cultural demise of the 60s and 70s spawned an obsession with the book of Revelation with dispensational apocalyptic productions and publications like those mentioned in the opening of this book. Did you notice that the election of the Democrat Bill Clinton went hand in hand with multimillion sales of the *Left Behind* series? Let's not just poke conservatives in the eye. "Apocalyptic" is an apt term for how many progressives reacted to the election of Donald Trump, though their apocalyptic mode of expression was not so tied to the book of Revelation. Maybe the correlations of Revelation with politics are why "apocalyptic" and "apoplectic" sound so much alike!

But because of all this, many today have turned down the knob on the music of the book of Revelation. The speculation approach is behind the ordinary dismay with this book, and speculation can be laid at the front door of what is called *dispensationalism* (see appendix 1, "Dispensationalism's Seven Dispensations.") Dispensationalism of the classical sort is a method of reading the Bible in which God forms seven (or so) different covenants with humans—like Adam, Abraham, Moses, David, and Jesus. Israel, the modern state of Israel, figures big in this scheme. What dispensationalism is known for even more is its belief in the imminent rapture that occurs before a future seven-year tribulation. Sometime near the end of that tribulation, Jesus will come back (the "second coming"), establish a literal one-thousand-year reign on earth, and then at the end of that millennium comes eternity. For dispensationalists the book of Revelation, at least from chapter four on, is entirely about that tribulation. The message of Revelation for many is, "You don't want to be there when it happens. So get saved and get ready!"

Bizarre Readings

For many, such a reading of Revelation also borders on the bizarre, and "bizarre" or "strange" may be the two most common adjectives stuck to the word "Revelation." Why? Because there are so many bizarre readings of the book. Here is one of the stranger ones I have seen, from Timothy Beal's *The Book of Revelation: A Biography.*

Since Trump's election in November of 2016, many have linked him to the beast of Revelation and the number 666, noting, among other portents, that his election year, 2016, is the sum of 666 + 666 + 666 + 6 + 6 + 6; that he frequently makes an "okay" sign that forms the number six; and that his son-in-law Jared Kushner's real estate company owns 666 Fifth Avenue in New York.

In 1971 in Sacramento, Ronald Reagan commented that the coup in Libya was "a sign that the day of Armageddon isn't far off. . . . Everything is falling into place. It can't be long now. Ezekiel says that the fire and brimstone will be rained upon the enemies of God's people. That must mean they'll be destroyed by nuclear weapons." He was not the only president shaped by such speculations.

The *Left Behind* series, building as it did on the approach of Hal Lindsey's *The Late Great Planet Earth* and other such readings, lends itself constantly to bizarre interpretations of Revelation.

For a concise set of criticisms of the *Left Behind* series, see Gorman.

What's the Problem Here?

Let's step back to ponder how the book of Revelation is read by these interpreters. Philip Gorski, in his exceptional book *American Covenant*, says the speculative, dispensational approach needs criticism not only for how it reads Revelation but also for what it does to the readers. First, it reads the Bible:

- Predictively, as an encoded message about future events that can be decoded by modern-day prophets;
- Literally, such that the mythical creatures of the text are understood as material realities;
- "Premillennially," with the second coming of Christ understood to precede the earthly 'millennium' of God's thousand-year reign on earth; and
- Vindictively, with the punishment of the godless occurring in the most gruesome and violent forms imaginable.

He presses on his readers another vital point: *this is not how the church throughout its history has read the apocalyptic texts of the Bible.* What was *apocalyptic* and *metaphorical* and *fictional* over time became *rigidly literal* for too many readers.

Gorski really helps us all when he zooms in on *what these kinds of readings do to people.* "First, it leads to hubris. It seduces its followers into claiming to know things that no human being can possibly know." Such persons consider themselves elect and special and insiders, and such confidence tends toward condescension. Gorski's second point stuns. This way of reading the Bible "leads to demonization of others. Our [the USA's] enemies become physical embodiments of evil. Third, it leads to fatalism, suggesting that wars and other calamities are beyond human control. Finally, and most fatefully, it suggests that the ultimate solution to all problems is a violent one involving the annihilation of one's enemies." Michael Gorman, who wrote one of the most important textbooks on Revelation, concludes that the discipleship of this approach is about

- believing in order to escape the Tribulation,
- evangelizing to help others escape,
- connecting current events to prophecies,
- and being ready to die for faith in Jesus.

Christopher Rowland, another world-class expert on all things Revelation, said something similar: "All that matters" for this view of Revelation "is to be found as part of the elect, who will enjoy the escape of the rapture." That is, the reading leads to either *withdrawal* from society or *resignation* to the evil arc of history. If you think this is exaggeration, Google this stuff, find the YouTube videos, go to a church where a pastor is preaching these themes, and you will find each of these characteristics flourishing.

Here's where we are then, and it pains us to say this, but we have students with these pains on their faces when Revelation is even mentioned. Nelson Kraybill puts it succinctly: "Many Christians in the West have shut out the book of Revelation after seeing it exploited by cult leaders, pop eschatologists, and end-time fiction writers." A big hearty "Amen!" is what we hear from our students.

No matter how misguided these readings of Revelation are, the *Left Behind* series has what Amy Johnson Frykholm calls a "tenacious grasp on the Protestant imagination" of millions. Hidden deep in the *Left Behind* plot is a conservative perception of American politics in an international context. Have you read any of the *Left Behind* books from a different location, like South Korea, South Africa, or South America? The language comes off as so profoundly American to them. Again, Gorski's project reveals that this approach to Revelation partakes far too often in nothing less than American Christian nationalism! "We" (America with Israel) win and "they" (usually Russia or the European Union) lose. Dispensationalism's reading of Revelation breeds confidence in America and not *dissidence about Babylon* (more on this later).

Dallas, we've got a problem.

Future Speculations, Excitations, and Frustrations

We've been using the term "speculation," so let's explain it a bit more. This reading of Revelation obsesses about *predictions about the future*. That is, one narrows down an image in Daniel or Ezekiel or Revelation to such-and-such leader or to some specific nation. The USA fits into the predictions, and that means *we (mostly Protestant, evangelical, white) Christians are the safe ones since we are the saved*. The sort of dispensationalism we are talking about specializes in knowing "signs of the times" that are imminent. The signs point to a world-shifting event in some nation, some leader, some international conference, or some decision in Washington DC or in Brussels with the European Union or in Rome at the Vatican. People get jacked up and then watch for a date or fulfillment, then they get disappointed, and then they get jacked up again over something else and then disappointment returns, over and over until they decide to give up on Revelation.

Countless students and friends and people have told us this. They've had their excitations about the imminent rapture, they've heard the predictions, and they've seen that every one of them was wrong. Every. One. No. Exceptions.

Do they stop and reconsider? Nope. Thomas B. Slater says that when these speculations and predictions and expectations turn out wrong, "cognitive dissonance goes on overdrive, and they merely recalibrate." There's got to be another way. But the way forward can't be mapped in Revelation—at least that's what so many have told us. They have all but excised Revelation from their Bible. We're not exaggerating. They are unaware that there is a far more *accurate* and profoundly *relevant* way to read Revelation.

We'll tie some of this into a knot of terms: Revelation connected to speculation leads to excitation, and excitations lead to expectations, and expectations unfulfilled lead to frustrations. Frustrations lead to realizations that have led many to say, "There's something big-time wrong with these speculations." They are right, and many are confused because the only way they know how to read this (to them) bizarro book is speculation, and they want another way of reading Revelation. Speculation eventually leads to stupefaction. Eugene Peterson once observed our very problem and found another way, the way of imagination instead of speculation:

> But for people who are fed up with such bland fare, the Revelation is a gift—a work of intense imagination that pulls its reader into a world of sky battles between angels and beasts, lurid punishments and glorious salvations, kaleidoscopic vision and cosmic song. It is a world in which children are instinctively at home and in which adults, by becoming as little children, recapture an elemental involvement in the basic conflicts and struggles that permeate moral existence, and then go on to discover again the soaring adoration and primal affirmations for which God made us.

Peterson's words offer for *the rest of us* a different way to read Revelation, and we will show that this way is what John wanted for his seven churches. The book is for all times because it is about all time. The flexibility of the book to give Christians a sense of direction and meaning throughout church history is the big clue to a different approach. The clue is that Revelation is timeless theology not specific prediction, and the moment it turns to specific predictions it loses its timeless message. It's timeless because history, instead of some idealist steady progress, is tragic. Or history is at least two steps backward for every three steps forward, and some of the backward steps are long indeed. The timelessness of history, and its rather cyclical nature, gives Revelation's sketch of Babylon a constant relevance. Predictive specifics—the pope is the antichrist, Russia (or the European Union) is Gog and Magog, Israel's rebirth as a nation—stifle the book's proclamation of how to be *discerning, dissident disciples* in the face of Babylon in our world.

> ### Why Is the Predictive Reading So Popular?
>
> 1. Fulfilled prophecies validate a person's faith.
> 2. It resolves theological tensions: this world is not my home, this world remains my home for a while; God is in control, but I can choose, etc.
> 3. Predictive theology is by the people for the people instead of professionals.
> 4. History has meaning and a plan.
> 5. It offers utopian hope with a perfected social order.
>
> Paul Boyer, *When Time Shall Be No More*, 293–324

So, Revelation for the Rest of Us

The Apocalypse is not about prediction of the future but perception and interrogation of the present. It provides readers with a new lens to view our contemporary world. What if Revelation is what another scholar on Revelation, Greg Carey, thinks it is? "Monsters characterize imperial brutality; cosmic portents reflect social injustice; heavenly glories display the rule of the transcendent over the ordinary." What if the book gives us eyes to see this world anew, as dissidents who spot and then resist the imperial powers ever with us? As Nelson Kraybill, in his exceptional study of this book, says it, "The last book of the Bible is not a catalog of predictions about events that would take place two thousand years later. Rather, it is a projector that casts archetypal images of good and evil onto a cosmic screen." Wow, that line leads us to a fresh reading of Revelation.

What we need is a generation, not of speculators about the rapture and the millennium and the role of Israel in the end times, but of double dissidents. A dissident is someone who takes a stand against official policy in church or state or both, who dissents from the status quo with a different vision for society.

We need a generation of dissident disciples who confront and resist corruption and systemic abuses in whatever locations they are found:

- corruption in the countries of the world,
- our churches' complicities in these corruptions,
- and the reading of Revelation as speculation, which blunts our prophetic voice.

The book of Revelation is for modern-day disciples who have eyes to see the power of the empire in our world and in our churches and in our lives and yours. Michael Gorman sums this dissident theme up in a tightly packed bundle he calls "uncivil worship," which opposes and resists the civil religion of ancient Rome as well as of those of today. The book of Revelation, when read well, forms us into *dissident disciples who discern corruptions in the world and church.* Conformity to the world is the problem. Discipleship requires dissidence when one lives in Babylon.

As Greg Beale says, Revelation may be the most relevant book in the entire Bible, speaking to us today with its exhortations for "God's people to remain faithful to the call to follow the Lamb's paradoxical example and not to compromise." But to discern its relevance we must stop our *speculations* and *excitations*—with their toothless approaches to discipleship—and our *obsessions* over being raptured or left behind, and we must go to prison with John. In Revelation we enter his incredible imagination and see what God wants his people to see. As Wes Howard-Brook and Anthony Gwyther say it, "To allow the interpretation of Revelation to be controlled by a particular group of Christians is to throw away one of the church's most powerful tools for inculcating and sustaining countercultural discipleship."

Revelation records a timeless battle between two cities: Babylon and new Jerusalem. It's a battle between two lords: The Lord of lords, Jesus, and the lord of the empire, the emperors of Rome. It's a battle between hidden forces: angels and those in heaven against the dragon and his many-headed beasts (or wild things), and armies on both sides.[1]

Babylon loses and new Jerusalem wins.

It takes imagination to believe this is true. It was a stretch for a first-century imprisoned dissident, tucked away on a remote island, to imagine the mighty empire of Rome losing out to a presently captive Jerusalem. But that's the message of Revelation then with implications for us now. If you open Revelation with the eyes of a discerning, dissident disciple, you can discover a renewed vision of following Jesus faithfully today.

---

1. You will notice that we translate what is often translated "beast" with "wild thing." Beast evokes something big, but the Greek term *thērion* evokes something wild. As a wild thing, it represents chaos and destruction and uncivilized behaviors.

CHAPTER 2

For Whom Was the Book
of Revelation Written?

(Take a Deep Breath)

Sometime in the last third of the first century, several inter-
locking events culminated in the writing of what we today call
the book of Revelation. Seven churches in today's western Turkey
were struggling with faithfulness to Christ. As the Roman way of
life was penetrating these churches, a prophet named John spoke
out against Rome's impact, and someone well connected to Rome
decided something needed to be done about John, so they put him
in prison on an island in the Aegean Sea called Patmos. Today,
very little remains of those seven churches. Nothing survives of
the Roman officials' decisions.

But John's response to the encroachment of Roman culture
on the church survives. It's called *The Apocalypse* (or Revelation)
of John, and what John wrote is in a form of literature (genre)
called "apocalypse." But in addition to following the apocalyptic
genre, the book is also a prophecy with several letter-like messages
for the seven churches. Whatever we wish to call it, the book
of Revelation is an orchestral arrangement of images, some of
which are difficult to understand and interpret. Yet John must
have believed his listeners, those who heard the reading of this
book, would comprehend what he had written. With one eye on

Rome and the other eye on these seven churches, John chose to communicate with them in a way that has had a lasting—and sometimes bizarre—legacy.

Long before he wrote Revelation, John had been teaching these ideas, and that made Rome very nervous. From our perspective today, Rome's response to John seems overdone. Why worry about an old religious man? He did not have a sword and there was no army to follow him, just a few pockets of insignificant people singing spirituals (more about that later) about Jesus, whom they claimed as their Lord. Yet someone with considerable power in the empire came down on John and shipped him off to a lonely island in the Mediterranean. The powers of that time lived in suspicion and fear, even fearful of this pocket of house churches. Their songs were subversive, pointing to a different hope, and their witness announced a different Lord. There was something about them that made those in power nervous, so they began at the top with a plan to eliminate the most influential Christian in western Asia Minor: a Jew who believed Jesus was the Messiah. They shipped him off to a remote island, no doubt thinking this would put an end to this dissident.

Except it didn't.

One Sunday, John was caught up in a vision. We don't know that this man named John was the apostle John, and we also don't know the exact date when John's response, our book of Revelation, was written, but it likely happened sometime after Rome's heartless, cruel destruction of the city of Jerusalem in 70 CE. As a consequence of that destruction, Rome became for Jews what Martin Goodman calls the "epitome of evil." The prophet John knew of the fire in Rome under Nero and how the emperor had persecuted Christians (and Jews) as a result. And as this persecution spread, a tradition of dissidence began to take root. One of the most memorable acts of dissidence is the story of Masada, a Jewish fortress atop a craggy mountainous area along the Dead Sea. To escape mass murder by the Roman soldiers, the Jews in that fortress committed mass suicide. They preserved their honor and Josephus, the Jewish historian, remembered their story.

In the book of Revelation John instructs the seven churches of western Asia Minor on how to live as Christian dissidents in an empire racked by violence, power, exploitation, and arrogance. "Follow the Way of the Lamb" thumps the drumbeat of this book. Yet many discussions of Revelation completely miss this key message. Michael Gorman is right: Revelation "is not about a rapture out of this world but about faithful discipleship in this world."

John wrote the Book of Revelation for dissident disciples. He wrote it for those, like the Jews at Masada, who were willing to die before they would compromise, who would resist the empire at any cost. This is a book that calls us to civil disobedience.

A dissident is a person of hope, someone who imagines a better, future world, and then begins to embody that world. It's someone who speaks to promote that better, future vision and against what is wrong in the present. And the Bible is filled with dissidents—from Moses to Amos to Jeremiah to the man on Patmos. This pattern of speaking out and confronting injustice provided a model for Jewish thinkers to criticize the gentile rulers. Many of these dissident disciples created their works in a clandestine manner, while others did it openly, right under the nose of their opponents. Or under their thumb, like John.

Imprisoned Dissidents

Imprisoning a dissident does not deter them. Because they are inclined against the cultural grain, prison often has a transformative effect, turning them from household complainers into international celebrities. In prison dissidents plot revolutions, write books and newspaper essays that rock the world, and correspond with the outside world in ways that unmask the lies of those in power. Some of those imprisoned form networks that work to bring the systems of power and oppression down. Some spend their time in prayer in God's presence, not only speaking *to* God but hearing *from* God, while others dream prophetic dreams and envision prophetic visions, calling for change and confronting the status quo.

- Gandhi formed his theory of resistance in prison and brought India to its knees.
- Aung San Suu Kyi was under house arrest for her resistance and fight for freedom in Burma.
- Fannie Lou Hamer fought with words and ballots against systemic racism in the USA.
- Dietrich Bonhoeffer was imprisoned in Tegel and elsewhere, where he wrote books that are read all over the world today.
- Nelson Mandela was imprisoned on Robben Island, where he spent decades plotting justice for blacks in South Africa, eventually becoming South Africa's president.
- Alexander Solzhenitsyn was in the gulag, where he brought to light injustices against free speech and freedom itself.
- Vaclev Havel was a former Czech dissident imprisoned for protesting for freedom, and his books are read the world over.
- Martin Luther King Jr. wrote a letter in a cell in Birmingham and spoke prophetic words at a memorial in the world's most powerful capitol.

By imprisoning them, the powers in charge hoped to render these dissidents powerless, hoping to marginalize them and render them incapable of influencing others. But history tells a different story, one where dissidents thrive in imprisonment. Leave one alone, and over time she will develop a vision that might change the world.

Not all dissidents are imprisoned. Some write books at home or at the office or in libraries that give others an imagination for a new way of life—

the way Harriet Beecher Stowe did in *Uncle Tom's Cabin,*
the way Alan Paton did in *Cry, the Beloved Country,*
the way Dee Brown did in *Bury My Heart at Wounded Knee,*
and the way Ralph Ellison did in *The Invisible Man* . . .

some make *Marvel* movies . . .

. . . and you may add others to the list. Each of these individuals saw a better world and turned their visionary gifts of writing, speaking, or activism against the powers controlling their present world. Dissidents tap into the mind of God and return with a vision that sees the powers of this world differently. Some dissidents have the gift of discernment, and we ignore their warnings at our own peril. Perhaps the twist of terms by Martin Luther King Jr. says it best. He once referred to Christians as "transformed nonconformists"—a perfect definition of a dissident disciple of Christ. King spoke of Jesus as the "world's most dedicated nonconformist," adding that each of us "is either a molder of society or is molded by society." We are either thermometers reflecting the temperature of the world or thermostats adjusting that temperature. But we are only nonconformists, he warned his audiences in Montgomery, if we have been transformed in Christ.

> *It was the tension between John's vision of the kingdom of God and his environment that moved him to write his Apocalypse.*
> —Adela Yarbro Collins, *Crisis and Catharsis*, 106

John Was a Dissident

The apostle John was on Patmos "because of the word of God." That is to say, he was there because of his witness about and for Jesus (Rev 1:9). Patmos was not a penal colony, nor was it a deserted, uninhabitable island. John was exiled to the island to remove him from any position of influence in western Asia Minor.[1] And his critical eye was not only turned toward Rome, but to the church as well. We might call John a *double* dissident because he had his eyes on the evil powers at work in the empire as well as those same powers at work in the church. He saw too much Rome in the church, and not enough church in Rome.

---

1. According to Eusebius, he was permitted to return after Domitian's death (96 AD) to Ephesus (*Ecclesiastical History* 3.20.10–11).

In a wonderful poem, Malcolm Guite relates an incident that helps us understand John's story. Once, while photocopying some poems for a talk, Guite's copy machine jammed and he yanked out what he could recover before leaving for his talk. Upon returning, he was told by the person tasked with fixing the jam, "Your poetry is jamming my machine!" Guite turned that phrase into a poem called, simply enough, "On being told my poetry was found in a broken photocopier." Guite's poem is an apt metaphor for us as dissident disciples: the poetic imagery and words of Revelation were written to jam the empire's machine. Guite's closing words in the poem take us to the heart of John's dissidence:

> My poetry is jamming your machine . . .
> With pictures copied from a world unseen.

A world unseen, but now seen and revealed to us by John. And if we read it again today, listening to the message John has for us, it will once again jam the machines of empire.

Author and Date

For the view that John was an otherwise unnamed early Christian prophet by the name of John, but not the author of the Gospel or the letters, see Koester, *Revelation*, 65–69; A. Y. Collins, *Crisis and Catharsis*, 25–49, 134–138; deSilva, *Discovering Revelation*, 29–32. For a recent discussion that concludes the Gospel of John, the letters of John, and the Revelation are from a similar circle of thinkers but not the same author, see N. T. Wright and Michael Bird, *The New Testament in Its World* (Grand Rapids: Zondervan Academic, 2019), 812–814. For the view that the apostle John wrote it, see Fee, *Revelation*, xviii–xix. Justin Martyr said it was by the apostle (*Dialogue* 8.14). For a fair-minded discussion of the connections between the Gospel of John and the Book of Revelation, see Rowland, "Revelation," 514–517.

On the date: Wright and Bird conclude it could be under Nero or under Domitian or edited later under Trajan, 814–81; Koester, *Revelation*, 71–79. Irenaeus said it was written at the end of Domitian's life (Irenaeus, *Against Heresies* 5.30.3). Certainty eludes us, but we think it was written at the end of the reign of Domitian, who ruled as emperor from 81–96 AD (deSilva, *Discovering Revelation*, 35–39), yet we recognize that Revelation 11:1–2 sounds like the temple is still standing and that 17:9–10 can be read to reflect the time just after Nero's death. See deSilva, *Discovering Revelation*, 149–150 for a sketch of the evidence. For a good discussion on date, see A. Y. Collins, *Crisis and Catharsis*, 54–83.

To find the right language to describe what he saw in those visions, John combed through his Bible's prophets, several of them proficient "empire jammers" like Nahum. Nahum speaks up and speaks out, targeting his own leaders as well as the evil Assyrian Empire. He does not hesitate to call leaders names and blame them for the chaos they had created, and he predicts their coming collapse. His dissidence is largely focused on the "nobles" and "great men" as he announces the imminent failure of their trusted gates, walls, and fortresses: "Your guards are like locusts, your officials like swarms of locusts that settle in the walls on a cold day—but when the sun appears they fly away, and no one knows where" (Nah 3:10, 17). John Goldingay, in his wonderful translation of the Old Testament called *The First Testament*, renders the common translation of "locusts" with the word "grubs" instead. You've got to have a big chest to call the powerful leaders of the world "grubs." But Nahum did this, and more, when he accuses the leaders of laziness, saying "your shepherds slumber" and "your nobles lie down to rest" (3:18). And the consequences of their neglect of pastoring the people? "Your people are scattered on the mountains with no one to gather them" (3:18). The final verse of his prophetic writings spells out the tragedy: "All who hear the news about you clap their hands at your fall" (3:19).

Nahum was a no-fear-'em prophet. Similarly, the prophet Amos calls his national leaders the "cows of Bashan" (Amos 4:1). And Jesus, too, used some spicy names in his own preaching, calling the Pharisees not only "hypocrites" but "whitewashed tombs" and "snakes" and "vipers" (Matt 23:27, 33) and giving Herod Antipas the name "fox" (Luke 13:32).

In writing the book of Revelation, John wasn't focused on the brutal empire of Assyria as his predecessor Nahum had been. Instead, John had his eyes on Rome, the empire of empires. But he, too, uses descriptive and derisive names for its leaders, referring to Rome as a beast and a dragon. We'll get to those soon. What's important to understand is that John, too, was a dissident, a prophetic voice in a long line of dissident voices speaking about the negative influence of Rome in the church. Too many of the churches were floating along with cultural buoyancy, wrongly assuming that all was fine. They believed they could follow Jesus *and* still be 100% culturally respected. They thought they could live like Rome *and* enter the new Jerusalem. John saw through their errant beliefs and spoke up and spoke out. It's one thing to talk trash about Rome—the obvious enemy—behind closed doors, but it's another to diss your own churches.

So what did John say that got those churches riled up?

To Ephesus—one of Rome's biggest cities at the time—he charges that the Christians there have "forsaken the love you had at first" (Rev 2:4).

To Pergamum—another prominent city with a long history —he accuses the Christians there of embracing the "teaching of Balaam" and food that had been offered to idols while practicing "sexual immorality" (2:14). John labels some in that church "Nicolaitans"—an insulting term similar to "grubs" for Nahum.

To Thyatira—John writes that they "tolerate . . . Jezebel," a false prophet, and warns that she too was leading them into idol-offered food and sexual immorality (2:20). Yet another grub.

To those in Sardis, John delivers a fatal blow with these words: "You are dead" (3:1). Everyone thought the church was alive and well, but John saw the truth.

To those in the beautiful valley overlooking Laodicea, John uses several labels. He calls them "lukewarm," telling them that Jesus himself would spit them out as unpotable, unpalatable water (3:16). Later he tells the people they are "wretched, pitiful, poor, blind and naked" (3:17).

But while he is dispensing grubs to the churches, he's also got his eyes on Rome and the other churches he pastors. Because John spoke against Rome, he became an imprisoned dissident. Because he spoke against the churches, some saw his imprisonment as a relief. This is one of the keys to reading Revelation well—that we understand the dual critique of the church and the empire. Reading Revelation well requires recognizing that Revelation has much to say; it makes no sense until we first see how it speaks a powerful encouragement to be dissident disciples.

And the first step in understanding this is learning to use our imagination.

CHAPTER 3

Revelation and Imagination

The book of Revelation interprets what John *saw*.[1] One of John's favorite books in his Bible, if not *the* favorite for John, was Daniel—especially Daniel's seventh chapter. There, Daniel shares a picture of one like a son of man, describing his visionary experience: "In the first year of Belshazzar king of Babylonia Daniel *saw a dream and the visions in his head*" (7:1, Alter; cf. Dan 2:28). Similar to Daniel, John too had a vision. It may have been a dream or a vision in his head while lying in bed asleep. We don't know all of the details, but we know that other prophets "saw" visions too (Mic 1:1; Amos 1:1; Isa 1:1). Most likely, these visions were images generated in the brain, perhaps approximating something like we would view on a movie screen.

And John not only "saw," he also *heard*.[2] The book of Revelation records a range of sensory experiences, such that John can call on his listeners and readers to "*Look!*"[3] Those listening to the performance of this book were summoned to an imaginative, sensory-laden, alternative world designed to reveal deep truths about God, the church, and the Roman Empire.

---

1. The term is used more than sixty times in Revelation. Here are a few: 1:2, 12, 17, 19–20; 4:1; 5:1, 6, 11; 6:1.
2. The term is used more than forty times in Revelation: 1:10; 4:1; 5:11, 13; 6:1, 3, 5, 6, 7, etc.
3. A term used twenty-five times: 1:7; 2:10, 22; 3:8, 9; 5:5; 6:2, etc. The NIV blunts this term often.

Like Daniel, John also wrote down what he saw and heard. How does one "transcribe" a vision or what you've heard other than putting it into words? And once the vision is communicated through words, those words interpret the sensory experience for the one reading or listening. Revelation is a visionary, auditory experience interpreted for the seven churches, the result of an artistic and graphic imagination. That's not to say that what John saw did not happen. It's simply to note that his experience was interpreted and mediated through what is written. One way of seeing this is by noting that the book of Revelation has more connections to the Old Testament writings than any book in the New Testament—yet it almost never quotes from it. What John *saw* and *heard* was interpreted using the language with which he was familiar—the language of his Bible. John was so soaked in our Old Testament that he could not describe his sensory experiences without using the Bible's language. Of course, he may have seen something similar to what Daniel saw and described, using similar language that echoed the Bible's similar visions.

> *A poet uses words not to explain something, and not to describe something, but to make something.*
> —Eugene Peterson, *Reversed Thunder*, 5

The key idea here is that *the book of Revelation doesn't simply transcribe what John saw.* We asked two world-class experts on the book of Revelation the same question: What does "saw" mean when we read that John saw something? Both of them immediately told us that "saw" refers to more than a visionary experience. It can mean he saw something with his "mind's eye," as in a dream, and then his "seeing" involved mentally pondering what was seen and interpreting it with the aid of the Bible's own language. In other words, seeing involves sight and interpretation. It likely worked something like this:

1. John had a visionary, auditory, revelatory experience.
2. John pondered that sensory-shaped experience.
3. John connected what he saw to familiar prophetic texts

from the Old Testament, the history of his people, and the Greco-Roman world.

4. John drafted, edited, and wrote up the vision to be performed.

Putting this all together is what we mean when we say John used his "imagination." We don't mean imagination in the sense of making something up—as in writing a fictional story. Instead, we mean the creative process of communication, where something real stimulated his imagination and then something he says to communicate that experience stimulates ours. Remember: it takes imagination to read Revelation rightly. There is nothing weird about reading Revelation this way. Imagination is used frequently by scholars and students to inform all kinds of readings about Revelation. For instance, that great New Testament scholar Bruce Metzger once wrote a wonderful little book called *Breaking the Code*. I (Scot) gave this book to both of my children to read when they were young adults. In his book, Metzger notes that Revelation "is unique . . . in appealing primarily to our *imagination*." Similarly, Michael Gorman writes that Revelation "can transform the imagination with respect to how we perceive and live in relation to God, others, and the world," pointing us to an expression by scholar Richard Hays, that reading Revelation requires a "conversion of the imagination." Christopher Rowland, one of the world's experts on apocalyptic literature, says, "Apocalyptic imagery beckons us to suspend our pragmatism and to enter into its imaginative world." But he concludes with a rebuke to our unexercised imaginative capacities: "Our imaginations are out of condition; we lack the skills to exercise our imaginations."

So how do you read Revelation with imagination?

Imagination

John's strategy was to write an "apocalypse" (the Greek *apokalypsis* means "unveiling," "revealing"). An apocalypse, by design, is an imagination-stimulating genre. Apocalypses reveal to humans

God's plan for the world. They inform readers that what they think is real is not *as real* as they think, that there is a deeper reality, that the world is not what it seems to be. And in reading, the unfathomable becomes clear.

Many, in an attempt to clarify the deeper message, succumb to a desire to translate the images into specific persons or events, but such hasty moves often work counter to the role our imagination is designed to play. This is because John collides the real world with the real-er world. "His purpose," Adela Yarbro Collins said long ago, "was to create the tension [of this world and the real-er world] for readers unaware of it, to heighten it for those who felt it already, and then to overcome it in an act of literary imagination."

> *[Revelation] is a classic example of art that stimulates rather than prescribes.*
> —Christopher Rowland, "Revelation," 513

An apocalypse is an art form (see appendix 2, "What's an Apocalypse?"). Art forms open doors to a new way of looking at life. Think of how you interact with a painting, a drawing, a sculpture, a mural, or another work of creative art. Or think of how you might view the Marvel Cinematic Universe films, like *The Black Panther*, or of works of fantasy and fiction. Richard Bauckham, one of the most gifted scholars of Revelation of the last half century, put it this way:

> Revelation is a book that in all centuries has inspired the martyrs, nourished the imagination of visionaries, artists and hymn writers, resourced prophetic critiques of oppression and corruption in state and church, sustained hope and resistance in the most hopeless situations.

Revelation excites our faith to imagine the victory of God over evil—and thus, how to live in our world *with* that kind of imagination. Some are understandably nervous about a word like "imagination," thinking it refers to something like a hallucination or childish, silly ideas. But as Trevor Hart has said,

On the contrary, careful analyses of the subject [of imagination] suggest that the capacity for acts of imagination lie at the root of our most reliable and fruitful ways of engaging with the world, in the sciences as well as in the arts and humanities, and furnish the conditions under which alone they [the, sciences, arts, and humanities] are possible.

Hart suggests that we distinguish the merely imaginative from the power of imaginary. Faith and imagination, he shows, are wound together in a tight thread in the Bible, such that the faithful person lives out a kingdom imagination.

Sometimes there is pushback when you connect Revelation to things like fiction or fantasy. Ironically, the pushback often comes from people whose primary understanding of Revelation has been shaped from fiction, readers of books like the *Left Behind* series or the multitude of movies and other novels about end-times eschatology. Could it be that these dispensational-inspired fictions gain some of their potency the same way the book of Revelation does, as *eschatology wrapped in imagination?*

We have all been shaped deeply by the imaginations of others. Think of the great Greek writer, Homer, or the comparable Roman writer, Virgil. They routinely stimulated the reader's and the listener's imagination and created a mythic narrative in which Greeks and Romans learned to live. Think also of Dante's *The Divine Comedy*, where your imagination is invited to comprehend the three levels of *inferno* (hell), *purgatorio* (purgatory), and *paradiso* (heaven). Dante's imaginative presentation was so brilliant many people believe that what he wrote about each of these levels depicts reality. Or consider John Milton's *Paradise Lost* or John Bunyan's *Pilgrim's Progress* and how influential those books have been in shaping Protestant views of heaven and hell. Harriet Beecher Stowe brought southern slavery to its knees with a novel. Dorothy Sayers took us behind the curtains in her mystery novels (I like *Gaudy Night*) to find another world, and her friend C. S. Lewis did this in his space trilogy and *The Chronicles of Narnia* series, which has excited the mind of faith for millions of people.

The list goes on: J. R. R. Tolkien's *The Lord of the Rings*, Ralph Ellison's *The Invisible Man*, J. K. Rowling's *Harry Potter*. Each of these writers usher us into a story that prompts us to imagine a better world. In this way, the aim of Revelation may be closer to Maurice Sendak's *Where the Wild Things Are* or Jonathan Swift's *Gulliver's Travels*, where imagination meets imperialism to critique and confront the powers of our age.

Our point is that good readers of Revelation will read it more like *The Lord of the Rings* than Paul's letter to the Romans. We should let the bowls empty out and the trumpets blast; we should visualize the fall of Babylon and the woman of Revelation zooming and leaping and spinning and twirling—if you want to read this book well. The writer John used his imagination to see what he saw, and it takes an imagination to engage his. Too many readings of Revelation are *flat-footed* and *literal*. But as Greg Stevenson, an expert on Revelation, says, "Revelation symbolically transforms the world into a battlefield in which the forces of the dragon are arrayed against the forces of God." He warns us of flipping the images into flat propositions: "Turning poetry into prose, however, destroys its power." And sadly, that is what has happened time and time again in interpreting the book. Speculators do this when they take the woman of Revelation 12 and look for the hidden meaning. Is she Eve? Israel? Mary mother of Jesus? The church? Both Israel and the church? The right answer is "Yes, and probably more than that too!" Forcing the woman of Revelation 12 into a single mold ruins the intentional morphing and ambiguity of the book. Instead, we should "take the time to feel the impact of the image and to adopt a receptive attitude in which feelings play as great a role as thinking."

Revelation was designed for performance. And we are invited to imagine our way into the vast and varied images at work in this book.

The Inner Workings of John's Imagination

John's Revelation was *performed* in each of the seven churches. But what did that look like? First-century folks loved to sit in rooms and on hillsides to hear someone reading from a book. But those readers didn't read the way we typically read Scripture passages in church, mispronunciations and all. Readers of that day performed a poem or a book or a story, and that's what happened with Revelation—someone performed it. The reader may have had the entire book memorized, knew to pause at all the right times, and likely changed voices for different characters speaking. They may have ramped up the tone with some texts and pastorally softened them at other times. All the while, they would have studied the eyes of their listeners and veered from the text if someone's brow was furrowed. Some in the audience were probably amen-ing and others were oohing and ahhing, clapping at times, booing at others. (This was not your father's church, unless you are like my father, who grew up in a Holiness Pentecostal church). The reader would have likely paused for questions. Be honest: How many questions do you think were asked in an oral performance of this book? (Lots.) It would have taken hours to get through this book with each church audience, and in some of these locations there was more than one house church. Think again about the opening words of this book and what they might have meant to those first-century hearers: "God's blessing for the *reader* and the *hearers* of the prophecy's words, and *observing* the matters written in it . . ." (1:3, author's translation). That blessing stimulated the imaginations of those listening.

Imagination does to this book what *music* does to words. John often gives us the image without telling us what to think, just as Bach or Mozart did with their music. His images enter our minds and do what only music and the imagination can do, *transcending words* by stimulating mental images that become our port of entry into an alternative world, the world of the dragon and the Lamb. All sorts of readers get messed up on this point—not just the speculators that we see in movies like *Left Behind*. How can you have God and the Lamb winning without having a battle and some losers? You can't. That's how John rolls and if we want to read him well, we need to become holy rollers.

Again, we want to emphasize that imagination does not equal

fiction. It is not opposed to truth or reality. No, images *convey truth* and speak God's deeper reality. With imagination we brush up against the Other Side, we enter (like the Pevensie children of Lewis's Narnia) through the wardrobe door and discover we are next to John in God's throne room. We can hear the swooshing and see the brightness of the twenty-four elders and the four living things and hear the timbres of the music, and we get blinded by the glory of it all. Reading Revelation with imagination is like the experience of Tolkien's character in his short story "Leaf by Niggle." Niggle's passion was painting leaves and trees. He dies and enters heaven—rolling downhill, of course, on a bike—to experience trees beyond trees and mountains and leaves that he ached to paint while he was alive. But now, in heaven, he sees them in all their fullness, those trees he was aching to paint just right are there in a way he had only glimpsed before.

Imagination *ignites the mundane.* Think of the bush where Moses witnesses the holy presence of God. Imagination invites us into a world that transcends our world so we can return to our world transformed by the conversion of our thinking. Imagination captures the uncapturable and leads into reverie, the pondering that loses us in the swirling visions. "Get lost" is the best advice for reading Revelation, and don't be left behind!

Imagination also comforts *the oppressed, the discouraged, the seeker, and the wanderer.* When we engage the flood of images Revelation offers us and experience them with our senses, it encourages us to trudge through the deep icy snows of discouragement and stimulates faith in the God who really is the

> *We need to ask not whether it is realistic or practical or viable but whether it is imaginable. We need to ask if our consciousness and imagination have been so assaulted and co-opted by the royal consciousness that we have been robbed of the courage or power to think an alternative thought. . . . It is the vocation of the prophet to keep alive the ministry of imagination, to keep on conjuring and proposing futures alternative to the single one the king wants to urge as the only thinkable one.*
> —Walter Brueggemann, *The Prophetic Imagination,* 39–40.

Lord of lords and King of kings—even when dictators and tyrants ruin our society. Imagination is more than fantasy or fiction, though an apocalypse like Revelation has much in common with those worlds. That imagination of John led him to produce a text filled with starts and interruptions and re-starts and more interruptions. And on the journey through his Apocalypse, John stimulates our imaginations to form and shape us into dissident disciples.

Imagination and the Hope of Dissidents

And that's one of the key takeaways from how we should read Revelation as it was intended to be read. Imagination empowers *dissidents*. An apocalyptic imagination aims at deconstruction of the status quo, perhaps even revolution. Dissidents aim to change the world. They do this through sometimes bizarre, almost cartoonish images, and they create battles where good characters conquer evil ones. Many of the fantasy novels mentioned earlier discerned the real presence of evil in the world and created characters who overcame that evil through a dissident hope. They rejected the stupefaction of social lethargy and perceived two ways in the world, two teams. One was for good and one for bad, one stood for evil and the other for justice.

John operates with two opposing sides as well. *On one side* is God and the Lamb and the Seven Spirits, the woman, the seven churches, allegiant witnesses, the four living things, the twenty-four elders, and the good angels—all of whom are marching toward the kingdom of God or the new Jerusalem. *On the other side* is the dragon, the wild things, and their demonic and human servants—all of whom are embodied in Babylon. To read Revelation well, we will need to get to know John's characters as our companions.

"Choose your team!" is one of John's rhetorical strategies. Choose *Team Lamb* and you become a dissident who resists *Team Dragon*. Dissidents soon learn how many are on Team Lamb, and they begin to discern the manifold ploys and plots of Team Dragon. They also learn, as they speak up and speak out on how to resist Team Dragon.

Three principles for reading Revelation well are now on the table:

1. It's not written for speculators—for those looking for a decoder ring to interpret newspaper headlines.
2. It is written for dissidents—for followers of Christ ready to challenge the powers of world and empire.
3. And it requires imagination—engaging our senses and minds with the performance that is Revelation, with all of its rich images and intriguing characters.

Now, we turn to a fourth principle, which brings all three principles together: *we must understand the Playbill, or the Cast of Characters, of Revelation.* The Book of Revelation puts a number of characters on the stage, each becoming a "character" in the drama. Each deserves to be understood for their role. To understand Revelation, one must grasp what John means—to take the first example of a character in the Playbill—with "Babylon." If you wait until you meet this character in chapter 17 to think about Babylon, you will have a thin reading of the first sixteen chapters. So before we go any further, we will devote two solid chapters to unpacking Babylon. You'll see why once we are finished. Babylon is a key character in the drama of this book, and as we meet Babylon we'll also meet a few other characters as well. Let's get started.

PART 2

The Playbill of Revelation

CHAPTER 4

Babylon's Identity

I (Scot) was attending a theater performance of *Hamilton*, and just before it began, I opened the playbill to find a list of characters with brief descriptions of each one. I was especially interested in reading about the main characters of the story, one of whom happened to be a nephew of a former student of mine from Nassau. (His voice and acting were excellent.) The playbill served a very helpful function: it introduced me to the characters. And if we want to understand what John is saying to us, we need something similar for Revelation. After all, it's a performance, and to read Revelation well requires knowing its cast of characters and the roles they play in this cosmic drama. *"Who is doing what?"* John's cast of characters are assigned to one of two teams, summarized in the playbill pages that follow:

TEAM LAMB: God and the Lamb and the Seven Spirits, the woman, the seven churches, allegiant witnesses, the four living things, the twenty-four elders, and angels, all designed for new Jerusalem

TEAM DRAGON: The dragon and the beasts, which I translate throughout as "the wild things"—there are two of them—all inhabiting Babylon (kings and merchants and sailors and anyone who chooses to have the mark of the wild thing, and John names some others: the Nicolaitans and Balaam and Jezebel)

37

THE PLAYBILL OF REVELATION
Team Dragon in Babylon

BABYLON Mission is to embody the way of the dragon. Rides on the wild thing. Characterized by royalty, idolatry, opulence, murder, status, arrogance, power, military might, murder, and economic exploitation. Kills those in the way of the Lamb. Gathers under her power the kings of the earth, merchants of the world, and sea captains. Serves as a timeless metaphor for empire and injustices and idolatries. In John's day, Babylon is Rome. Babylon falls. Also known as the great prostitute.

THE DRAGON Has a mission of accusation, deceit, death. Chases the woman but loses her. Wages war with the woman's children. Battles Michael the angel and loses. Has control of the wild things, significant control with the political powers embodied in Babylon. Defeated by the Lamb and by the allegiant witnesses. Bound for one thousand years, released, and then destroyed in the lake of fire. Also known as Satan, the devil.

WILD THING #1 (FROM SEA) Mission is to embody the will of the dragon. Represents chaos, power, deception, and opposition to the Lamb. Ruler of evil empires. One of the dead-heads of the wild thing is raised from the dead. Worshiped by humans. Its rule is temporary. Makes up one third of the unholy trinity: dragon, wild thing #1 and #2. Aka the beast from the sea.

WILD THING #2 (FROM EARTH) Mission is to embody the will of wild thing #1 and dragon. The sycophant in chief, the propagandist. Looks like the Lamb, acts like the dragon. Forces worship of wild thing #1, does fraudulent miracles, deceives the world. Forces humans to accept the "mark of the wild thing." Its name is its number, 666. Aka the beast from the earth.

666 Represents Roman Emperor Nero and many others.

OTHERS Jezebel and the Nicolaitans/ Nicolaus and Balaam. These are representative names, serving as stereotypes for idolatries and sexual immoralities and false teachings.

THE PLAYBILL OF REVELATION
Team Lamb in New Jerusalem

GOD ON THE THRONE The God of Israel, the Father, the sovereign God over all, who orchestrates the events of history toward the new Jerusalem. God's might is matched by God's gracious love. This God will defeat the dragon, banish death, and establish life in New Jerusalem. To God belongs all worship and praise and honor and glory because this God brings salvation through the Lamb. Trinity: Father, Son (Lamb), and Spirit.

THE SEVEN SPIRITS Though some question this, the Seven Spirits are John's language for the Holy Spirit. The number represents perfection or completeness, and it corresponds to the missions of the Spirit.

THE LAMB In the center of the throne room and the center of the action in Revelation. The Lamb is the Lord Jesus Christ, who has many names and attributes, including: Jesus, Messiah, faithful witness, first born from among the dead, ruler of the kings of the earth, loves us, liberates us, Alpha and Omega, who is-who was-who is to come, like a son of man, first and last, living one, holds keys of death and hades. Lion, Lamb, Logos, Light: all of these represent the Lord over all lords and King over all kings. He is the Savior/Redeemer by his blood.

THE ALLEGIANT WITNESSES These are the believers and followers of Jesus in the way of the Lamb. The seven churches are faithful (allegiant) witnesses in life and word to the way of the Lamb and the rule of King Jesus. They suffer for their witness. They are known for their works of goodness and love and kindness.

THE WOMAN She appears to morph in Revelation 12 from Eve to Israel to Mary, mother of Jesus, and finally to the church. She is opposed by the dragon, who tries to kill her and the baby boy born to her (Jesus). She escapes under protection from God. Her offspring is opposed by the dragon.

ENVOYS/ANGELS Abundant in Revelation, they perform missions for God in this world for the redemption of humans.

TWENTY-FOUR ELDERS They surround the throne, wearing white clothing with gold crowns. The number twenty-four suggests two times twelve, representing Israel and the apostles. Altogether they represent the redeemed people of God in worship of God.

FOUR LIVING THINGS They surround the throne, cover their eyes, have six wings, and praise God endlessly. They intercede, and at times guide John through the three times seven judgments/disciplines. They echo the living creatures of Isaiah 6 and Ezekiel 1's four living things and represent all creation worshiping God.

MYRIADS Those who worship God are innumerable.

NEW JERUSALEM This future, ideal city is the world as God designed it to be. It is inhabited by those who want to dwell in God's presence and with whom God dwells. It is better than the visions of the Greco-Roman visions of society (Plato, Aristotle, Cicero), it fulfills the expectations of Israel's prophets and more, and it takes the old Jerusalem and becomes the heaven-with-us kingdom of God.

These two teams are engaged in a cosmic battle with one another, what Paul Minear refers to as "sovereignties in conflict." One can't read Revelation well or make Revelation come alive in our world until we understand John's multilayered cosmic universe and the characters who are both visible and invisible.

God on the Throne vs. Babylon

Let's begin with God on the throne. Following the messages to the seven churches in chapters 2 and 3, there is an abrupt shift as we open chapters 4 and 5. We are ushered into the presence of God on the throne, and this glorious God is surrounded by worshiping elders and lightning flashes and four living creatures singing 24–7 "Holy, holy, holy is the Lord God Almighty, who was, and is, and is to come" (4:8).

David Mathewson, another expert on Revelation, offers an important clue for us in reading this book. When John's original listeners would have heard this read in their churches, they would have heard the throne-room scene as "a parody of the Roman court scene" because it "counter[s] imperial claims." Today, we miss this parody because of our distance from that culture and time and our own comfortable political positions in the West, but this was clear to those early churches. Among those listening you might have heard the equivalent of oohing and aahing, perhaps a few claps and "booyah"s as hope suddenly swelled across those gathered. The throne room, along with the vision of the Lamb in chapter 5, abruptly changes when we hit chapters 6 and following. The judgments of those chapters unfurl and descend from the throne room and find their climax in the judgment of Babylon in chapters 17–19.

It's important for us to see that this throne-room vision fundamentally determines the message of the entire Apocalypse: *God is on the Throne, Caesar is not, Babylon will go down, and someday justice will be established in the new Jerusalem.* All of this unfolds naturally when the book is read to an audience dwelling under the power of Rome, aka Babylon. But for us today to grasp the real impact this had on the original audience and understand the rest of the book, we would benefit from *reading Revelation backward,*[1] or at least somewhat backward, by reading chapters 17–19 first.

From Grub to Babylon

Remember when the Old Testament prophet Nahum called the leaders of the oppressing cities "grubs." Well, here John one-ups Nahum. He calls Babylon "the great prostitute," a common insult used by the prophets to imply immorality, idolatry, and infidelity (Hos 1–3; Nah 3:4; Isa 23:16–17), yet still a harsh word in his day. John's concern is not prostitution, however. The woman appears rather ghastly: she's in the wilderness, sitting on a bloodshed-evoking scarlet beast (or wild thing) that is "covered with blasphemous names and had seven heads and ten horns" (Rev 17:3). To picture this, imagine her on a wild beast with what looks like four unicorn heads! If you are familiar with Maurice Sendak's famous book *Where the Wild Things Are* or some of the ghastly images of Gollum in *The Lord of the Rings*, you might begin to comprehend John's image here. Those who read this as literal, physical beings that will be alive at some future time in history are making a colossal mistake. John here is not offering us prediction, but *revelation*, making an appeal through our *perception* and engaging our *imagination.*

And John's insulting descriptions continue. Our unicorn-riding woman is dressed up in the clothes and jewelry of opulence, royalty, status, and power. She has a big cup in her hand "filled with abominable things and the filth of her adulteries" (Rev 17:4). And she gets a name from John, a secret (or a "mystery") now disclosed (17:5):

---

1. In reading any book of the Bible, it often helps to *begin with the end in mind.* Put differently, it helps to *read backward.* Turning to the ending of Matthew's Gospel, the closing chapters of Paul's letters, or the final chapters of Revelation will ensure that we understand the overall direction and purpose of the work. Knowing the direction and purpose shapes our reading of the materials.

BABYLON THE GREAT
THE MOTHER OF PROSTITUTES
AND OF THE ABOMINATIONS OF THE EARTH

John is telling us that Babylon spawns immoralities and idolatries. And now we begin to see the significance of Babylon for
reading Revelation. This prostitute was intoxicated, not with
alcohol, but the blood of the faithful witnesses to Jesus. Her idea
of a fun night on the town was finding some Jesus followers and
draining their blood into a bowl to drink and feed her raging lust
for power.[2]

Babylon sits on the wild thing, and the wild thing has seven
heads, which are "seven hills" (it would have been clear what this
meant, since Rome is the city of seven hills) and "seven kings," five
of whom are dead, one is on a throne, and one not yet enthroned.
The wild thing is, thus, the eighth king. *Ah, the plot thickens.*
Seven hills, seven kings plus one. The ten horns are ten kings
who will be short-reign kings with the wild thing, and their entire
mission is to accumulate power and glory for the wild thing. The
centralizing of all this power has one purpose: to fight the Lamb.
The Lamb will win, of course, and John tells us this in 17:14 to
calm down our excitations. Yet Babylon rules over John's most
universe-encompassing expression: over "peoples, multitudes,
nations and languages" (17:15).

Still, despite her great power and authority, Babylon begins to
experience cracks in her governing system. Dissension breaks out.
The wild thing and its kings "will hate" Babylon, they will strip

---

2. John's use of images of women—the woman of Revelation 12 and the bride
of Revelation 21 along with Jezebel and the whore of Babylon—mixes goodness
with evil. The either-or rhetoric is easily comprehended while the images harbor
potential dangers of abuse for women. They must be then either guarded carefully
or deconstructed. One important reminder is that these women are not literal
women but people and cities. The women of chapter 12 and 21 are the people of
God, and the woman of Revelation 17–18 is a city that replaces the woman imagery,
said explicitly in 17:18. John is blasting away at economic exploitation, arrogance,
militarism, and idolatries in the woman Babylon; prophetic criticisms are of much
value in our world today.

her and eat her and "burn her with fire" (17:16). This is classic language found in Jewish imaginative literature ("apocalypses") used to speak about the destruction of cities (like Babylon). John ups and tells us what he means: "The woman . . . is the *great city* that rules over the kings of the earth" (17:18, italics added). So we now have everything in this vision identified:

the woman is Babylon,
the woman is sitting on the wild thing,
the wild thing operates on seven hills with seven kings
    (make that ten more kings),
and the wild thing is a king too!

The wild thing hates the Lamb, but the Lamb will be victorious, and Babylon, "the great city," will burn to the ground. It would have taken very little imagination in John's day to recognize that *this so-called great city is Rome*, but it may shock today's reader to know that this is the most repugnant, hostile portrait of the "eternal city" in the ancient world. What Rome had done to other nations, also depicted as women at times, would be done to her. We know that this understanding of Rome was commonly used by others in the early church as well. For example, not that long before the writing of Revelation, Peter is in Rome and he calls Rome "Babylon": "She who is in Babylon, chosen together with you, sends you her greetings" (1 Pet 5:13).

There is something else, though, about this woman of Revelation 17–19 that is not as widely known. Rome had a goddess named *Roma*. And many interpreters believe the whore of Babylon is John's way of blasting away at *Roma*. She is both the city of Rome's and the empire's public image of Roman glory. John has morphed *Roma*—an image of Roman pride and glory—into "the mother of prostitutes, Babylon the great." If so, John turns Rome's own image of itself inside out and upside down. If Babylon is Rome, and Rome's public image is *Roma*, then the satirical sketch of Babylon in Revelation 18 would have been heard by those listening as a potent act of dissidence, resistance, and prophetic criticism. Indeed, it would have been seen as sacrilegious, blasphemous, and traitorous.

But why go undercover with "Babylon"? Why not just say "Rome" or get right to the point by calling out "*Roma*"?

Why Babylon?

These two-and-a-half chapters in Revelation (17–19) are all about Rome, and John makes that clear in the last verse of Revelation 17 when he says Babylon is the "great city" (17:18), the city of "seven hills" (17:9). A first-century person would have quite naturally connected the woman sitting on seven hills to the common Roman coin depicting *Roma*, the goddess, sitting on seven hills.

But again, why not just say this? Why call her Babylon? And the answer is because John isn't just speaking about Rome, but he is connecting Rome and the empire to the ongoing story of God's people. *Babylon became for Jews and early Christians the most graphic image, metaphor, or trope for a city filled with arrogance, sin, injustice, oppression of God's people, and idolatry.*

Today, if you want to insult a leader you would call him a "Hitler" or "Stalin." If you want to insult the integrity of an athlete you might call them a "Pete Rose." In the Jewish world of John, you would insult a woman with the label "Jezebel" and a man by calling him "Balaam." But if you wanted to insult an entire city and mock its powers, you pulled out the "Babylon" card.

For Jews, Babylon was the city known for its hubris and pride and insufferable arrogance. In 587 BC it captured Jerusalem, enslaved the Judeans, and took them as captives to Babylon. A nation's history is marked by its major events. One such mark is Israel's *slavery in Egypt*, followed by the exodus liberation of the children of Israel, deliverance through the Red Sea, the wandering in the wilderness, receiving the law at Mount Sinai, wandering some more, and then crossing the Jordan River into the land. Another mark was the *exile* to Assyria for the Northern Kingdom. And yet another mark was the *exile and captivity* of the Southern Kingdom to Babylon. This experience of captivity in Babylon eventually became the *paradigmatic experience of captivity and exile*. It was, of course, followed by the return to the land under Ezra and Nehemiah.[3] But for the Jews, this experience was etched in their collective consciousness and became an enduring paradigm of the enemies of God's people.

So it should not surprise us that in the first century, when Jews experienced captivity again as they did at the hands of Rome in 70 AD, they understood their experience as *Babylon all over again*, as the violence of an evil empire against God's good people. John himself experienced this pain when Jerusalem was sacked by the Romans, and John shared the prophetic anger of his fellow Jews who saw Rome as Babylon all over again. Labelling Rome as "Babylon" was also resistance language. It named the problem, Rome, and it gave that problem a label—systemic sinfulness and injustice and idolatry and opposition to God. To use "Babylon" to refer to the reigning powers of the world was very, very Jewish.

Contemporary Jewish Texts about Babylon

We want to share two examples from Jewish texts roughly contemporary to the time of the book of Revelation, both of which identify Rome with Babylon. These help us see how "Babylon" was a trope—a metaphor, an image, a figure—for *any* empire filled with arrogance, oppression, violence, immorality, and idolatry.

In the *Sibylline Oracles*, a text with apocalyptic overtones like Revelation, we read in book 5, dated to around 70–80 AD, about the death of many Jews at the hands of Nero:

> But when after the fourth year a great star shines which alone
> will destroy the whole earth, because of the honor which

---

3. There were four major captivities: Assyria, Babylon, Rome (63 BC under Pompey) and Rome again in 70 AD (Vespasian was emperor, Titus the commander). In the Old Testament violent captivity at the hand of Israel's enemy was also described as God's discipline against the people of God for covenant unfaithfulness. In the book of Revelation there are no hints that Rome's violence is divine discipline. John has moved beyond that to divine discipline and judgment against Babylon itself, a theme found often in Isaiah, Jeremiah, and Ezekiel.

they first gave to Poseidon of the sea, a great star will come from heaven to the wondrous sea and will burn the deep sea and **Babylon** [=Rome] itself and the land of Italy, because of which many holy faithful Hebrews and a true people perished. (5.155–61)

In the next passage in the *Sibylline Oracles*, we read of Rome's destruction in (or by) Hades, a passage that sounds at times like the book of Revelation. And we know this is about Nero because earlier in book 5 (5.143) we read about Nero fleeing from Babylon!

Another source from around this same time is called 4 Ezra. It was written somewhere between 100–120 AD and probably from Jerusalem, and it too has its eye on Rome, which is identified again as Babylon. Again, this shows how prevalent the term "Babylon" was for depicting Rome:

[A prediction-shaped reading of Revelation] does not call readers and faith communities to the closed-end task of deciphering, of trying to determine which nation or other corporate entity is Babylon. Rather, it calls readers to do, in their present contexts, precisely what John sought to do in his own: to discern what is Babylonish about the domination systems in the midst of which they live . . . and then to discover the ways in which they can both divest themselves of participating in and bear prophetic witness against the same.

—David deSilva,
Discovering Revelation, 166

In the thirtieth year after the destruction of our city [Jerusalem, thus =100 AD], I, Salathiel, who am also called Ezra, was in **Babylon** [=Rome]. I was troubled as I lay in my bed, and my thoughts welled up in my heart, because I saw the desolation of Zion and the wealth of those who lived in **Babylon**. (4 Ezra 3:1–2)

In chapter 15 "Asia" too is like Babylon:

And you, O Asia, who share in the glamour of **Babylon** and the glory of her person—woe to you, miserable wretch! For you have made yourself like her; you have decked out your daughters in harlotry to please and glory in your lovers, who have always lusted after you. (4 Ezra 15:46–47)

If all of this sounds somewhat like Revelation, that's our point. We could give several more texts,[4] but these should be enough to illustrate how Babylon served as a trope for an empire's embodiment of arrogance, oppression, and captivity.

> Babylon is chosen because that specific city from that specific time in Israel's history became a trope for the powers that oppressed, took captive, and killed the people of God.

Babylon for All Times

This leads us to an important observation and another principle for reading Revelation well: *Babylon is a timeless trope.* Jews knew of the original city of Babylon as a specific event from their own story. But from that time onward they had their eyes open for the presence of the next Babylon and other Babylons to follow. Whenever they saw an oppressing nation or an enslaving power, they saw Babylon all over again. Whenever they saw their country besieged and their city (Jerusalem) attacked or exploited, they remembered Babylon. Babylon was more than a one-time event—it was timeless for Jews. And because John grabbed that timeless trope in his message to the churches . . .

> Each century has its Babylons, each country has its Babylons, and each state and city and—yes, church institutions and churches—has the potential to release the powers of Babylon.

One of America's prophets, William Stringfellow, observes, "The moral pretenses of Imperial Rome, the millennial claims of Nazism, the arrogance of Marxist dogma, the anxious insistence

---

4. For instance, *2 Baruch* 11:1–3; 67:1–9; and in the Dead Sea Scrolls: 4Q163 f4 7ii.1–21; 4Q168 f1.1–6; 4Q386 f1 iii.1–6; 4Q553 f3 + 2ii + 4:1–7.

that America be 'number one' among the nations *are all versions of Babylon's idolatry.*"

Chronological and speculative readings of Revelation popular among many Christians over the last century understand Babylon as a colossal city in some future worldwide empire. Those who read Revelation 17–18 as predictive prophecies have a suitcase full of speculations about which city that will be. Could it be Moscow? Rome again? Berlin? Washington DC? Beijing? Tehran? Baghdad? Yet another suitcase of speculation is filled with the names of people who might be the final wild thing of history, the antichrist. Is it Hitler? Stalin? Saddam Hussein? Often enough, in recent American readings of these chapters the names inevitably include whoever rules Russia, or perhaps Iraq or Iran. But speculations based on predictive prophecy miss the whole point of what John is saying—and they have always been wrong.

> Babylon is as present to John as Patmos.
> Babylon was not some future city for him.

There is nothing in the description of Babylon in Revelation 17–18 to make one think he is referring to some future empire. Babylon for John was very present and very now. He feels it in his feet because where he stands and writes and prays is a location determined by Babylon.

Babylon is always here—even today. Babylon is an image, a metaphor, a trope Jews used for empires that oppress and persecute the covenant people. As a trope, Babylon names empires that oppress those who walk in the way of the Lamb. When we turn later in this book to the story at work in the book of Revelation and look at its timeline, we will need to depict Babylon as timeless. And this means:

> Babylon accompanies the church as it
> moves through church history.

Babylon is a moving factor in history. Babylon is both a city and at the same time the history of empires. As Howard-Brook and Gwyther observe, "Babylon exists wherever sociopolitical power coalesces into an entity that stands against the worship of YHWH alone."

This can't be stressed enough: Babylon is timeless. So, yes, we glimpse the wild thing and its sycophants in the Caesars of Rome, in Constantine and even more in Theodosius I, in Charlemagne, in Napoleon, in Stalin, in Hitler, in Mussolini, in Churchill, in Roosevelt, in the apartheid creators, in Mao, and in various powers in Washington DC.

We will meet the dragon's violent ways in the militaries of major empires and nations—in airplanes, in submarines, in warships, in bombs, in nuclear warheads, in nerve gasses, in alliances of nations, and in internet terrorism. We encounter the dragon and Babylon in spiritual, moral, cultural, political, economic, and educational degradations that bring death, that block freedoms, that are designed by the wild things to yield allegiance to the dragon. The speculators, who read Revelation as predictive prophecy, promote reading all this stuff as something future, yet to come, and those who read in this way fail to form a *Babylonian hermeneutic* for the church today. They miss what John is doing—developing a discipleship for dissidents.

May this be the slogan for dissidents seeking to discern the dragon's Babylon in our world today. As Richard Bauckham says: "Absolute power on earth is satanic in inspiration, destructive in its effects, idolatrous in its claims to ultimate loyalty." *This is the slogan that should shape the way dissidents discern Babylon today.* Yes, we see Babylon in the evil slave trade of the eighteenth and nineteenth centuries, in the systemic degradation of a people based on skin color and race, in the corrupted systemic residues of slavery, and in the hideous displays of privilege, power, and attempts at supremacy in the monstrous culture war in the USA. Many of those reading Revelation speculatively point their fingers at Russia or Iran or Iraq and fail to see Babylon in their own country. Yet as Michael Gorman has gone to pains to demonstrate, the USA has earmarks of empire in its exceptionalism, nationalism, colonialism, and militarism. Gorman, deepening his accusations of American imperialism, points his finger at America's sacred symbols and spaces and rituals and language and music and texts and leaders and heroes. We'll have more to say on this at the end of the book.

A Word for the Church Too

The biggest problem facing the seven churches was Babylon. And the biggest problem we still face in our churches today is Babylon. Babylon is *past* and it is *now*; it is *tomorrow* and it is *future* as well. But it is only the future because Babylon is *always*.

There is far more in this term "Babylon" than just a good ol' image from the Old Testament prophets that caught on in the first and second century to describe Rome as the place that destroyed Jerusalem and took God's people captive. When we read Revelation well, we develop our ability to discern the presence of Babylon in our world and in our own churches, and then we learn to resist its creeping powers. But for us to develop this ability, we need to go one step further and sketch the "character" of Babylon.

What are Babylon's chief personality and character traits?
What makes a place a new version of Babylon?
And how can we discern the Babylons of our world?

CHAPTER 5

Babylon's Characteristics

Babylon means military might, exploiter of the economy, and oppressor of the people of God. But there's more to this image than just an external threat to God's people. Babylon is also present in the various sins of the seven churches. The storyline of the book of Revelation is about wiping out the sins of Babylon so there can be a new Jerusalem. Dissident disciples have their eyes trained to discern the signs of Babylon, and they recognize the sinister symptoms of something disordered.

Babylon is far more sinister than a large city or an evil empire. John discerns the face of evil in Rome, but that evil penetrates deeper than empire or city. He knows the real problem is the dragon and its sycophants, the wild things, and all those who are seduced by the wild things. The signs of Babylon are visible disorders, like exploitation of bodies in slavery and sexual corruptions, but eliminating the disorders does not get to the root of the problem. The root is the dragon, who works through the wild things to create Babylon.

Revelation reveals the plan of God to wipe the world clean of evil by defeating the dragon, wrangling the wild things, and taking down Babylon. It takes readers into the heart of evil, defeats it, and leads us triumphantly to the world's true destiny: *the new Jerusalem, the city that flows with peace and justice.*

But we aren't there yet. We still live in Babylon today. What then are the signs of Babylon? John's theme verse for Babylon is found in Revelation 17:2 and it reads:

> With her the kings of the earth committed adultery, and the inhabitants of the earth were intoxicated with the wine of her adulteries.

Babylon attracted the political powers of the world into her orbit, and once drawn into that circle they became intoxicated with Babylon's poisoned wine. What is life like inside Babylon's circle? A straightforward reading of Revelation 17–18 reveals the following *seven signs* of Babylon. These seven signs manifest idolatries and injustices, but if one wants to reduce them to their core they express *a corrupted, corrupting civil religion and spiritualized politics.* To quote again from Richard Bauckham, here is his thematic statement for the seven characteristics of Babylon:

> Absolute power on earth is satanic in inspiration, destructive in its effects, idolatrous in its claims to ultimate loyalty.

In one word: *domination.* The one who follows the Lamb toward new Jerusalem discerns and resists the claims to absolute power by Babylon. These seven characteristics of Babylon provide for us today a template for growing in discernment as we become dissident disciples of Jesus.

1. Anti-God (for Jews and Christians)

Babylon formed an anti-God way of life into a rigid system. Jews and Christians had long denounced common idolatries (Isa 40–55; Wis 13–15; Acts 12:21–23; Rom 1:18–32). What they witnessed throughout the ancient world were gods *and* kings, even kings *as* gods, revered in temples. They were convinced their Roman neighbors "deified" their emperors. They used names for the emperors like "god" or *divi filius,* "son of God," as Octavian (Caesar Augustus) did because his father Julius Caesar was exalted to a position among the gods. For Jews and Christians, however, this was blasphemous. Stories abounded about the emperor Caligula (aka Gaius Caesar Augustus Germanicus!) demanding an image of himself in Jerusalem's temple.[1] The story, exaggerated or not, was the word on the street in John's time, confirming the empire's idolatry.

Participation in idolatry is not always the same for everyone. One can become an idolater by betraying God in worshiping another god, by rebelling against the covenant that God made with his people, by worshiping a god of our own making, representing, imaging, projecting, or imagining, by becoming allegiant to lesser gods like spirits and demons and angels, by worshiping a "strange" god or offering some "strange" form of worship. There is no reason to think that one or only one of these idolatries was in view when John wrote Revelation. Rather, paganism had a rich supply of idolatries, and Babylon encompasses them all.

For Christians there is but one true God—Father, Son, Spirit—and there is but one true Son of God, Jesus. For Rome, *pietas* or piety ran straight from the family hearth into the public piazza and to the shrines and temples and all the way to Rome itself. There was no distinction made between military might, political rulers and emperors, politics, and religion. Empire and religion were woven together into a seamless whole.

To become a dissident living against the grain of the Babylons of our world, Christians need to have eyes to detect the presence of anti-God systems and institutions.

2. Opulent

Babylon luxuriated in opulence, indulgence, entertainment, and games. John tells us that Babylon "was dressed in purple and scarlet, and was glittering with gold, precious stones and pearls" (Rev 17:4). The rich got richer as the poor remained in their crowded, beggarly, and ignored condition. Rome itself was a city of both wealth and squalor, power and powerlessness. Consider,

---

1. Josephus, *Antiquities* 18.261–309; Tacitus, *Histories* 5.9.

for example, the fashionable, over-the-top, Great Gatsby-like banquets of Romans showcasing status that we read about in the famous "Feast of Trimalchio" (see Petronius's *Satyricon*, 26–78). The guests began with a bath of hot steam. With slaves attending and scurrying about to obey their every command and with entertainers singing and playing instruments, the guests at the banquet enjoyed *hors d'oeuvres*, observed or participated in games, and then began to eat succulent, extravagant foods like peahens' eggs. They washed their hands with wine, and then vintage wines were served. Then a dish: ram's-head chickpeas, beef, kidneys and animal testicles, figs, muffins and cakes, fish, crawfish, goose, mullets, and honey. Then a meal of fowl and sow and rabbit and more! It goes on and on, the indulgences running deeper, their desires intoxicated, the stories growing bawdier and the talking louder. Is this a stereotype? Yes. Satire? Yes. Is it similar to Revelation's language? Yes. One of the best ways to communicate the ugliness of opulence is through hyperbole!

Dissidents rightly perceive opulence for what it really is: showy disdain for the normal way of life, followed by the rest of the population. It is a showcase of rampant indulgence, with lustful desire and conspicuous consumerism on full display. And running right through the heart of it all is a sense of superior status.

3. Murderous

What Rome called *pax Romana*, or the peace of Rome, was really the subjugation of enemies through violent conquer or surrender. To be emperor over a large empire, one needed the chops of military victories, and the more impressive the enemy, the more status accrued to the emperor. Emperors with less than impressive victories magnified puny military conquests to establish their own glory. Adrian Goldsworthy specializes in the study of the so-called *pax Romana*, and here is his description of it:

> Precision is impossible, but we can confidently state that over the centuries millions died in the course of the wars fought by

Rome, millions more were enslaved, and still more would live under Roman rule whether they liked it or not. The Romans were imperialists.

Writing Rome's history means composing a history of war. The way of Rome was to inspire fear through murder and terror. In John's terms, "The woman [Babylon, Rome] was drunk with the blood of God's holy people, the blood of those who bore testimony to Jesus" (Rev 17:6). Even during John's time there was enough opposition to the Christians that some in western Asia Minor were killed for speaking up and speaking out for Jesus. A man named "Antipas," John tells the church in Pergamum, "was put to death in your city" (2:13). In one of John's many interludes (more on these later) we are told there was an innumerable host from across the world who had "washed their robes and made them white in the blood of the Lamb" (7:14)—these individuals were put to death for their witness to Jesus as the world's true Lord. They were dissident disciples, now deceased.

Dissidents of Babylon discern attempts to scatter the ashes of death over anyone and anything that dares to resist.

4. Image

By all accounts Babylon impressed the watching world with its strategies, engineers, and architecturally brilliant temples, palaces, buildings, theaters, and sporting spectacles. Roads and aqueducts crisscrossed the empire. Marble-shaped-images were everywhere. The monumental buildings testified to the impressive glory of Rome, its victories, and its leaders.[2] Those who saw the power and glory and reach of Babylon (=Rome) were stunned—everyone except the dissidents, the oppressed, the slaves, those captured, and the poor. In other words, most everyone! John makes this very point when he says that humans were "astonished" (17:8).

---

2. You can see a theoretical (and impressive) reconstruction of ancient Rome at this website: https://www.romereborn.org/. I admit to getting lost in wonder at this website every time I visit.

That's exactly what Babylon wanted (and has always wanted)—to be an object of awe, astonishment, and praise.

Babylon continues its efforts through many today who spend their time cultivating an image and a persona. They construct platforms on which they perform with their cultured persona so others will adore them. They live into a self-created image instead of the image of God in Christ. Dissidents of Babylon learn to discern and resist the intoxicating allure of cultivating image and persona.

5. Militaristic

Rome accumulated all it had through military might and power. Rome tellingly rejected the use of "king" (*rex*) for its premier leader, instead preferring the title "emperor," a translation of *imperator*, referring to military commanders. The ruler of Rome was the most powerful man in the world, and as the world's mightiest man he was a militarist. On each coin was the emperor's bust, often with a laurel wreath, the symbol of a military victory. In Revelation 17:13 we read that the kings of the world "will give their power and authority to the beast." It didn't take much imagination for John's readers in the seven churches to know this truth: Rome was the center of the world, had the blessing of the gods, and the glory of the people—and it had all these things because of its ruthless power and relentless strategy.

Galgacus, a Caledonian [British] chief, speaking of the Roman army and its ruthlessness, calls them the "robbers of the world" and says, "To robbery, slaughter, plunder, they give the lying name of empire" and they call it "solitude" and "peace."[3] Closer to the time of the book of Revelation, and no doubt lingering in the memory of John himself, is what the Jewish historian Josephus said about Vespasian after his victory over Jews along the Sea of Galilee. Some wanted the whole lot of Jews killed on the spot.

---

3. From Tacitus, *Agricola* 30.14, in Everyman's Library; A. J. Church, W. J. Brodribb.

Vespasian hesitated, then marched south to Tiberias, trapped the Jews, moved them to the stadium, and this is what happened:

> [Vespasian] then gave orders for the execution of the old and unserviceable, to the number of twelve hundred; from the youths he selected six thousand of the most robust and sent them to Nero at the isthmus [at Corinth, as slave labor]. The rest of the multitude, numbering thirty thousand four hundred, he sold, excepting those of whom he made a present to Agrippa . . . and the king in his turn sold them. (*B.J.* 3.532–542, quoting 539–541)

This is but a foretaste of the violence of Titus against Jerusalem in the siege of AD 70. He broke apart all he could (including the temple), burned all he could, and killed all he could (Josephus, never afraid of exaggeration, estimated more than a million deaths), and he did so with as much blood and gore as a Roman army could muster. The Romans mopped up their victory at Masada.

All of this is fresh in the memory bank of John as he describes Babylon and its military might. This background puts the words of Revelation 18:13 in bold face: "human beings sold as slaves." The Greek text has "bodies, the life-forces of humans." Slavery is about owning and exploiting bodies involuntarily. Dissidents discern in the exploitations of other humans—whether man, woman, or child—a mark of Babylon.

6. Economically Exploitative

Rome, aka Babylon, aggregated, accumulated, exploited, taxed, and traded—and this was a daily experience throughout the empire. Mosaics in Pompeii show that on the houses you could read on the floor "Hello Profit!" or "Profit is Happiness!" The poor resented the wealthy as much, if not more, in western Asia Minor as they did anywhere else, and the poor agitated for redistribution. The blistering criticisms of Revelation 18 then fit quite well with the social conditions of the time. The injustices of exploitation simmered just below the surface of Roman society.

There are several indicators of Babylon's economic exploitation in John's words: "The merchants of the earth," he says, "grew rich from her excessive luxuries" (18:3). Rome's party spirit was an unstoppable, unsatisfying treadmill of desire and indulgence craving a never-ending demand for titillating supplies. The trade market, known from other writers of the time like Strabo and Pliny (*Natural History*), was extensive. The Mediterranean Sea today is filled with sunken ships that didn't deliver, and we read about new discoveries every year.

Closer to home, one of the main routes for trade was the Great Trunk Road, which passed by the home of the traditional author of Revelation, the apostle John, in Galilee. The writer, whomever he was, probably knew the luxuriant items on this list from childhood. In Revelation 18:11–13, reformatted here, the list typifies Roman trade at the time:

> The merchants of the earth will weep and mourn over her
>   because no one buys their cargoes anymore—
> cargoes of gold, silver, precious stones and pearls;
> fine linen, purple, silk and scarlet cloth;
> every sort of citron wood,
> and articles of every kind made of ivory, costly wood, bronze,
>   iron and marble;
> cargoes of cinnamon and spice,
> of incense, myrrh and frankincense,
> of wine and olive oil,
> of fine flour and wheat;
> cattle and sheep;
> horses and carriages;
> and human beings sold as slaves.

One writer even quipped that you could travel the world to see what it has to offer or you could go to Rome and see it all there. The merchants sold what Babylon was buying with a ceaseless flow toward Rome. Dissidents today are also attuned to recognize the excesses of economic exploitation and consumerism.

The Rulers of Rome

The Republic (50 BC–14 AD)
Julius Caesar
Augustus, or Octavian

The Julio-Claudians (14–68 AD)
Tiberius
Gaius (Caligula)
Claudius
Nero

The Year of the Four Emperors (69 AD)
Galba
Otho
Vitellius
Vespasian (see below under "Flavians")

Flavians (69–96 AD)
Vespasian
Titus
Domitian

---

7. Arrogant

The previous six signs of Babylon could all be rolled up into this one. Rome turned its arrogance into a virtue. "In her heart," John knows by discernment, "she boasts, 'I sit enthroned as queen. I am not a widow; I will never mourn'" (Rev 18:7). The Old Testament prophet Isaiah says nearly the same thing about the original Babylon: "You said, 'I am forever—the eternal queen!'" (Isa 47:7); and she said "I am [that's blasphemy in the highest], and there is none besides me. I will never be a widow or suffer the loss of children" (47:8). Arrogance begins at the top of the empire, or rather, the system rewards the arrogant and lines up everyone else in a hierarchy of status.

At the end of his life the emperor Augustus wrote up his accomplishments and someone inscribed them in front of his mausoleum (the original has unfortunately not survived.) His account, called in Latin *Res Gestae Divi Augusti*, or "The Acts of the Divine Augustus," put on record the arrogance of the empire. Of his thirty-four sections, we will cite just one. This first selection trots out his military successes, his parading of victims from his victories and public honors, always omitting the violence, bloodshed, and savagery:[4]

> Twice I have celebrated triumphal ovations and three times I have driven triumphal chariots and I have been hailed twenty-one times as victorious general, although the senate voted me more triumphs, from all of which I abstained. I deposited the laurel from my *fasces* [rods of office] in the Capitoline temple, in fulfillment of the vows which I had taken in each war. On account of affairs successfully accomplished by land and sea by me or through my deputies under my auspices the senate fifty-five times decreed that thanksgiving should be offered to the immortal gods. Moreover the days during which thanksgiving has been offered by decree of the senate have amounted to 890. In my triumphs nine kings or kings' children have been led in front of my chariot. I had been consul thirteen times at the time of writing, and I was the holder of tribunician power thirty-seven times [AD 14]. (*Res Gestae* 4.1–4)

This boasting falls directly opposite the cross of Jesus and his way of life. Jesus's victory came by means of a hideous crucifixion—the way of the Lamb. Augustus exposes for all to see the way of the dragon—*self-adulation, human accomplishment,*

---

4. All translations are of the Latin text by Alison E. Cooley, *Res Gestae Divi Augusti: Text, Translation, and Commentary* (Cambridge: Cambridge University Press, 2009).

and false humility. His rule and way of life exist through power, through violence, through murder, and through the exploitation of others for the sake of indulgence and opulence.

By Augustus's own design, there is nothing precious about his family, nothing to be said about morals or character. Instead, all that matters is his mighty power, his annexation of other countries' land and produce, his undeniable benevolence (or redistribution), and the display of marble in a new Roman forum. This is the naked ego of one man on full display, yet at the same time it is representative of the ego culture of Rome and its empire. Dissident disciples will learn to discern all forms of narcissistic arrogance.

Summary

If we had to choose a single term for Babylon, we'd focus on the militaristic drive to conquer and select the term "domination." Domination unto death is the way of the dragon. In fact, a later emperor, Diocletian, required his subjects to call him *dominus*, and some historians refer to a transition with Diocletian changing from an "empire" to a system called "dominate." Domination bundles all the signs of Babylon into one:

Anti-God
Opulent
Murderous
Image
Militaristic
Economically exploitative
Arrogant

When John calls the seven churches to exit or "come out" of Rome (Rev 18:4), he's pressing against this status system.

These are the signs of Babylon that come to the surface in Revelation 17–18. And while we can discover more of these signs in the series of judgments found in chapters 6–16, these remain the primary "character traits" of Babylon, whom John calls "the great prostitute." These set the tone for how Babylon penetrated the seven churches, and we should reflect on how they continue to be expressed in churches today.

Remember, dissidents discern Babylon—they develop a *Babylonian hermeneutic.*

In truth, Babylon today is not all that different from John's own Babylon, and later in this book we will take a closer look at how to discern Babylon today.

CHAPTER 6

The Dragon
and Its Wild Things

Babylon presents itself as the powerful order of strength, but behind Babylon are the dragon and the wild things. We've offered a brief introduction to each of these characters in the playbill, but here we want to unpack that further. Babylon, in short, is the *systemic order of power* created by the dragon and the wild things.

The dragon enters Revelation 12 to attack a woman with a son, and that son is none other than Jesus, God's Son. No good reading of Revelation will ignore the dragon as *the* sinister force behind evil, the one who attacks the son of the woman. In John's Old Testament, the dragon was a symbol for the monstrous, hostile powers that oppose God (Jer 51:34; Ezek 29:3; 32:2–3), and the book of Revelation will explicitly identify the dragon as Satan (Rev 12:9; cf. 2:9, 13, 24; 20:2, 7). This includes Genesis 3's serpent, and as the Bible rolls onward, Leviathan and Beelzebul and other demons that serve as henchmen for the dragon. John will also call the dragon the "devil" (12:9; cf. 2:10; 20:2, 10). In bringing the dragon on the stage, John wanted our imaginations fired with all sorts of ideas about the shadow side of God's good creation. He wants his hearers to envision a cosmic battle between good and evil, between God and the dragon.

Notice that John calls the vision of the dragon a "sign," and the sign is "in heaven" (Rev 12:1). He describes a great fire-red sea dragon. Like Babylon in chapter 17, the dragon has seven heads and ten horns and seven crowns. Its tail is so big that it sweeps a third of the stars, which is probably John's language for political rulers (or perhaps fallen angels of heaven or the saints), and they are flung down to the earth. The dragon's mission is clear: *it wants the woman's baby boy, the Son of God who is to rule, and it wants the Son dead.*

The war is on between *Team Dragon* and *Team Lamb.*

Notice the astounding opening in Revelation 12:7: there is a war in heaven! One can't read that and not think of John Milton's battles in *Paradise Lost*, or those of J. R. R. Tolkien or C. S. Lewis between good and evil. This is the stuff of the world's great stories and myths. The dragon goes toe to toe with Michael and his army of angels, and the dragon is defeated in heaven (12:8). John often interrupts readers and hearers with callouts from the deep reality of heaven, and this time he announces through "a loud voice in heaven" that the dragon, "the accuser of our brothers and sisters" (12:10), has been tossed from the divine courtroom and its day of accusations are over. But that heavenly defeat spells problems for the earth because God now hurls the dragon to the earth.

The dragon immediately prowls for the woman, but with God on her side she is protected from the dragon's gushing stream of water, his attempt to drown her. God rescues the woman, and the dragon loses this battle too. This should remind us of the words of Genesis 3:15:

> And I will put enmity
> > between you and the woman,
> > and between your offspring and hers;

> *For those who were sorely tempted to make their peace with Rome, Revelation unveiled truth about empire. It revealed empire as both a seductive whore who offered the good life in exchange for obedience and a ravenous beast that devoured any who would dare oppose it.*
>
> —Wes Howard-Brook and Anthony Gwyther, *Unveiling Empire*, xxii

> he will crush your head,
>   and you will strike his heel.

The escape of the woman strikes the heel of the dragon-serpent, so the dragon turns to attack a third enemy: the faithful of "her offspring." These are those who observe the commandments of God and hold to the witness of Jesus (12:17).

All seven characteristics of Babylon in the previous chapter dramatize the deathly realities of the work of the dragon and the wild things. That last verse we cited, Revelation 12:17, speaks of going to war with the offspring of the woman. The seven characteristics of Babylon manifest the *way of the dragon*, which battles against the *way of the Lamb*. One can't read Revelation well without embracing the cosmic, even mythic, battle between Team Dragon and Team Lamb.

Dissident disciples are the first to realize they are in a battle—not with flesh and blood, but with the principalities and powers that snake their way into the seven churches. Some readers of Revelation, however, turn Revelation 12 into little more than a symbolic battle between abstract good and abstract evil. But the dragon can't be reduced to a *symbol* of evil. The dragon is the ultimate *agent* of evil. Cities matter, politics matter, and governments matter; and Babylon is the public face of the dragon's dominating power. But how does this happen? The dragon works its evil way into the land through the wild things of Revelation 13.

The Wild Things: #1 and #2

One of the biggest mistakes we can make in reading Revelation is spending too much time speculating on the precise predictive identity of the wild thing (or the antichrist; see appendix 3), the mask of the dragon. Who will it be? Luther and Calvin thought it was the pope, as have many zealot Protestants since (and some still today). When I was in college, I (Scot) read a book that proclaimed with certainty it was Mikhail Gorbachev, and his birthmark excited much speculation. Others thought it was Henry Kissinger, and then it was Saddam Hussein. These speculators were all wrong, and they've all been wrong because they lack the kind of imagination a faithful reading of Revelation requires, wanting to reduce everything to literal predictions. But as we have seen, we should not look for one, single end-time wild thing. Instead, dissident disciples should discern the dragon behind the wild things of every age, including our own day. We are not looking for figures by predicting specific persons in the future; rather, we are looking for images of dragon-like leaders at work in all societies and all times. They are puppets, whose strings are pulled by the dragon. Remember, *these images are not about predicting the future, but about shaping our perceptions of the present.*

There are two wild things in Revelation 13, one from the sea and one from the earth. Wild thing #1 emerges from the sea, a picture of chaos and the ancient abyss (see 11:7). Wild thing #1 is all about *power* while wild thing #2 is about *propaganda.* Both of them do their work behind closed doors in the dragon's Babylon, creating a propaganda machine to control and dominate. Participants on Team Dragon include the famous enumerated figure, 666, and corrupted leaders in the church, whom John refers to using names like "Jezebel" and the "the Nicolaitans." We do not dismiss these characters, but the focus of the book of Revelation falls on the dragon and his masked bandits, the two wild things.

666

Many readers of Revelation today get snagged in the 666 web of speculation (Rev 13:16–18), wondering what such a number means, how numbers like this worked in John's world, and to whom 666 might apply today. The NIV's number "666" at Revelation 13:18 in Greek reads "the number is six hundred sixty-six." It's wise to begin with the undeniable: if 777 is triple perfection, 666 is triple imperfection or falling short. It is the number of a human (vs. God). In Greek there were no numbers; letters were used both as letters and numbers (think of how Latin writes its numbers, what we today call "Roman numerals"). That number in Greek would be *chi/xi/sigma* (χξϲ). Letters easily became numbers and the art of turning them into numbers is called "gematria." So 666 is the numerical value of three letters. This means the reader is encouraged to play with the numbers to find something suitable, usually a name. *Who will it be?* is not the right question to ask, though. Rather, we should ask *Who was it for John?* and *Who might it be for us?*

To begin, we go back to the time when the Book of Revelation was written. Nero Caesar, in Greek *Nerōn kaisar*, adds up to 666 when translated into Hebrew: 50+200+6+50+100+60+200 = 666! Some manuscripts of Revelation here do not have the number 666 but instead 616, and if one drops off the second "n" in *Nerōn* that name then totals 616! So it seems clear that 666 is gematria for emperor Nero. But Nero is not alone in satisfying such a calculation, because 666 is also the numerical value of the word *thērion*, which is the Greek word for "beast" or "wild thing." This was likely all great fun for the first readers of Revelation.

Calling someone 666 requires imagination—as well as flexibility. That number can be used for any of the anti-God beastly powers that design strategies for death and destruction. Like Babylon, 666 does not point to one person at one future moment in history but to all political tyrants who have the powers to establish the way of the dragon and oppress Team Lamb.

But what about the "mark"? Just what the "mark" (*charagma*) was physically is now hard to know (Rev 13:16), but it is something placed, like the law of God referred to in Deuteronomy 6:8, on both the right hand and the forehead. That mark also permits commercial transactions (Rev 13:17)—and it obviously represents allegiance to 666. The mark could be a branding, like coins stamped with the image of the emperor, or it could be more metaphorical than physical. Regardless, the mark seems to be a parody of the seal of the living God (7:2–3; 14:1) and to function, as David deSilva says it, as "the beast's stamp of approval, [which] provides access to participation in the Roman economy and the enjoyment of physical security."

So that's Team Dragon. Team Dragon dwells in Babylon, plotting the destruction of the Lamb and his followers—Team Lamb. This team is headed for the new Jerusalem, and that's where we turn in the next chapter.

CHAPTER 7

———

The Lamb

The believers to whom Revelation was originally written lived in Babylon—that is, the Roman Empire. Their entire lives—bodies, minds, and spirits—were swamped by Babylon. Those believers become faithful witnesses to Jesus as Lord by following the Lamb *as residents in Babylon.* And faithful discipleship, a life that mirrors Christ, who is the Lamb, is still about being a witness to Jesus as a resident in this world. Discipleship is about Lamb-like living. Thomas B. Slater, one of our favorite writers on Revelation, says this perfectly: "Just as the slain Lamb has replaced the Lion of Judah" so also "witnessing faithfully even unto death has replaced making war for the Apocalypse."

For John, the ultimate image of discipleship is found in chapter 14. Here we have a vision of a group with a number: 144,000, which is twelve times twelve thousand, another of John's perfect numbers. No one has a better epitaph than this group: "They follow the Lamb wherever he goes" (14:4). They perfect their verbal witness because they speak up and speak out for the Lamb amid life in Babylon. A similar expression is given to those connected to the white horse and its rider in chapter 19 (the rider's got to be Jesus): his robe has been dipped in blood and his name is the Word, or Logos, of God. The rider is accompanied by the "armies of heaven" who are "*following* him" (19:14). This term, *following*, is used in the Gospels for the disciples as well. The faithful follow

Jesus in the way of the Lamb—into a witness that can lead to suffering and even death, and into the way of victory over those who oppose the Lamb.

Too much interpretation of Revelation speculates about the antichrist or such newsy items as the rebirth of the nation of Israel. Because speculation drives interest (and sales!) such interpreters silence the magnificent images of Jesus and how those images should form our teaching and discipleship. Instead of forming a Lamb-shaped discipleship that discerns how to live amid a timeless Babylon, this speculation generates specialized knowledge about the future and encourages people to spend time looking for a cloud-rider in the skies.

But if discipleship is really about following the Lamb, what are the characteristics of the Lamb that we are to follow? John gives us a multifaceted depiction of Jesus in the book of Revelation, and he is the one whom disciples are to follow by resisting Babylon.

Colors in Revelation

White: purity, God's presence, victory
Red: blood and violence
Purple: royalty, but especially corrupted powers
Black: death
Green: death

Seven Plus Terms for Jesus

A collage of seven or more terms for Jesus (numbered in what follows) is found in the opening chapter of the book of Revelation. Here are the first three words of this book, translated literally as "revelation Jesus Christ," and "Jesus Christ" means

[1] Jesus
[2] the Messiah, or "King Jesus."

These are the first and second terms John uses for Jesus. The NIV's "from" in "the revelation *from* Jesus Christ" is an unnecessary interpretive move. It's simpler to translate the "revelation of Jesus Christ" or even the "Jesus Christ revelation." Is this apocalypse from Jesus? *Yes.* Is the whole book about Jesus? *Yes.* Is this a Jesus-Christ kind of apocalypse? *Yes.* John may have avoided precision so we could see all three of these and perhaps even more! But as Revelation moves along, we will see that the entire book for John is a "testimony *about* Jesus Christ" (1:2). Besides knowing that "Jesus" is "king," who then is this King Jesus in the opening chapter? He is the

[3] faithful witness,
[4] the firstborn from the dead, and
[5] the ruler of the kings of the earth!

That's who John tells us he is in 1:5. Jesus is the One

[6] who loves us and
[7] has freed us from our sins by his blood,
and has made us to be a kingdom and priests to serve his God and Father, and this Jesus is to be glorified eternally. (1:5–6)

Then Jesus is the one who says that he is the

[8] Alpha and Omega,
[9] who is, and who was, and who is to come,
[10] the Almighty. (1:8)

Pause with us for a moment. While we don't know with certainly who the author of Revelation may have been, if it was John, the son of Zebedee, who was with Jesus from the beginning, and if John had to be convinced that the charismatic man from little ol' Nazareth was more than a typical Jewish teacher, that he was in fact the Messiah of Israel—and if John saw him, walked with him, listened to him, was with him until he was crucified, and saw him after he was raised, it still takes some imagination to believe that the man in sandals from Nazareth is all this and more! We are only through the first eight verses of this book, and already Jesus fills a theological textbook with ideas and concepts about his identity and mission!

"On the Lord's Day" (1:10), which may well indicate Sunday, John is in exile on Patmos because he spoke up and about Jesus in the midst of "Babylon." Behind him he hears a great trumpet-like voice. He turns, and what he sees must be read in its entirety if we are to fully grasp the Jesus he wants us to meet in this book:

> I turned around to see the voice that was speaking to me. And when I turned I saw seven golden lampstands, and among the lampstands was [11] someone like a son of man, dressed in a robe reaching down to his feet and with a golden sash around his chest. The hair on his head was white like wool, as white as snow, and his eyes were like blazing fire. His feet were like bronze glowing in a furnace, and his voice was like the sound of rushing waters. In his right hand he held seven stars, and coming out of his mouth was a sharp, double-edged sword. His face was like the sun shining in all its brilliance.
>
> When I saw him, I fell at his feet as though dead. Then he placed his right hand on me and said: "Do not be afraid. I am the [12] First and the Last. I am the [13] Living One; I was dead, and now look, I am alive for ever and ever! And [14] I hold the keys of death and Hades. (1:12–18)

We now have four additional terms for Jesus, making a total of fourteen in this opening chapter. Because of the density of focus on *who* Jesus is, the first three words of this book must be translated as *about* King Jesus. In other words, the book of Revelation is first and foremost a revelation *about* Jesus. Ian Paul describes this first chapter as "a breathless account in which the images tumble out on top of one another in a kaleidoscope of color and sensation which threaten to overwhelm us." He says these images bring together terms found in Exodus, Daniel 7 and 10, and from pagan deities as well. It not only takes imagination to read Revelation well. It takes time, turning back in our Bibles to the prophets of the Old Testament, if we wish to capture the fullness of John's images.

John's Jesus is altogether splendorous. And again, his words are soaked in Old Testament imagery: a long, priest-like robe with a golden sash, snow-white hair like Daniel 7, eyes of fire and glowing feet like Daniel 10, and a resonant, reverberating voice like Ezekiel 1. He's in the midst of seven golden lampstands and holds seven stars and has a double-edged sword proceeding from his mouth like we see in Isaiah 49. His face has the brilliance of the sun like Moses in Exodus 34.[1]

What John sees and the words he uses to describe his vision combine to turn the reader's imagination back to the Old Testament prophet Daniel and his famous son of man vision. Location matters, and we should note that Jesus the Son of Man is in the middle of the churches. Nothing could be more important for Christian witness than knowing this: *he's in the middle of the assemblies called by his name.* He stands there in full glory as the one raised from the dead. What these believers and churches face in opposition to their witness will not be tolerated as the final word. The final word will be his: "I hold the keys of death and Hades" (1:18). The Lord of the churches is the Lord of life and death. How to summarize all this? We can say that Jesus is *indescribable with any one set of images.* It takes the whole Bible for John to communicate the fullness, splendor, and glory of Jesus he saw on the Lord's Day. We will start by summarizing the terms he has given to us into the following major identities of Jesus in Revelation.

---

1. For specifics, see Isa 11:4; 49:2; Ezek 1:13, 24–27; 9:1–11; Dan 7:9–10, 13–14; 10:5–10; Zech 4:1–14.

The Lord

Because of the flow of this book, we need to always keep our eyes on what John said in 1:5: Jesus is "the ruler [*archōn*] of the kings of the earth." He is, in other words, the Lord of lords. Living into this requires both a comic and cosmic imagination, especially for those living outnumbered as allegiant witnesses to Jesus. In today's terms, you might hear an echo of someone in these churches yelling out "Booyah!"

John uses the images from the vision he saw of Jesus in chapter 1 when he begins each letter to the seven churches:

These are the words of him who holds the seven stars in his right hand and walks among the seven golden lampstands. (2:1)

These are the words of him who is the First and the Last, who died and came to life again. (2:8)

These are the words of him who has the sharp, double-edged sword. (2:12)

These are the words of the Son of God, whose eyes are like blazing fire and whose feet are like burnished bronze. (2:18)

These are the words of him who holds the seven spirits of God and the seven stars. (3:1)

These are the words of him who is holy and true, who holds the key of David. What he opens no one can shut, and what he shuts no one can open. (3:7)

These are the words of the Amen, the faithful and true witness, the ruler of God's creation. (3:14)

John is saying that Jesus is there with them, alive and speaking, and they should hear him speaking as the one true ruler of the world, the Lord of lords! They should declare allegiance to him, walk in the way of the Lamb, and resist the dragon by refusing to walk in the way of Babylon.

Pause with us one more time: what strikes the reader of Revelation 1 is not speculation about *who will be whom, who will do what,* in *which nation,* and *at what date.* What strikes the reader is the overwhelming majesty of Jesus, God's Son, the Messiah, the King of kings and the world's only true Emperor of emperors. The followers of the Lamb hearing this book performed are over the moon in joyous rapture at the prospect of a world run by Jesus—a world John calls the new Jerusalem. This Jesus is the one who calls people to follow him by resisting the lords of Rome and walking in the way of the Lord of lords.

The Lion

The vision of John shifts from Jesus to the churches in chapters 1, 2, and 3, and then to the Throne-God in chapter 4, and then back to Jesus all over again in chapter 5. But in chapter five the lordly images describing Jesus in Revelation 1–3 morph from a Lion into the Lamb. We'll start with the Lion. In the Throne-God's right hand is a scroll with writing on both sides, glued tight with seven wax seals. This image of a sealed scroll begging to be read has a history in Israel. In Isaiah 29:11–12 we read,

> For you this whole vision is nothing but words sealed in a scroll. And if you give the scroll to someone who can read, and say, "Read this, please," they will answer, "I can't; it is sealed." Or if you give the scroll to someone who cannot read, and say, "Read this, please," they will answer, "I don't know how to read."

Some of those listening to this in the seven churches may have thought of Isaiah when John describes this similar scene. But here something new happens. Will there be someone who can open this new scroll, someone who can read this scroll?

We see a "mighty angel" who asks this colossal question with intense desire and anxiety, a question that had no answer in Isaiah's day, but can now be asked and answered: "Who is worthy to break the seals and open the scroll?" (5:2). The answer comes quickly: "No one in heaven or on earth or under the earth" was worthy (5:3). And just like Isaiah, John wept. But John's tears are about to be dried up with a surprise. "One of the elders" from the previous scene (4:4) says the magical words:

> See, the Lion of the tribe of Judah, the Root of David, has triumphed. He is able to open the scroll and its seven seals. (5:5)

Joseph's famous blessing to Judah in Genesis 49:8–12 refers to Judah and his descendants as a "lion's cub," and this is given new life here alongside Isaiah 11:2's royal image of the Root of David. The covenant pattern of the Old Testament is fulfilled in the line of David—who will, like a lion, capture and rule the nations. Victory is to be found in the One who deserves to crack the seals of this little scroll.

A lion is the image of someone who is lordly. It's easy to follow a lordly lion. No one messes with a lion. Get behind one, follow one, and the lordly lion paves the path forward. To be a disciple of Jesus means following this lordly Lion, but there's more than his lordliness in the mix of images about Jesus here.

The Lamb

Something odd happens in chapter 5 that transforms the message of the book of Revelation. One of the elders informs John that only the Lion of the tribe of Judah, the Root of David, had triumphed and so only he can crack open the scroll (perhaps "little scroll"). John wants us to see with the eyes of our imagination again—to picture the Lion romping forward to grab hold of the scroll. But no, that's not how it happens. Instead, there is a morphing, a transformation: "Then I saw a *Lamb*, looking as if it had been slain, standing at the center of the throne" (5:6, italics added). G. B. Caird highlights the reversal: "What John *hears* is couched in the traditional messianic imagery of the Old Testament; what he *sees* constitutes the most impressive rebirth of images he anywhere achieves." The Lion becomes the Lamb. And it is a bizarre lamb, with three sevens: "seven horns and seven eyes, which are the seven spirits of God sent out into all the earth" (5:6). The Lamb "took the scroll from the right hand" of God (5:7). Then two groups (four living creatures and twenty-four elders) erupt into worship of the Lamb.

Why the transformation? It's easy to follow a fierce lion, but who wants to follow a lamb? The Lamb, they sing, is *worthy*, not because he headbutted someone off the stage. No, he is worthy because he was slain, and by being slain, the Lamb "purchased" a universal people of God, and they—not Babylon's lords—will be a "kingdom and priests to serve our God." What's more, the Lamb's followers "will reign on the earth" (5:10). The Lord of Revelation 1:5, you will remember, is the "ruler of the kings of the earth." That Lord, that Lion, *is* the Lamb. The four living creatures and twenty-four elders with innumerable angels along with "every creature" in all creation praise the Lamb. The original two groups then close the worship service down with a responsive "Amen!" (5:14). And this is not the only time the throne room's choir praises the Lamb (cf. 7:10; 14:1, 4; 15:3).

Pause for a moment here. Again, we have found that too many readings of Revelation know the Lion is the Lamb, *but then they ignore the significance of the Lamb in the book of Revelation.* Their Lamb is really a Lion who wins with a sword in his fist in a noisy, bloody battle at Armageddon. Their Christology distorts the book, because they are driven by speculations about *when this will happen, where it will happen,* and *who will be the antichrist.* The Lion is a Lamb who wins (as we are about to see) not with a sword in a bloody battle but with a nonviolent weapon, namely the Word of God. John presents us, as Bruce Metzger once wrote, with the "choice between the power that operates through inflicting suffering, that is, the power of the beast, and the power that operates through accepting suffering, namely, the power of the Lamb."

The morphing continues as the lordly images of Jesus in

Revelation 1–3 applied to the Lion are now applied to the Lamb in chapter 5, but there is a new morph here that deserves even more attention. The Lamb John sees has been slain or slaughtered. Let's dwell on this. Being slain is used of Jesus four times in Revelation (5:6, 9, 12; 13:8). But what does it mean to say that the Lamb was a slain lamb? Remember how we morphed from a fierce, powerful, death-dealing Lion to a vulnerable, defenseless Lamb? Many of us think instinctually of Isaiah 53:7's words: "He was led like a lamb to the slaughter, and as a sheep before its shearers is silent, so he did not open his mouth." Biblical imaginations think like that. But lambs had other connotations in the Bible-reading world, and the Passover lamb of Exodus 12:6 also comes to mind, a slaughtered lamb that liberated the children of Israel from Egypt. Notice that in Revelation 1:5 Jesus "has freed us from our sins by his blood." This slaughtered lamb evokes *both* the Passover liberation *and* the forgiveness of sin. And that's how artists operate. *They evoke, they don't define.* If they want to tell us something *particular,* they do. But if they want us to use our minds and imaginations, they paint something for us and then ask us, "What do you see?" Note that there is a difference between evocation and instruction, and John utilizes the former.

Two more observations about the slaughtered Lamb. Jesus's way of life, the Lion-Lamb way of life, forms the paradigm for his followers, so it comes as no surprise that followers of Jesus are *also* slain or slaughtered. Notice these two verses:

When he opened the fifth seal, I saw under the altar the souls of those who had been slain because of the word of God and the testimony they had maintained. (6:9)

In her [Babylon] was found the blood of prophets and of God's holy people, of all who have been slaughtered on the earth. (18:24)

Babylon's way is the way of sword and violence. The way of the Lamb is to speak up and about Jesus in the midst of Babylon, come what may. What may come is the Lamb's way of ultimate witness: *martyrdom*. The Lamb wages war, not with a sword in his fist, but with a sword coming from his mouth and with a life that embodies resistance to the lords of Babylon.

Along with this, we would also point out that at times in the book of Revelation, the dragon and the wild things try to *imitate* the Lamb. In 13:3 we read that the wild thing from the sea had seven heads and that one of the heads "seemed to have a fatal wound." But the NIV translation fails to lead readers to the connection John is making here. You could also translate this by saying "one of its heads" appeared to be "slain to death," as it is the same word used to describe the Lamb in Revelation 5. The wild thing is the biggest copycat of all, aiming to appear as *Lamb-like* as possible, even faking the very act of Jesus: *dying for others and coming back to life.* John depicts a cosmic battle by his careful choice of terms, implying that the slaughtered Lamb and the slaughtered witnesses to the Lamb are being copied by the slaughtered wild thing! In this, John yearns for the seven churches to become more aware of the fraudulence of idolatry.

The Logos

John's Jewish contemporaries prayed and memorized the book of Psalms as their prayer book. Words from Psalm 44 formed in the memories of God's people a picture of God as warrior and Israel's "victories" coming not because of their own power or swords but from God. There are several expressions that help us see this as we read Revelation:

> We have heard it with our ears, O God;
>> our ancestors have told us
> *what you did* in their days,
>> in days long ago.
> *With your hand you drove out the nations*
>> *and planted our ancestors;*
> *you crushed the peoples*

and made our ancestors flourish.
It was not by their sword that they won the land,
nor did their arm bring them victory;
it was your right hand, your arm,
and the light of your face, for you loved them.

You are my King and my God,
who decrees victories for Jacob.
Through you we push back our enemies;
through your name we trample our foes.
I put no trust in my bow,
my sword does not bring me victory;
but you give us victory over our enemies,
you put our adversaries to shame. (Ps 44:1–7)

If this is how you were taught to pray, you probably won't stumble over the language of military victory in Revelation or insist on a literal bloody battle in a massive valley with blood flowing up to the horses' noses and filling their nostrils. Sensitive readers will spot a metaphor when the author uses one!

In Revelation the Lamb wins the war. The splendorous woman of Revelation 12 gives birth to the Son, who will "rule all the nations with an iron scepter" (12:5), an expression that echoes what John told us at the start, that king Jesus would be "the ruler of the kings of the earth" (1:5; cf. Pss 2:9; 89:27–28). That Son is the Lion who is the Lamb. But there's something profoundly disruptive about the Lamb's weapon.

In this book, there are three cycles of seven judgments: the seals, the trumpets, and the shallow bowls. Their graphic images are the stuff of apocalyptic fictional battles. Jews knew these images from their prophets and John makes use of them as the judgments come cascading down from God. There is a gruesome battle with a paradox: the "deaths" at the hand of the Lamb are by the Word, the Logos, and not by a sword in the king's fist.

And here's why. The way of the Lamb is not the way of Babylon and its dragon. The latter is the way of power and might, violence and bloodshed, murder and arrogance, and the exploitation of human bodies. In a previous chapter we looked at the militarism of Babylon. Militarism is not the way of the Lamb. Instead, the Lamb wins by *losing*, and his *losing* liberates others. The Lamb liberates by giving his life, and the Lord wins the battle with the Word, the Logos.

Some interpreters of the book of Revelation relish the battle descriptions as literal, physical, military battles with incalculable bloodshed held at a place called Armageddon. When we read such interpreters, we should wonder if their heart has been cauterized. Because while the images of battle in Revelation 6–18 look like physical battles, they are really apocalyptic fictions, images that dance before our eyes and imaginations to tell us that the Lamb will win. And the Bible tells us the Lamb wins *with the Word*. Winners with the Word deconstruct winners with the sword, and they will win at the parousia of Jesus, or his second coming or return (see appendix 4, "Armageddon").

A Summary Passage

There is a key passage that shows us how John works all this out. In Revelation 19:11–16, we find one of John's versions of the second coming, or what scholars call the parousia.

> I saw heaven standing open and there before me was a white horse, whose rider is called Faithful and True. With justice he judges and wages war. His eyes are like blazing fire, and on his head are many crowns. He has a name written on him that no one knows but he himself. He is dressed in a robe dipped in blood, and his name is the Word of God. The armies of heaven were following him, riding on white horses and dressed in fine linen, white and clean. Coming out of his mouth is a sharp sword with which to strike down the nations. "He will rule them with an iron scepter." He treads the winepress of the fury of the wrath of God Almighty. On his robe and on his thigh he has this name written:

KING OF KINGS AND LORD OF LORDS

The Rider is called "Faithful and True," which is what Jesus is called in 3:14: "the faithful and true witness, the ruler of God's creation." Unlike Babylon, who is drunk on the blood of God's people, Jesus will bring justice, as was predicted of the Messiah in Isaiah 11. Like Daniel 10:6 and Revelation 1:14, he has fiery eyes. This image means that he is coming to purge evil from God's creation. He is not wearing "crowns," as the NIV has, but rather "diadems," which are worn as a symbol of kingship. Roman emperors wore wreaths, not diadems, because the former symbolized victory and the latter kingship. The way of the Lamb is not the way of the dragon or Babylon.

From the Faithful and True Rider on the white horse, from the Word of God's mouth comes a "sharp sword" that will "strike down the nations," an image that is also characterized as the "winepress of the fury of the wrath of God Almighty" (19:15, 21). The battle is won by a sword that comes from the mouth of the Lion, the Lamb, the Logos.

The Word is the weapon of the divine white horse Rider.

The Lion is the Lamb, the Word of God, who is the Emperor and Lord over all the earth's lordless lords. He will win and he will reign. There will be a great victory feast, a final judgment, and a splendorous city descending from heaven, the new Jerusalem. Smack-dab in the middle of new Jerusalem is the Lamb and God—they are the sanctuary or temple, where the Lamb will replace the sun and moon, and from God's and the Lamb's throne will flow the river of life's water. The longing for the new heavens and the new earth is the longing for the presence of God with us, for the Son—who morphs and morphs in this book—to come back to earth and undo injustice, defeat evil, and establish the new Jerusalem.

By the Word, not by the sword.

Disciples follow Jesus by waging a battle with evil by the Word of God, even if it means suffering in nonviolent witness. Such disciples are dissident, allegiant witnesses, and they form part of Team Lamb. If the Lord, Lion, and Lamb gains victory by the Logos-sword from his mouth, disciples of the Lamb must also learn to wage their battle by a similar logos, by the witness of their life and lips.

CHAPTER 8

The Faithful Witnesses

The Throne-God wins, the Lord-Lion-Lamb-Logos wins, and
the Seven Spirits win. The dragon and the wild things lose.
The book of Revelation, however, is not just about a spiritual
battle in the heavens, as was sketched out for us in Revelation
12. The apocalypse takes place on earth too, as the battle for
allegiance, truth, and *power.* Babylon and new Jerusalem form the
two encampments while the dragon and the Lamb lead troops of
wild things and faithful witnesses.

The faithful witnesses declare their allegiance to the Lamb and
walk in the way of the Lamb as dissidents of Babylon. Faithful to
the Lamb, they witness to the Lamb, speaking up and speaking out
and sometimes suffering. While we will not cover every reference
(which occupies nearly every page of the book of Revelation), we
will try to identify the various groups of faithful witnesses and
describe each of them briefly. Duke Divinity School professor
Richard Lischer tells the larger story of Revelation when he says
this of John's vision: "I have seen the future, and it belongs to
God." As we have seen before, the book of Revelation has a diverse
cast of characters who, once understood, reveal to readers the full
message John is seeking to communicate.

The Woman

As we saw with the Lord, Lion, and Lamb, there are images that
will morph and shift in Revelation. This is what we see happening

with the woman of Revelation 12. She is first Israel or perhaps Eve, and then she becomes Mary, mother of Jesus, and then she becomes the church. She's one woman, but she's a bricolage of images:

- She's clothed with the sun.
- She's got the moon at her feet.
- She wears a crown of twelve stars (she's now Israel).

"Twelve" evokes Israel's twelve tribes—or perhaps the twelve apostles. Twelve is also connected to the twenty-four elders, the twelve gates, twelve angels, the names of the twelve tribes on the gates, and twelve foundations with the names of the twelve apostles of the new Jerusalem. The number "twelve" is obviously important for John. We also learn that:

- She's pregnant (she's now Mary).
- She's in the agony of giving birth (she's Israel—Isa 26:17–18; Jer 4:31).
- She gives birth to a Son (she's Mary, her baby is Jesus).
- Her son is the Son of God who "will rule the nations" (she's Israel and Mary—Ps 2:9).
- The cosmic dragon wants to kill that Son.
- Her child was raptured (yes, that's the term) to God and the throne.
- She flees into a prepared place in the wilderness (the place for refuge, instruction, and divine discipline—is she now Israel? The church? Or still Mary? Exod 19:4–6; Isa 40:30–31).
- She's protected for three and a half years (or 1,260 days, or a time, times, and half a time, see Dan 7:25; 12:7).
- The dragon hunts the woman to kill her, but the dragon loses.
- The dragon now wages war with her offspring (sounds now like she's the church) (Gen 3:15).

Like a mother, the woman protects her baby boy. And God, like a father, has a protective instinct for this woman. She's a nation and she's a mother and she's the church. She is a faithful witness to Jesus as the one who gave birth to Jesus.

She flees (12:6), and God cares for her. When God hurls the dragon down to earth after the dragon loses the battle of heaven, it goes after the woman. She flies on her wings for protection (12:13–14), perhaps recalling the words of Psalm 55:5–8 and uttering them herself:

> Fear and trembling have beset me;
>> horror has overwhelmed me.
> I said, "Oh, that I had the wings of a dove!
>> I would fly away and be at rest.
> I would flee far away
>> and stay in the desert [wilderness];
> I would hurry to my place of shelter,
>> far from the tempest and storm."

Remembered or not, these words express her desire. So, the dragon gushes at her with a torrent of water, but the earth helps her survive (12:16–17). Losing yet again, the dragon surrenders to the woman and chooses to battle "the rest of her offspring" (12:17). These children of the woman are the faithful witnesses of the seven churches: "Those who keep God's commands and hold fast their testimony about Jesus" (12:17). It's correct to say the woman *is* the faithful of the seven churches. She's a nation and she's a mother and she's the church. She, like the good followers in the seven churches, faithfully and publicly witnesses to Jesus.

It takes a fun-filled imagination to read this woman well. Instead of asking "Is the Woman Eve, Israel, Mary, or the church?" we should be watching her begin as one character and over time become other characters. Only when we do this do we enter the story of the woman. We should let her *be* who John described her to be. Some of those listening to the book of Revelation read in churches of western Asia Minor may have connected these images to the mythologies of their world (see appendix 5, "Ancient Mythologies"). Notice, too, that John thinks of the people of God and the people of the dragon as women—the woman of Revelation 12, the woman of Revelation 17–18, and the bride of Revelation 21.

The Seven Churches

One of the most unfortunate developments among readers and interpreters of Revelation is an approach that treats the seven churches of chapters two and three as a prediction of the history of church. One can find this approach in the (old) *Scofield Bible*, my (Scot's) first Bible, which is still on a bookshelf in my library. In this scheme, Ephesus describes the apostolic church and Smyrna the persecuted church until about AD 312, when Emperor Constantine "embraced" the Christian faith. With Pergamum comes the Constantinian or compromised church, one that combined church and state for three hundred years. Then we encounter in Thyatira a gross stereotype called the worldly medieval church until we finally reach Martin Luther's Reformation in the church at Sardis. The Reformation era churches (of Sardis) last through about the middle of the eighteenth century, followed by Philadelphia, the missionary church of the eighteenth through twentieth-century church, which leads finally to the lukewarm or faithless church of today, Laodicea.

This approach to Revelation distorts the meaning of what John wrote in a number of ways, not least these two. First, these are wildly inaccurate descriptions of the periods themselves. And second, John thinks of these churches as coexisting and contemporary. There is not a shred or scrap of evidence that John sees them as future churches. Everything about Revelation speaks directly to John's own day and how John's churches can live faithfully in Babylon (Rome). The biggest problem with this interpretation also damns the entire approach: it fails to comprehend the historic global church. The red-hot power of God at work in churches in Africa and Asia and South America and Central America is disgracefully unacknowledged by this periodizing scheme of reading the seven churches. And in more recent centuries, there has been a third distortion—namely, that the entire history of the church being imposed on the seven churches is American-centric and reeks of nationalism. What about the history of the church in China or Africa or South America or Australia or India? Let's agree to move on from this deeply mistaken approach.

Jesus, we must recall, looms large in Revelation 1 and in the opening words to each church. There's a basic pattern with his messages starting with affirmations about that church. The Lord, the one standing among the lampstands with searching eyes and piercing judgments, announces the following affirmations (and we italicize the principal terms and provide our own translation):

2:2   I know your *works* and your *labor* and your *resilience* and that you are *unable to carry the bad ones*, and you *tested* the ones who say they are commissioners and are not, and you found them falsifiers, and you have *resilience* and *you carried [the load]* because of my name and have not become labored.

2:9   I know your *trouble* and your *poverty* (but you are wealthy) and the *insult* from the ones saying of themselves they are Jews and are not but are Satan's assembly hall.

2:19   I know your *works* and *love* and *allegiance* and *service* and your *resilience*, and your last *works* are greater than your first.

3:1   I know your *works*, that you have a name that you live, and you are dead.

3:4   But you have a few names in Sardis *who didn't soil their robes* . . .

3:8   I know your *works*. Look! I have given before you an opened door that no one is able to shut because you have *a little power* and you *observed* my word and *didn't deny* my name.

Note that John has nothing good to say about the church of Laodicea. Each church has its own calling, so we would need to probe each in its own context, but our aim here is not to delve into those particulars. Instead, we want to highlight the big idea—which is often missed. What Jesus affirms in the churches can be summarized as a call to be an *allegiant or faithful witness*. The words that occur most often here are "works" and "resilience" (or perseverance, endurance). Being an allegiant witness of enduring works is about the public expression and embodiment of the lordship of King Jesus. These believers are, as it were, prophets in Babylon, Christians living publicly while remaining utterly faithful to Jesus. They walk in the way of the Lamb. They *will* dwell in the new Jerusalem and are *already* living as if they were in the new Jerusalem.

Early Christian Prophets in Revelation

But in the days when the seventh angel is about to sound his trumpet, the mystery of God will be accomplished, just as he announced to his servants the **prophets**. (10:7)

The nations were angry,
 and your wrath has come.
The time has come for judging the dead,
 and for rewarding your servants the **prophets**
and your people who revere your name,
 both great and small—
and for destroying those who destroy the earth. (11:18)

Rejoice over her, you heavens!
 Rejoice, you people of God!
 Rejoice, apostles and **prophets**!
For God has judged her
 with the judgment she imposed on you. (18:20)

> In her was found the blood of **prophets** and of God's holy people,
> of all who have been slaughtered on the earth. (18:24)
>
> The angel said to me, "These words are trustworthy and true. The Lord,
> the God who inspires the **prophets**, sent his angel to show his servants
> the things that must soon take place." (22:6)
> —Adela Yarbro Collins, *Crisis and Catharsis*, 34–49

This brief sketch of the major characters in the cosmic drama called "The Book of Revelation" sets us up for a good reading of the book. You have to know who's doing what to catch all the scenes as they are meant to be caught. This is a book for dissidents whose imaginations are stimulated by the cosmic images tossed onto their mental screens as they listen to the book being performed. They are the ones who know *who is who* in this book and *who does what*. The imaginative drama becomes their storied universe, shaping their worldview and their understanding of what happens on the streets of Ephesus and Smyrna and Sardis. Unfortunately, Revelation isn't always read this way. More often, it is read as a map filled with detailed predictions of what's going to happen just before God defeats the dragon's earthly nations. But what John gives us is something far better—a drama that wraps the characters in the playbill into a new narrative, one that explains everything.

PART 3

The Dramatic Narrative for the Characters

CHAPTER 9

The Drama of Revelation

The book of Revelation has several parts. It begins with a prologue (1:1–8) and a vision of Jesus Christ (1:9–20) that introduces us to the Jesus who addresses the seven churches in western Asia Minor for two chapters (2:1–3:22). These messages are followed by visions of the throne and the Lamb (4:1–5:14). The first five chapters of the book form the background for what follows: three cycles of seven divine judgments.

We encounter:

the seven seals (6:1–8:1),
the seven trumpets (8:2–11:19),
and seven shallow bowls (15:1–16:21).

Three plus ten. Ten interludes interrupt three cycles of seven judgments (7:1–8, 9–17; 8:3–5; 10:1–11; 11:1–14; 12; 13; 14:1–13, 14–19; 15:2–4). We will say more about the special significance of the ten interludes later, but for now we need to note that the three cycles of judgment listed above are followed by the defeat of Babylon (17:1–19:10) and the establishment of new Jerusalem (19:11–22:5). Revelation is then zippered up with an epilogue (22:6–21).

There's nothing controversial about breaking the book of Revelation into these major sections. The controversy begins when we ask, *How are we to read the book's narrative plot and flow?*

How do the characters of the playbill come together to form the plot? Previously, we noted four basic principles for reading Revelation well: (1) it's not for *speculators*; (2) it is for *dissidents*; (3) it requires *imagination*; (4) and we need to know the *basic characters*. Now we add a fifth principle: (5) it is vitally important that we locate these characters within the *dramatic narrative*.

Chronological Readings

One of the most common approaches to reading Revelation is to see a chronological plot at work, a view peppered with predictions. This is the approach that drove classical dispensationalism. For those unfamiliar with this term, here is a brief introduction. Dispensationalism has many flavors, so here we are concentrating on its classic form because that is what nearly everyone we meet believes. This is true even of those who don't know what dispensationalism is!

The three most significant elements of classic dispensationalism are:

> First, an emphasis on a *literal* reading of Revelation. And it must be added that those who urge this claim that they alone read Revelation "literally." Not a few of us would describe this as flat-footed.
>
> Second, classic dispensationalism teaches a *prophetic or prediction-heavy* reading that seeks to locate Revelation on the world's stage. Think of looking for the signs of Revelation as you scroll through your Twitter feed.
>
> Third, add to these first two a *chronological* reading that sees chronological steps progressing all the way from chapter 6 to the end of the book.

Following the double introduction of chapter 1, the messages to the seven churches and the vision of the throne and Lamb, dispensationalists see a basic chronology: the literal seven seals are followed by seven trumpets and then by the seven shallow bowls, all leading to the literal defeat of Babylon and the literal establishment of new Jerusalem on earth. For some, these judgments overlap with one another, telescope into one another, or simply follow one after another. But there is agreement among dispensationalists that these three cycles of seven judgments are all predictions—and they all lie somewhere in our future. They are literal—word for word as you read them on the page—and very graphic. For example, some literal interpreters spend time calculating out the details of what will happen to the environment when the sun loses its light and the world is under darkness.

These chronological readings of the seven judgments assume they all happen as part of the future great tribulation and all occur within the space of seven years (after the rapture, before the millennium; for more on the rapture, both historical and theological, see appendices 6 and 7). Taken together, Revelation's three times seven judgments and the great tribulation could begin as soon as now.

But there are several reasons why this reading is most unlikely. To begin with, the word "prophetic" does not have to mean "prediction." Pick up your Bible, read the prophets of Israel, and you will see immediately that they are speaking to their own day as much as they are speaking to the future. It's a both-and way of speaking. Furthermore, dispensationalists often argue their reading is "literal" and other views are "spiritual," but the scare tactic of calling one's reading "literal" and the other side as either "spiritual" or "symbolic" doesn't mean every image in Revelation happens exactly as described, word for word, in the letter. No one *literally* thinks any of these beasts have seven heads or that some sword will zoom from Jesus's mouth when he speaks. Some things are "literal" and others "symbolic," and both sides interpret in both ways. Not to mention that John himself does not see what he is describing as *future* but considers himself to be a *fellow participant* in the so-called great tribulation (1:9).

We believe there is a better way to read and interpret Revelation, one more attuned to the Old Testament prophets and to apocalyptic literature, more attuned to the powerful use of imagery and its appeal to imagination, and one more in tune with the context of first-century Judaism, the Roman Empire, and Christianity.

Here is that better way.

The Story of Everything

Christianity, in the words of Duke professor C. Kavin Rowe, is the "story of everything." We can miss the importance of his words if we don't pause long enough to let them sink in. Christianity is not one religion among many (religious pluralism), nor one philosophy among others (philosophical pluralism), and it is not one worldview that counters other worldviews (perspectivalism). Rather, it is a robust, confident story of everything, from God to God's creation to God's providential guiding of history to God's wrapping up all of history and all creation. The book of Revelation is about *the story of everything*, and this is why we say Revelation is *cosmic*. Its scope is, well, everything.

Life—past, present, future—is not a product of random chaos, nor is it the result of fate or blind luck. No, in the story of everything, the world is God's world, time is in God's hands, history has a beginning, and God guides history toward its divine intention: the new Jerusalem or the kingdom of God. Such a worldview colors one's perception of every moment and counters every other worldview. To the degree that those seven churches lived according to the story of everything, they had to live in two worlds. Summoned from their preoccupation with Babylon, Craig Keener observes they were called "to recognize, in light of [God's] ultimate plan for history, what really matters and what really does not."

The anchor to the story of everything is the story about Jesus. At the center of his story is the resurrection. His life and his death are all reshaped by conquering death. By virtue of that resurrection, Jesus was raised and becomes in Revelation the Lamb in the center of the throne. The Lamb conquers the dragon, and the feast in the new Jerusalem celebrates that victory.

The other side of this story of everything is the story of sin, of evil, of injustice, of war, of death. That is, it includes the story of the way of the dragon, the wild things, and Babylon. The story of everything promises that the Lamb's resurrection will guarantee their defeat.

Here is the only secret you need to reading Revelation: *this book is about the Lamb's final, complete defeat of the dragon and its Babylons and the establishment of new Jerusalem.* In the plot of this book, Hades (the god of the dead) is the place where God sends evil (the way of the dragon) so the kingdom of God can be fully and finally established. For there to be an uncontested new Jerusalem, there must no longer be a Babylon warring with the Lamb. Far too many readings of Revelation depict hell (or Hades) in lurid colors and seem to take joy in the final destiny of unbelievers. But this lacks the imagination of Revelation. The book is not about finding joy in unbelievers getting their comeuppance, but about the defeat of the dragon and the systemic evils in Babylon. The celebration is not personal vengeance but cosmic justice. It's a colossal cosmic relief for the dragon to be defeated so the splendor can all go to the Lamb and the One on the throne.

Every story, including the *story of everything*, has a backstory. And John was soaked in that *backstory*, but it's a backstory that decisively shifted with Jesus into what we call *the story so far*, which sets the stage for the *final story*. Each of these is worth further explanation because each element of the story shapes the book of Revelation.

Revelation's Backstory

For Jews and Jewish Christians, the story of Israel was their one and only backstory. For the gentiles, the backstory to understand the world was found in two dominant traditions. For the Greeks it was found in Homer's *The Iliad* and *The Odyssey*; for the Romans it was *The Aeneid* of Virgil. Cicero and Demosthenes shaped the gentile conception of great oration, while Moses did this for the Jews—and he wasn't an orator as much as a lawgiver. The Greeks' and Romans' stories of war and conquest and glory turned more and more toward the Eternal City, Rome. But for those new on the scene—the Christians—the Gospels and the apostolic writings began to gradually update the Old Testament narrative with a fresher version of the backstory.

> Embracing Jesus as their new backstory formed
> the core of early Christian conversion.

Everything in the New Testament, from Matthew to Revelation, utilizes the backstory of Israel. John alludes to the Old Testament prophets constantly because *their story is his story.* Well, that's not quite right. It's better to say their story *becomes* his story, and his story takes that backstory and reframes the entire story of Israel as one headed toward the new Jerusalem. John alludes to several Old Testament prophets, listed here in descending order based on the number of allusions he makes in Revelation: Isaiah, Ezekiel, Daniel, and the Psalms. Some have estimated there are as many as one thousand allusions, while a more cautious estimate (like that found in the standard Greek text) lists more than six hundred cross references! Others place the estimate of allusions to the Old Testament writings at somewhere between two and three hundred.

So what is the backstory? And how does it relate to the story so far and the final story of Revelation? There are several elements included in each, and as those are updated we see how the larger story of everything is filled out.

The Backstory of Israel
Includes: Creation, promise, covenant, the plagues and the exodus, law, temple, kings and prophets, exile, and return.

It's essential in reading Revelation to have some familiarity with the backstory of Israel. This means readers of Revelation need to know the *characters* and *formative events* of the Bible: Adam and Eve, Abraham and Sarah, Israel, Moses, David, Solomon, and the prophets. Along with these characters, readers of Revelation also need to know about the events of the backstory: creation, promise, covenant, law, tabernacle and temple, kings and prophets, law, exile, return, and how specific events like Passover, the plagues, the exodus, and entering the land became paradigms for God's redemption in this world.

To repeat what we said earlier: when John writes this book, he not only records visions but he writes them up, and that writing up involved recollection of the vision, meditation on that vision, imagination of its meaning, pondering the significance of the vision, connecting the vision to other events in Israel's history and the prophets, and then making a presentation that would be performed in each of the seven churches. Revelation's abundant resonances with countless texts in the Old Testament only happened with meditation and imagination. In doing so John re-actualizes Israel's prophetic imagination. A big mistake often made by those who read the book literally is thinking that each of the texts captured by John from Israel's story is to be read as a prophecy and fulfillment of the vision. No, John soaks his visions in the prophets' words and puts them into a new song, one that plays an octave higher and stronger.

But it's not just Israel's story that is at work for John. There are some adjustments as well.

The Story So Far

Jesus radically adjusted the backstory of Israel in two ways. First, he added several events with his own life and actions. And second, the entire backstory became a new story because Jesus taught his followers that the backstory anticipated and was fulfilled in him! The "first" testament becomes a "second" testament because of Jesus, and John updates Jesus's and the other apostles' versions of the backstory into the story so far.

The Story So Far
Includes: Creation, promise, covenant, law, temple, kings and prophets, exile, and return.
Adds Jesus: His birth, life, teachings, miracles, apostles, last week, death, resurrection, ascension, and second coming.

Out of the backstory and the Jesus-and-apostles story so far, John creates a new version of the story of everything. Like that of Jesus and the apostles, John's story so far has a double edge. For Jesus and the apostles, the kingdom of God was both now *and* not yet. The predicted future of the kingdom was not just some future, far-off utopia but was already unleashed; it was *already* here now, *yet* not completely here. Theologians and scholars call this *inaugurated eschatology.* This means the seven churches of Revelation already embody in western Asia Minor the inauguration of the kingdom of God. Those churches have one foot in Babylon and the other foot already in new Jerusalem. As the face of the Lamb, the seven churches of John's time were called to embody the future realities of the new Jerusalem as allegiant witnesses in the present presence of Babylon—embodied by the empire of Rome.

The Final Story

Just as Jesus adjusted the story of Israel, so the final story provided by John in the Apocalypse adjusts the story so far yet again! But there's something in John's story that also tells us where we are in the story and how we should live as allegiant witnesses in today's Babylons.

Revelation's Final Story
Includes: Creation, promise, covenant, law, temple, kings and prophets, exile, and return.

> **Adds Jesus:** His birth, life, teachings, miracles, apostles, last week, death, resurrection, ascension, and return.
>
> **Adds some final details:** Babylon, dragon, and wild things; One on the throne, Lamb, Seven Spirits, three times seven judgments, Babylon defeated, and new Jerusalem.

In the final story there are new characters and old characters in new clothes. John tells us about the dragon, wild things, Babylon, *and* he talks about the throne and the Lamb and Seven Spirits and twenty-four elders and four living things and angels on top of angels zooming from heaven to earth. He has an innumerable host of allegiant witnesses who die for their witness, and he has corrupted church people like the Nicolaitans, Jezebel, and Balaam. He's taken the characters of Israel and the church and given them each time on the stage!

The events in this drama shift into cosmic events. Revelation 12's vision of a battle in heaven that defeats the dragon, who is tossed down to the earth, becomes a battle over the woman and her baby boy (the Messiah, the Lamb, the Lord). The churches of Revelation 2–3 receive the challenge to a faithful witness in an empire called Babylon, and the dragon and the wild things seduce Babylon to march humans away from the Lamb so they can launch their death program. Babylon seems to be winning but in the final story, Babylon loses to the Lamb, to the Logos of God who slays death itself. One act of God after another attempts to persuade Babylon to surrender to the Lamb, but Babylon will have none of it, so the judgments increase until the whole shebang is tossed to the powers of Hades, the god of death. The dragon and evil are finished, and the new Jerusalem descends in its glory to the earth.

The Timelines on the Timeline

In the "timeline" of Revelation (below), you will see both a horizontal axis and a vertical axis—two timelines on the timeline.

The horizontal timeline is the progress of God's work in history from creation to the new Jerusalem. The vertical line, which is really a series of timelines, moves from the throne, the Lamb, and the Seven Spirits downward through those present in the throne room to the woman, to those faithful to the Lamb and the seven churches down onto the world's stage and into the world of the dragon, where we meet Babylon and Babylon's various representatives (kings, merchants, sailors), and finally down through the wild things to the dragon itself. This vertical line is *not* locked in time. It encompasses from the first century through to the future when the New Jerusalem is fully established. And this is what those who speculate about the future get completely wrong—the vertical axis *moves through time.*

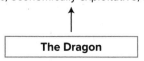

The Vertical Line: Always present, always moving in time, always at work.

The Horizontal Axis: The progress of history from creation to new Jerusalem.

Babylon is present until the dragon is tossed into the fiery lake, and God's Lamb is at war with the dragon and Babylon throughout history. The vertical axis is the ever-present battle of God and the dragon, of the presence of Babylon and the yearning for new Jerusalem.

Three Stories in Which We Find Ourselves Today

The Bible's *story of everything* transcends what the world offers us. In a recent and brilliant study of the stories told by Americans, Philip Gorski proposes the existence of three basic storylines: radical secularism, Christian nationalism, and civil religion.

First, and the easiest for most Christians to reject, is *radical secularism*. This storyline explicitly wants God out of the public square and Christians to cease with their God-shaped moral visions. Instead, it wants a secular ethic rooted in reason that engages all people neutrally in the public square. For believers this is impossible, not least because everything we think and do flowers from our faith (or at least it ought to).

The second story popular today flips this first script on its head: *Christian nationalism*. In this story, the USA is a Christian nation, and its laws and government ought to reflect to one degree or another their Christian foundations. Accompanying this story is the necessity of violence wielded to maintain this Christian foundation and framework. Such an approach finds affinity, according to Philip Gorski, with the conquest narratives of the Old Testament, especially those we read in Joshua. Christian nationalists read the book of Revelation as the paradigm of earthly war and defeat, and their perspective on the place of government and its role emerges from the premillennial dispensational approach to Revelation. However extreme it was, January 6, 2021, illustrates such an approach.

Gorski himself contends for a third storyline, what he calls *civil religion*, which he contends draws from both the secular

Western world of "civic republicanism" but also the biblical world of "prophetic religion."

These are the current options we in the West either grow up with or into. Three stories that help us make sense of the world around us and how we should engage in the public square—yet none of them offer us what Jesus and the apostles and John's story of everything offer. Each of these stories has something to teach us, but none of them are fully satisfying. John thinks of the world in a very different way, seeing the redeemed and the rebellious, where the redeemed are those walking the way of the Lamb and the rebellious are walking the way of the dragon. Life is certainly complex and far more complicated than simple binaries, but John's strategy forces us to see a stark contrast between the Lamb and the empire, leading us to choose Team Lamb. He declares the final defeat of Team Dragon and predicts a New Jerusalem in which justice and peace will flow from the throne of God and the Lamb. John's story of everything can work alongside a vision of civic republicanism and even civil religion, but it does so with a church-based way of life that discerns throughout the prophets and the apostles the realities of life in Babylon.

> John does not adjudicate how to engage in politics.
> Instead, John instructs Christians how to discern the moral
> character of governments and politicians and policies and
> laws. John takes the stance of a dissident disciple who
> lives out of a story unlike anything the world has to offer.

The story of everything is John's challenge to his hearers and readers—even to us today—to turn from Team Dragon and live out the story of Team Lamb.

CHAPTER 10

An Interlude about
the Interludes

Have you ever noticed that the book of Revelation is filled with *interruptions* or *breaks* in the narrative flow? Why are there so many of these interruptions—we count ten of them—interrupting the flow of John's story in chapters 6 and following? It's like traveling on a road trip with someone who wants to stop at every fresh fruit stand along the way. If you open your Bible and scan the section headers in Revelation 6–16, you'll likely notice the interludes and see them as interruptions. Does John think the seven churches need interruptions as he tells this story? Perhaps he has a reason. The story he tells is ghastly, with three times seven judgments on the world. Might John be concerned for his audience, hoping to keep them from succumbing to fear or depression?

We believe this is exactly what is happening. Just as we get to the point where we want to put our hands over our eyes, John lifts us into the presence of God, a place of worship and revelation. These interruptions are called *interludes* and they perform one key function: *they lift the listeners in the seven churches out of the horrors of the dragon and the wild things and Babylon into the heavenly throne room to experience God as the real story behind the story of everything.* The new Jerusalem, the interludes remind us as listeners, is not yet here, and the life we now experience may feel like the dragon is winning. But Good Friday became Easter morning, and new Jerusalem will one day replace Babylon. John wants his hearers (and us, too) to remember our Easter faith, that Jesus defeated death in the resurrection. That story announces that the Lamb and justice win, and the dragon and death lose. Here is a list of all ten interludes:

> Interlude 1: Marking 144,000 (7:1–8)
> Interlude 2: Universal Acclamation by Witnesses (7:9–17)
> Interlude 3: Petitions of the Devout Ones (8:3–5)
> Interlude 4: Little Book Eaten (10:1–11)
> Interlude 5: Two Witnesses (11:1–14)
> Interlude 6: Woman and Dragon (12:1–17)
> Interlude 7: Dragon's Two Wild Things (13:1–18)
> Interlude 8: Allegiant Ones (14:1–13)
> Interlude 9: Judgment Announced (14:14–19)
> Interlude 10: Conquerors (15:2–4)

Each of these interludes are sudden but relieving revelations of the truest reality of all for those living in Babylon. Their purpose is to suspend our fear about Babylon and form within us a deeper allegiance to the Lamb, who reigns from the middle of the throne. The positive messages are striking. In the first interlude (7:1–8), John sees 144,000 who have been marked, protected from the "four winds" and destined for redemption. That number is not literal, but clearly symbolic: 144,000 equals 12,000 × 12, and twelve is the number of tribes in Israel, so 144,000 represents a perfect or complete number of Israelites. Brian Blount calls this the "human wing of God's cosmic army" and Richard Bauckham reminds the reader of the "lavish use of militaristic *language* in a non-militaristic *sense*." John, so one reading goes, wants the seven churches to imagine a horde of Jewish believers in Jesus as Messiah, and to know that they are protected during these judgments, just as Israel was in Egypt (cf. Exod 12:26–27).

What the Interludes Do

The interludes function as *digressions in speech*, departing from the sequence of the argument to call attention to something important. Revelation was written for oral performance (Rev 1:3), and the interludes capture the hearers' attention with their unexpected shifts in focus.

The interludes enhance the *emotional appeal*: while the visions awaken fear, the interludes offer hope for salvation, inviting confidence.

The interludes *create delay* by disrupting the seemingly inexorable movement toward God's judgment.

The interludes *create intensity*.

The interludes *pull us from the disorientation* that is intentionally created by the seals and trumpets.

—Cited and adapted from Craig R. Koester, 356–57

Another interlude follows the 144,000, who are outnumbered by an innumerable crowd (7:9–17). This reminds those in the seven churches who are worn down by Babylon that their numbers are not as small as they may think. So who are these 144,000 and the innumerable groups of people? Many see them as Jewish believers and gentile believers, but one could also see them as the church militant, living on earth and battling for the Lamb (144,000), and the church triumphant, in heaven soaring in praise.

The seven churches may have needed some imagination to embrace their connection to the universal, innumerable followers of the Lamb. So John carries them away from the realities of Babylon to the reality of the presence of God. Even those who die for their faith, the martyrs, will be vindicated, John tells them (7:11–17) here and in the eighth interlude (14:1–13). Revelation 14:1–5's interlude will tell us that their "mark," the registration badge name on the believers' foreheads, contains the name of the

Father and the Lamb. They are marked, reminiscent of how the dragon utilizes the marks of the wild thing (13:16–18).

Another interlude reveals people in heaven praying for the earthly believers (8:3–5), while in another interlude an angel tells John to eat a little scroll—sweet to taste but bitter to digest (10:1–11)—a reminder to him that judgment precedes the new Jerusalem. In the fifth interlude (11:1–14), we hear of two witnesses for the way of the Lamb who, as John's scroll indicates, will be defeated. We have already taken a brief look at the woman, the dragon, and the dragon's two wild things (12:1–13:18). These interludes reveal to the seven churches that the battle is already fought in the heavens, and the dragon's defeat is sure.

Over and over in these interludes we find the pattern of the ninth interlude (14:14–19). One like the Son of Man from Daniel 7 has a sickle in his hand and will harvest the earth in a way that defeats the dragon and its armies of evil.

What now looks like a dragon victory will
eventually be the Lamb's victory.

The seven churches are invited to join those who conquered the wild thing by being a faithful witness to the Lamb (15:2–4) and participating in worshipful celebration. Babylon runs along as if there is no Lamb, as if Rome's current emperor is the world's true king, and as if they have nothing to worry about. But in many of these interludes, the seven churches get sensory experiences of the realest of realities in the presence of God. A reality that someday will be New Jerusalem.

The doom of the dragon, the wild things, and Babylon is sure.

The interludes pull back the curtain, unveiling God's world, and because of this they are *the most significant feature* of the book of Revelation for those hearing this message in the seven churches. These glorious interludes mediate the victory of the Lamb for those who remain allegiant to him. Those living in

Babylon *need* the interludes. This is the truth from behind the curtain, now pulled back for a brief moment of revived hope and encouragement. The interludes lift their listeners in the seven churches away from the horrors of the dragon, the wild things, and Babylon into the heavenly throne room where they can experience God as the real story behind what is happening:

As church, a community for those marginalized in our society;

as compassion for those suffering from sicknesses and diseases;

as music bringing hope to the downtrodden;

as the gospel, good news for those systemically abused and oppressed.

The interludes interrupt the flow of John's central chapters, chapters driven by one judgment after another. They lift the listeners in the seven churches out of the horrors into the heavens to experience God as the real story. The horrors of these chapters are interrupted for the people of God, but the judgments remain central to understanding the final story.

CHAPTER 11

Three Times Seven = Completion

Scenes of judgment fill up chapters 6–20 of the book of Revelation. Various interludes interrupt those scenes, but the plot of Revelation fixes the listeners' attention on these judgments. John depicts three sets of seven of them, and that's a lot of judgment, some of it lurid. Yet few readers ponder what the three times seven judgments—seals, trumpets, shallow bowls—are intended to accomplish in the larger storyline.

If you haven't noticed, John loves numbers. Many readers and interpreters of Revelation have noted that John never gives us a number that is free from symbolic value. *Seven* is the number of perfection, implying something done according to the divine design, the number of completion. *Three* implies the greatest or ultimate expression of something. So seven times three indicates triple perfection!

These judgments describe the complete, perfect erasure of evil.

Though these scenes may seem graphic to our modern sensibilities, the judgments are not scenes of bloody revenge as much as graphic depictions of God establishing justice. (We'll have more on this later.) John introduces four themes that help us see the intent behind these graphic judgment scenes.

They Are "Imminent"

The prophets of the Bible, including Jesus, *describe the next event on the horizon as the last event—even, it seems, as the end of history.* The word "imminent" rightly captures this tone, which underlies scads of prophetic announcements. Urgency drips from the words because the time is short. In Matthew 24 Jesus predicts nations battling nations, famines and earthquakes, and persecutions of his followers, followed by the "abomination that causes desolation" (something blasphemous in the temple) and then great distress. And then we get this:

Immediately after the distress of those days

> "the sun will be darkened,
>   and the moon will not give its light;
> the stars will fall from the sky,
>   and the heavenly bodies will be shaken."

Then will appear the sign of the Son of Man in heaven. And then all the peoples of the earth will mourn when they see the Son of Man coming on the clouds of heaven, with power and great glory. And he will send his angels with a loud trumpet call, and they will gather his elect from the four winds, from one end of the heavens to the other. (Matt 24:29–31)

That word "immediately" can only mean immediately—that is, imminently. Attached to these verses are parables that tie these cosmic events to what sounds like the final events of all history (Matt 24:32–25:46). But what historic event are these scenes tied to? Jesus connects them directly to the destruction of Jerusalem in 66–73 AD. The words of Jesus are aimed at that event and then expressed in terms that characterize the end of history. *That's how apocalyptic language works.*

The best explanation we have ever seen for how biblical prophecy works requires understanding two things: *resistance* and *affirmation*. What must be *resisted* is thinking that the prophets are announcing in precise detail what will happen in time and space in the immediate future. What must be *affirmed* is that rhetorically the prophets ramp up imminency to press upon their readers the urgency of responding to their message. Notice how not all that was predicted in both Isaiah 40–55 and Ezekiel 40–48, two texts especially important for Revelation, was fulfilled in their "fulfillments"—that is, when the temple was restored. Those prophets inspired their audiences to act by utilizing language that turned the next event into the end of history. But that end of history didn't occur and—this is so important—no one was squawking about the prophets being wrong. Rather, their audiences understood how prophetic language worked.

Revelation operates like this too. Revelation 1:1 and 22:26 speak of what "must soon take place." As Daniel told his readers to seal up the book of prophecies (8:26; 12:4, 9), John opens the book up and tells his hearers not to seal up the book (Rev 22:10). John's sense of imminency is found in other places as well (1:3; 2:16; 3:11; 22:7, 12, 20).

Was John wrong? Answering "yes" utterly fails to deal with apocalyptic and prophetic language. The next event is framed as the last event to motivate hearers to repent and follow the way of the Lamb. Prophet after prophet in the Old Testament did the very same thing, so John frames these judgments as something about to happen just over the horizon, and we are to receive them the same way—knowing that God's time is God's time, as Jesus taught his followers (Matt 24:36). In my own life, I (Scot) experienced something similar as a youngster listening to parents and pastors and preachers. They threatened and reminded me that *this* day, *this* week, *this* year was likely the end of time and my death could be imminent, so I needed to repent and get right with God. I never once thought they were false prophets, even with their dispensational speculations. Did I find it intrusive and annoying? Yes, at times. Well-intentioned? Nearly always.

The Three × Seven Judgments
Are a Bitter Sweetness

In the interlude in the second part of chapter 10, an angel, or "a voice from heaven" (cf. Rev 10:4, 8), instructs John to eat a scroll (10:8–11). The voice tells him, as was done by Jeremiah (15:16) and Ezekiel (2:8–3:3), to gobble the book down, informing him that it "will turn your stomach sour" but, ironically, in his mouth "it will be as sweet as honey." The honey comment comes to John either from Ezekiel 3:3 or (less likely) from Psalm 119:103, a treasured psalm for serious Bible readers. The stomach is embittered because the message indicates either suffering for their faithful witnesses (Rev 11:1–18) or judgment against evil (Rev 6:1–19:10). Regardless, the consequence will be the sweet taste of justice. What is the point of this "bitter sweetness" that characterizes God's judgment?

These judgments do not simply elicit celebration, but instead
they usher the listener into an embittered joy, a painful truth
that the world must experience for it to be redeemed.
These judgments are a necessary but bitter
reality. They are a bitter sweetness.

There is something profoundly wrong and unchristian about readings of Revelation that take delight in the so-called great tribulation's severities and judgments. John's narrative is not intended to titillate moderns into the joy of knowing they will escape these scenes, nor are they shaped to lead us into vindication or revenge as we see our nation's enemies crushed. These scenes are not the stuff of world wars or nuclear holocausts. They are images of God's justice being established by erasing the evils of injustice.

The Three × Seven Judgments Are
Answers to Prayers for Justice

There is a tendency on the part of some Christian readers to become squeamish about these judgments, and there are legitimate reasons to cover our eyes at times. Some peek through their fingers while others skim them, turning away in disgust. For sure, these descriptions are like a horror show, and for some they depict God as a cosmic monster pouring out wrath. For others there is a sense of joy, what the Germans called *Schadenfreude*, a delight in the destruction of one's opponents. But while the privileged and powerful may ignore or delight in these scenes, those who suffer oppression ache for God to make things right.

Some people read each of these judgments as graphically precise, literal judgment. As a college student I (Scot) read a book that said the locusts of chapter nine (9:3, 7) were the only category John had for airplanes, and the author of the book said there was no doubt these were B-52 bombers. (They're now military history, by the way.) The locusts were simply John's way of describing the planes. Rather than seeking one-to-one correspondence between modern machines, we should let John's image do what it does. Literal readings of the judgments have also led some to calculate what happens to the earth when the sun or moon is struck, or what happens to fish and the abundance of stink when the rivers of the world turn blood red. These kinds of calculations are colossally unimaginative blunders that do not understand how apocalyptic literature and the imagery of this book work. These graphic accounts of horrors will not happen literally on planet earth. One can think of them as fantastical or fantasy (see appendix 8, "Is Revelation Fantasy?"). They have a very real purpose: to portray the pain of the oppressed and show how it is finally resolved by God.

All of this to say: we are to see these—yes, triply—complete judgments as *the deepest desire of the oppressed for justice*. The specific judgments in the seals, trumpets, and shallow bowls are common tropes recognizable by those who have studied the Old Testament. Think of them as graphic images similar to those we see in John Milton's *Paradise Lost* or J. R. R. Tolkien's *The Lord of the Rings* or even science fiction. Think of them then not so much as literal events that God will cast forth onto the world but as rhetorical displays of warning for the dragon and comfort for the oppressed. They are visions for the oppressed that therapeutically provide momentary relief and generate hope for justice. Slater expresses this well, saying, "Often it is difficult for persons who have not been hopeless to understand how precious hope (and judgment, that is, *justice*) can be for those without hope." Privileged people tend to abuse Revelation with their misreadings, while the abused of this world find hope for the coming day.

The oppressed want to hear from God, and they want to experience his justice. They want to see judgment on evil, they want oppression to end, and they want injustices to be undone. They want to hear that their oppressors are scheduled for a date with the divine. They want to know that racism will end in equality, that starvation will end in a banquet, that exclusion from the city will end in open gates for all. The oppressed have felt the piercingly violent eyes of Babylon upon them and have stared into the face of the dragon in the wild things. They know evil when they see it, and they long for the light found in the Lamb's eyes.

For justice they *pray*, and these three times seven judgments *are God's responses to their prayers*. Notice two passages (the italics are ours to show the emphasis of prayer). The first is one of the seal judgments and the second introduces the seven trumpet judgments:

> When he opened the fifth seal, I saw under the altar the souls of those who had been slain because of the word of God and the testimony they had maintained. *They called out in a loud voice, "How long, Sovereign Lord, holy and true, until you judge the inhabitants of the earth and avenge our blood?"* Then each of them was given a white robe, and they were told to wait a little longer, until the full number of their fellow servants, their brothers and sisters, were killed just as they had been. (6:9–11)

> Another angel, *who had a golden censer, came and stood at the altar. He was given much incense to offer, with the prayers of all God's people, on the golden altar in front of the throne. The smoke of the incense, together with the prayers of God's people, went up before God from the angel's hand.* Then the angel took the censer, filled it with fire from the altar, and hurled it on the earth;

and there came peals of thunder, rumblings, flashes of lightning
and an earthquake. (8:3–5)

John frames the three times seven judgments as answers to the
prayer requests of the oppressed people of God. Their prayers
are How-long-O-Lord prayers that fill the throne room of God
with the incenses of petition and plea. That the angel takes that
censer, fills it with fire, and hurls the fire to the earth indicates
the divine answer to the prayers. The answer is symbolized in the
language of divine judgment that brings justice: "peals of thunder,
rumblings, flashes of lightning and an earthquake."

As a reminder, most of the ten interludes that routinely interrupt these graphic judgments remind the seven churches that
new Jerusalem is coming, and their prayers will be answered.
Whether it is:

- the 144,000 or the innumerable host of chapter 7
- the twenty-four elders falling down before God in thanksgiving that God alone is the world's true Lord who will
  bring justice (11:16–19)
- the 144,000 playing their guitars and singing a new ode
  (14:1–5)
- angels anticipating before the whole world that Babylon is
  coming down and that those who worship the wild things
  will be judged (14:6–13) and that the Son of Man is coming
  on a white cloud hurling his sickle to the earth to judge it
  (14:14–20)

All these and others remind the oppressed people of God that it
may not look good today, but tomorrow brings new Jerusalem.

The Three × Seven Judgments
Are Divine Judgment

There is no avoiding that the three times seven judgments are
orchestrated by God. The violent images reveal what God on

the throne will do, and they directly follow the scenes about the throne room of God and the centrality of the Lamb (Rev 4–5). It is the Lamb who alone is worthy to open the seals and who therefore unleashes the seal judgments (5:1–14). The Lamb opens the judgment seals in 6:1, 3, 5, 7, 9, 12, and 8:1. The seventh seal opens the seven trumpets (8:1–2). The trumpets are blown (as it were) by angels who "stand before God" (8:2), and this is repeated for us at the sixth trumpet (9:13) and in a different way for the seventh trumpet (11:15–19). Angels, commissioned from God's throne, open the seven final bowls.

Behind all these judgments is an acknowledgment of God's superintendence and orchestration. The book of Revelation exhales the air of God's judgment in hot gusts—and we must not diminish divine involvement. A mistake is sometimes made by those who press these judgments into literal earthly realities in which God supposedly makes havoc of his own creation. Rather, these are all—each and in totality—graphic images of judgment on the dragon, the wild things, and Babylon. These judgments have a clear purpose as well: the elimination of evil in the world so the people of God can dwell in peace in the new Jerusalem. They spring from John's vision, which he connects to the plagues and the prophets, and they stir the imagination of the oppressed in their hope for justice and of the sinful as a warning that God will eventually pay back all injustice.

Let's take a closer look at the seven seals (6:1–8:1), the seven trumpets (8:2–11:19), and the seven bowls (15:1–16:21).

	Seven Seals	Seven Trumpets	Seven Bowls
1.	White horse: war	Hail, fire, blood: 33%	Sores on humans
2.	Fire red horse: peace	Fiery mountain in sea: 33%	Blood in sea: death
3.	Black horse: famine	Wormwood star in rivers: 33%	Blood in rivers

4.	Pale horse: death	Sun, moon, stars, day: 33%	Sun scorches
5.	Martyrs praying	Woe #1: locusts unleashed	Beast's throne
6.	Cosmic signs	Woe #2: 33% of humans	River, frogs
7.	Silence	Woe #3: victory acclamation	Air: acclamation

Notice that some of the judgments in one column parallel judgments in another column, as we see comparing the trumpets and the bowls. The seals, however, are more general warnings about war and the absence of peace and famine and death. The martyrs plead with God. Cosmic signs typified for the Jews divine judgment. Each of the seventh judgments announces the end, that is, *each of the three times seven judgments lead us right up to the eradication of evil and the establishment of new Jerusalem.*

> *The Apocalypse is the literary equivalent to a book burning or a food riot or a violent revolutionary takeover. . . . Apocalyptic literature is an outlet of responding to political repression.*
>
> —Tina Pippin,
> *Death and Desire, 20, 28*

The more general warnings of judgment on evil in the seals are followed in more graphic form with the judgments of the trumpets and bowls. The trumpets are partial judgments (as their frequent 33% indicates), while the bowls are the consummate, final act of divine judgment on the dragon, the wild things, and Babylon. Thus, these last two sets of seven judgments increase in intensity. They are not chronological judgments, where each one follows the other, but are *three overlapping revelations of the eradication and elimination of evil from God's world.*

Noticeably in Revelation, the divine judgments are announced as *right or righteous.*

And I saw what looked like a sea of glass glowing with fire and, standing beside the sea, those who had been victorious over the beast and its image and over the number of its name. They held harps given them by God and sang the spiritual of God's servant Moses and of the Lamb:

> "Great and marvelous are your deeds,
>   Lord God Almighty.
> Just and true are your ways,
>   King of the nations.
> Who will not fear you, Lord,
>   and bring glory to your name?
> For you alone are holy.
> All nations will come
>   and worship before you,
> for *your righteous acts* have been revealed." (15:2–4)

The third angel poured out his bowl on the rivers and springs of water, and they became blood. Then I heard the angel in charge of the waters say:

> "You are just in these judgments, O Holy One,
>   you who are and who were;
> for they have shed the blood of your holy people
>   and your prophets,
>   and you have given them blood to drink as
>   they deserve."

And I heard the altar respond:

> "Yes, Lord God Almighty,
>   *true and just* [right] are your judgments." (16:4–7)

Morally, the core issue is justice, and God is the One and Only who always does what is right. We are to see the three times seven judgments as an indication that God is making the world right by eliminating the arrogant, anti-God, exploitative, dominating ways of Babylon. Nothing thrills the heart of the oppressed and unjust sufferers more than hearing that God will make everything right—that he will bring justice. To put it practically, this means:

- Racism condemned and made right is justice.
- Economic exploitation made right is justice.
- Trafficking bodies of humans made right is justice.

To understand the three times seven judgments requires that we encompass all of them as prayers for justice, acts of God, and the establishment of justice. These judgments are not revenge, they are not given to inspire *Schadenfreude*, and they are neither triumphalism nor colonialism. No, God makes things right because injustices are horribly wrong. The three times seven judgments are not lurid chronological timelines of revenge, but are three separable, but at times overlapping depictions, of God establishing justice so that the evils of Babylon disappear and the goodness of new Jerusalem becomes a reality.

John has thought long and hard about how best to present what he saw and witnessed. The interruptions of the interludes are one of his literary strategies, but he (and his readers) would have also perceived profound connections to other passages in the Bible when they read of these judgments.

CHAPTER 12

A Prophet Spinning Plates

When an Old Testament prophet's prophecy comes to pass and is fulfilled—though not in every single detail—some are tempted to characterize such prophecies as partially fulfilled. A "fuller" fulfillment is expected. For such readers, Revelation is the depiction of that final fulfilment, completing the missing aspects of many lingering, incomplete Old Testament prophecies. This, too, is a mistake. *Here's why*: the seeds of John's visions were planted in Israel's past but only bloom with the arrival of the Lamb. Put differently, our wonderful writer's imagination grows out of his memory. His book is not a prediction-fulfillment scheme based in Isaiah or Ezekiel or Daniel. Rather, John uses the images of these prophets to interpret the present *and* anticipate the future.

How Prophets Prophesied

Many people today are taught to read the Old Testament prophets as predictors and the New Testament authors as fulfillers of those predictions. But it's not that simple. Careful reading of Scripture teaches us that it takes time to read the Bible in its historical context. And what we find is that later authors capture the present by utilizing the language of prophets before them. This is not to imply prediction and fulfillment so much as using the right image at the right time—experiencing it all over again, as if for the first time. Here are a few examples of prophets using the prophets before them, and you can look up and check the cross references in your own Bible:

> Isaiah used Amos (Isa 1:12–17; 5:8–23) and Hosea (Isa 1:2–3, 21–26; 9:18). Jeremiah had read Micah (Jer 26:17–19).
> Daniel drew from Jeremiah (Dan 9:2).

It takes time, but if, in reading Isaiah, one carefully looks up the cross references in a common study Bible, one will see regular uses of similar language borrowed from earlier prophets. At times the prophets depict events fulfilling previously predicted events, and at other times they find images and language from the earlier prophets that they pick up and reuse for their own time and message. For example, Jesus connected his prophecy of Jerusalem's destruction, which occurred in the war with Rome in 66–73 AD, with the prophet Daniel (Mark 13:14). Peter saw Pentecost in the language of Joel (Acts 2:14–21).

> When prophets spoke like this, they said
> something old and new at the same time.

John's three times seven judgments express something new, but their newness flows from something old. Many of the judgments call to mind the plagues of Moses and the warnings of Israel's prophets. The old becomes new, and in that newness, there is often something surprisingly new.

The Prophets

Eighth Century	Amos, Hosea, Isaiah, Micah
Seventh Century	Joel, Jonah, Nahum, Habakkuk, Zephaniah

Sixth Century	Jeremiah, Lamentations, Obadiah, Haggai, Zechariah 1–8
Fifth–Fourth Century	Zechariah 9–14, Malachi
Sixth or Second Century	Daniel

How John Prophesied

John was soaked in the language of prophets like Isaiah and Ezekiel and Daniel, and at times there is a prophecy-fulfillment scheme at work. But most of the time John's scheme is *not* prophecy-fulfillment. Instead, it is perhaps better described as *re-actualization.* David Mathewson says John's major themes drawn from the prophets above are like watching someone spin plates, or like listening to an orchestra, or like contemplating a painter using broad strokes and nuanced coloring.

As a general example of how John dips his visions into biblical imagery and texts, consider Isaiah 27:1:

In that day,

> the LORD will punish with his sword—
>> his fierce, great and powerful sword—
> Leviathan the gliding serpent,
>> Leviathan the coiling serpent;
> he will slay the monster of the sea.

Notice the terms "sword," a "gliding [or perhaps slippery] serpent," and "the monster of the sea." While this passage from Isaiah is not the same as the vision of the wild thing from the sea in Revelation 13:1, the serpent is the dragon (20:2) and is being slain with a sword (19:15). Again, these are not identical, but they are close enough to make us wonder if John spent time pondering Isaiah 27:1. (Answer: Yes, he did.) We are not to think that John created what he says about the wild things or serpent or the sword solely from this text, but rather that this text *informed John* as he described the visions that he saw.

Or consider the prophet Zechariah. What Zechariah saw in his vision was a man on a red horse, behind which were red and brown and white horses (1:8–11), and in 6:1–7 he adds a dappled horse. All of this helped John describe the four horses of the first four seals (Rev 6:1–8). Zechariah's horses are not John's horses, but Zechariah's are enough like John's to know that John re-actualized Zechariah's horses.

The cosmic disturbances of the sixth seal (6:12–17) remind John of the words of Jesus in Mark 13:24–27. Here is what we read in Mark:

> But in those days, following that distress, "the sun will be darkened, and the moon will not give its light; the stars will fall from the sky, and the heavenly bodies will be shaken."
>
> At that time people will see the Son of Man coming in clouds with great power and glory. And he will send his angels and gather his elect from the four winds, from the ends of the earth to the ends of the heavens.

Now, when we read Revelation 6:12–17, we think of the words of Jesus:

> I watched as he opened the sixth seal. There was a great earthquake. The sun turned black like sackcloth made of goat hair, the whole moon turned blood red, and the stars in the sky fell to earth, as figs drop from a fig tree when shaken by a strong wind. The heavens receded like a scroll being rolled up, and every mountain and island was removed from its place.
>
> Then the kings of the earth, the princes, the generals, the rich, the mighty, and everyone else, both slave and free, hid in caves and among the rocks of the mountains. They called to the mountains and the rocks, "Fall on us and hide us from the face of him who sits on the throne and from the wrath of

the Lamb! For the great day of their wrath has come, and who can withstand it?"

One could say John is recording the fulfillment of Jesus's own words, and that would be partially right, but we should also note that Jesus's own words echo the prophets before him. John is echoing echoes! Take a look at these texts from Isaiah and Joel as well:

> The stars of heaven and their constellations
>   will not show their light.
> The rising sun will be darkened
>   and the moon will not give its light. (Isa 13:10)

> All the stars in the sky will be dissolved
>   and the heavens rolled up like a scroll;
> all the starry host will fall
>   like withered leaves from the vine,
>   like shriveled figs from the fig tree. (Isa 34:4)

> Before them the earth shakes,
>   the heavens tremble,
> the sun and moon are darkened,
>   and the stars no longer shine. (Joel 2:10)

> The sun and moon will be darkened,
>   and the stars no longer shine. (Joel 3:15)

We move from Isaiah to Joel to Jesus to John, seeing much of the same language. Different contexts, but similar ideas. These cosmic disturbances are apocalyptic language for divine judgment against political powers. John's uses of these texts are not "fulfillments" but the *re-actualizing of former prophecies*.

Let's look at one more. John re-actualizes the plagues of Egypt when he describes the seven trumpets and seven bowls. As the plagues were divine judgment and as John is describing the ultimate divine judgment, so his trumpets and bowls re-actualize those history-forming divine-justice plagues:

> as the Nile became red with blood, so the trumpets and bowls;
> as Egypt experienced a plague of frogs, so the bowls;
> as Egypt experienced a plague of sores, so the bowls;
> as Egypt experienced a plague of hail, fire, and thunder,
>   so the trumpets and bowls.
> As Egypt experienced a plague of locusts, so the trumpets;
> as Egypt experienced a plague of darkness, so the trumpets
>   and bowls, and
> as Egypt experienced a plague of death, so the trumpets.

This is neither accidental, nor is it prophecy being fulfilled. John captures his sensory experiences in the language he knew best: the plagues of Egypt.

For some, this may be too much to take in, but all this (and probably more) is involved when we seek to understand the "meaning" of the three times seven judgments (seals, trumpets, bowls). And in case you are wondering, we have ignored the seven thunders of Revelation 10:4 because John was told not to tell anyone about them!

In Summary

To sum up the previous chapters, we can say that the three times seven judgments are bittersweet scrolls for John to digest, and they are the answer to the prayers of the suffering, oppressed people of Jesus. The judgments map onto one another but also accumulate and intensify toward the final erasure of evil in the defeat of the dragon, the wild things, and Babylon. The judgments make things right for the people of new Jerusalem. What John has seen he must now describe, and he cannot describe what he saw without turning to his favorite sources: the Bible and his Lord Jesus. His descriptions are at times like Isaiah, Zechariah, Ezekiel, Joel, and Exodus. Yet they are also like the words of Jesus, who himself was re-actualizing the words of Isaiah and Joel in his own preaching and teaching. John cannot describe what he sees without using the language of his Bible!

But why do we continue calling these events "judgments"? Maybe we need to re-think and more closely examine a word we have used over and over. Does it mean what we think it means?

CHAPTER 13

Divine Judgments or Disciplines?

We believe more careful, nuanced thinking is needed to ascertain what is happening with the divine three times seven judgments in Revelation. These "judgments," are perhaps better described as divine disciplines which establish justice, *not* vindictive judgments of retribution. The difference matters. These acts of God on the stage of history are not retributions or the venting of a divine spleen. They are acts of God with the purpose of transforming people.

There is a routine refrain in the book of Revelation that enlightens our understanding of the "three times seven" as disciplines instead of retributions. The refrain is often ignored because many are carried away with the ecological or earthly impacts of the seals, trumpets, and bowls. But here are three examples (italics added) of the refrain we are referring to:

And they sang a new song, saying:

"You are worthy to take the scroll
and to open its seals,
because you were slain,
and with your blood you purchased for God
*persons from every tribe and language and people
and nation.*" (Rev 5:9)

After this I looked, and there before me was *a great multitude that no one could count, from every nation, tribe, people and language,* standing before the throne and before the Lamb. They were wearing white robes and were holding palm branches in their hands. (Rev 7:9)

Then I saw another angel flying in midair, and he had the eternal gospel to proclaim *to those who live on the earth—to every nation, tribe, language and people.* (Rev 14:6)

Can you hear the refrain? Here, John speaks of tribes and nations and peoples and languages. There is no more all-encompassing expression like this found in the entire Bible. At the time John is writing the Apocalypse, the church can only be found as small pockets of Jesus followers scattered throughout the Roman empire. And we'd emphasize *small* pockets. It exists as house churches. As Paul says, the Christian community possesses not many wise and not many noble and not many wealthy (1 Cor 1:26). But John knows through God's revelations that there will somehow and someday be myriads beyond counting (7:9)—waves beyond waves of human beings gathered in praise of God. How do we get from those little house churches in western Asia Minor to this massive movement of myriads?

A Time of Divine Discipline

Before we can answer that question, we need to once again consider the prophets. The prophets frequently expressed the end time as the return of the scattered northern tribes of Israel and their joining with Judah. For instance, the famous vision of the dry bones rattling and coming back to life in Ezekiel 37:20–28 was a prediction of that rejoining. But Revelation sees something bigger and broader at work. Instead of whistling to summon the lost ten tribes home, God is at work among gentiles who will also enter into the new Jerusalem. John envisions not just a return of the northern tribes, but a throng of gentiles from the whole world.

How does this happen? That's the question we need to ask. But it's a question many have ignored.

> The period of these three times seven "judgments" is a
> time of worldwide evangelism because what God is doing
> in these three cycles is "discipline" not judgment.

It is a biblical blunder to reduce the great tribulation to a future period when God is doing nothing but pouring out wrath for the purpose of retribution. Instead, we should read the so-called great tribulation as a time of the greatest evangelistic impact in history, a reaching-out that occurs in the midst of clashing empires. Babylon's persecutions are met by faithful witnesses and martyrdoms, and the flying angel of 14:6 that we just read about is a summons to the entire globe to "fear God and give him glory" (14:7). Even those committed to the dragon and the wild things convert!

A Time for Witness

During the three times seven disciplines, the people of God witness. Let's rehearse Revelation 11, John's fifth interlude about two witnesses who re-actualize "the two olive trees" (as in Zechariah 4:3–14). They are also "two lampstands," which indicates they are standing before God in worship and witness. God protects and empowers them to reenact plagues. The wild thing from the abyss kills them, and they lay open to public gaze and triumphal gloating for three and a half days in the "public square of the great city" (11:7–10). John interprets this as "Sodom and Egypt," language that here indicates Jerusalem, as John adds "where also their Lord was crucified" (11:8). God cuts the wild thing's murder celebration short and "raptures" the two witnesses in full view of their once-gloating persecutors (11:12).

What happens next? "At that very hour there was a severe earthquake and a tenth of the city collapsed. Seven thousand people were killed in the earthquake, and the survivors were terrified *and gave glory to the God of heaven*" (11:13). God somehow orchestrates out of the persecution humans who praise him. The language used here, "gave glory to the God of heaven," resonates with the language of conversion. Of course, many read this as a future, physical event in a future Jerusalem. Perhaps that is true, but we doubt it. More likely, John sees a vision that paints the story of persecution as one leading to *gospeling* and *conversions* of the church's oppressors.

Turn with us to a second text, to Revelation 15:1–4. John has a vision of angels holding the seven last bowls of divine discipline. But out of nowhere they are interrupted by a vision of those who had themselves conquered the wild things, its image, and its mark. They reactualize the song of Moses toward the victorious Lamb with these final words: "All nations will come and worship before you, for your righteous acts have been revealed" (15:4). *Again, we see conversion* occurring in the midst of the divine disciplines. For this reason, it is unwise to reduce the seals, trumpets, and bowls to the word "judgments"; rather, these are *divine disciplines*. There is an intent for them that goes beyond vindication and punishment. God uses these three times seven disciplines to warn followers of the dragon about God's coming judgment while also calling them to surrender themselves to the Lamb.

> God's disciplines turn humans away from their idolatries
> and sins and toward allegiance to the Lamb.

As a third text, let's consider the song of Moses in Exodus 15 as it is re-actualized in Revelation 15:3. Those who found victory over the wild thing

. . . sang the song of God's servant Moses and of the Lamb:

"Great and marvelous are your deeds,
    Lord God Almighty.
Just and true are your ways,
    King of the nations."

When we think of the original song of Moses, however, we need to remind ourselves that this song asks one big question: "Who among the gods is like you, LORD?" (Exod 15:11). And as another reminder, we should note that this very question was corrupted by the dragon in Revelation 13:4 by the wild thing's devotees, who asked their own question: "Who is like the beast? Who can wage war against it?" The answer to that question comes two chapters later in Revelation 15: *the Lamb is, and the Lamb is even more powerful!* The Lamb is beyond superior to the wild thing. (Brian Blount invented the term "sLambed" for this very idea.) The Lamb will conquer the wild things and the dragon, and their "battle" prompts some dragon followers and wild thing followers and Babylonians to turn from the way of the dragon to the way of the Lamb.

Putting this all together can feel a bit complicated, but here is our best attempt: *John has re-actualized the song of Moses and turned it on its head.* The expert on this interpretation, Richard Bauckham, has observed, "The effect [of John's version of the song of Moses] is to shift the emphasis . . . from an event by which God delivers his people by judging their enemies to an event *which brings the nations to acknowledge the true God.*" The martyrs who sing the new ode of Moses sing a song not of their own liberation from Egypt or their own salvation but of the *impact of their witness on the world around them.* Their witness led a mass of people to praise the God on the throne and his Lamb. John's ode is *like* Moses's ode, but it's also altogether *new* at the same time.

Let's consider a fourth indicator that these are disciplines and not retributive punishments. In Revelation 21:3 we read this: "And I heard a loud voice from the throne saying, "Look! God's dwelling place is now among the people, and he will dwell with them. They will be his people, and God himself will be with them and be their God." We would first point out that phrases like "his people" and "their God" are language used for and about *Israel.* So far this all looks fairly normal. But notice then that John says people *from the whole world* are now part of this covenant relationship with God.

Here, we'd like to make two more observations. First, remember that when John writes the book of Revelation to the people of Jesus, it is easy to count them—let's call it "easily numerable." (Won't take long.) Yet when he describes new Jerusalem, those same people have become innumerable. Notice, too, that the "kings of the earth," defeated as they were in 19:19–21, suddenly are welcomed into the new Jerusalem! Here is what John says in 21:24: "The nations will walk by its light, and the *kings of the earth* will bring their splendor into it." That is, instead of cargo ships and the honors of military victors all heading to Rome, these nations and kings *reverse their direction* and offer it all to God and the Lamb on Mount Zion.

When did this happen?
Answer: during these disciplines.

John's core chapters (6–19) tell us, and this concludes our observations, that the three times seven judgments are disciplines designed by God to woo people from the way of the Dragon to the way of the Lamb.

Not All Repent

We have saved two explicit texts for last. There are two tragic texts, and we show our emphasis in italics:

> The rest of mankind who were not killed by these plagues *still did not **repent*** of the work of their hands; they did not stop worshiping demons, and idols of gold, silver, bronze, stone and wood—idols that cannot see or hear or walk. Nor did they repent of their murders, their magic arts, their sexual immorality or their thefts. (9:20–21)

> The fourth angel poured out his bowl on the sun, and the sun was allowed to scorch people with fire. They were seared by the intense heat, and *they cursed the name of God*, who

had control over these plagues, *but they refused to* **repent** *and glorify him.*

The fifth angel poured out his bowl on the throne of the beast, and its kingdom was plunged into darkness. People gnawed their tongues in agony and *cursed the God of heaven because of their pains and their sores, but they refused to* **repent** *of what they had done.* (16:8–11)

If some convert to the Lamb through the divine disciplines, others are hardened and turn more vitriolic in their rejection of God. The term that stands out to us here, which we have emphasized in bold italics, is "repent." The whole world is called to repent.

Myriads will enter the new Jerusalem—but not all humans will repent. In his vision of the new Jerusalem John says that some people—those who maintain their allegiance to the dragon—will be excluded. Thus,

the cowardly, the unbelieving, the vile, the murderers, the sexually immoral, those who practice magic arts, the idolaters and all liars—they will be consigned to the fiery lake of burning sulfur. This is the second death. (21:8)

Nothing impure will ever enter it, nor will anyone who does what is shameful or deceitful, but only those whose names are written in the Lamb's book of life. (21:27)

Outside are the dogs, those who practice magic arts, the sexually immoral, the murderers, the idolaters and everyone who loves and practices falsehood. (22:15)

To these we should add the following as well:

Then I saw another angel flying in midair, and he had the eternal gospel to proclaim to those who live on the earth—to every nation, tribe, language and people. He said in a loud voice, "Fear God and give him glory, because the hour of his judgment has come. Worship him who made the heavens, the earth, the sea and the springs of water."

A second angel followed and said, "Fallen! Fallen is Babylon the Great, which made all the nations drink the maddening wine of her adulteries."

A third angel followed them and said in a loud voice: "If anyone worships the beast and its image and receives its mark on their forehead or on their hand, they, too, will drink the wine of God's fury, which has been poured full strength into the cup of his wrath. They will be tormented with burning sulfur in the presence of the holy angels and of the Lamb. And the smoke of their torment will rise for ever and ever. There will be no rest day or night for those who worship the beast and its image, or for anyone who receives the mark of its name." (14:6–11)

The tragedy of the story is that some *refuse* the signs of God in the divine disciplines. Some of those in the nations "will walk" in the light that shines forth from the Lamb (21:24), while others will choose, as Pharaoh responded to the plagues in Egypt, not to repent and turn to God or to follow the Lamb and will therefore experience the judgment of God.

The point of the seven times three divine disciplines can be seen clearly if one simply reads the book of Revelation as an unfolding plot from chapter 6 on. The divine intent of the disciplines is *to clear out the rubble*, the evil manifestations of the dragon and its wild things in the corrupted city of Babylon. Only then can new Jerusalem arrive without the fear of violence and the corruption of the dragon. Until one reads chapters 6–19 as the preparation for chapters 20–22, one doesn't read Revelation well. But when you read them as an unfolding story, they all fit together. Before new Jerusalem descends to the earth, the debris, the rubble, and the garbage must be cleared away. The garbage dump of Revelation is a fiery pit where bad things burn up, and this fiery pit completely eliminates the way of the dragon, doing away with the dragon, the wild things, and Babylon itself.

And Yet We Need to Consider the Church Too

If one reads (again) the messages to the seven churches and locates each of the negative consequences, we also see a disciplinary theme at work. The revelations of negative consequences combine with a threat of judgment and provide an opportunity to repent—which means there is discipline in the divine act of judgment.

> If you do not repent, I will come to you and remove your lampstand from its place. (2:5)

> Repent therefore! Otherwise, I will soon come to you and will fight against them with the sword of my mouth. (2:16)

> But if you do not wake up, I will come like a thief, and you will not know at what time I will come to you. (3:3)

> I am coming soon. Hold on to what you have, so that no one will take your crown. (3:11)

These statements are warrants for repentance and transformation, not simply warnings of inevitable judgment. The theme of discipline is at work in the warnings of judgment and is characteristic of biblical prophecy. We believe it deserves more attention.

CHAPTER 14

Visions of Final Justice

For the oppressed people of our world, the words "Babylon is fallen!" declare the end of the dragon's corruption (18:1–19:10). They are an announcement of the gospel itself. Not as an encouragement to delight in vengeance but as relief that the ache for justice is ended. Faithful allegiance will be rewarded in the world as God designed it, in the new Jerusalem. All that the dissidents have been resisting will come to an end, and evil will be defeated. John sketches these final scenes by providing a series of images, beginning with the white horse Rider.

The Rider on the white horse is one of seven visions in the last chapters of Revelation, all beginning with "I saw" (19:11, 17, 19; 20:1, 4, 11; 21:1). These seven visions overlap with one another in various ways, each revealing what will happen when God establishes final, lasting justice. As Ian Paul has observed in his insightful commentary, many want to read the seven visions in sequence, one followed by another, but this approach creates more problems than it solves, not least of which is more than one return of Jesus to earth (hint, there aren't multiple "second" comings). It is better to see these seven visions as various angles or perspectives on the return of Christ.

Rider on the White Horse

We begin with a new version of what appears to be the second coming of Christ, pictured for us in the image of a Rider on the white horse, whose name is "Faithful and True" and the "Word of God" (Logos of God). Anyone can figure this one out: it's Jesus! He comes, not with a sword in his fist (as with Babylon), but from his mouth. On his uniform, which is a robe and not military gear, there is another name: "KING OF KINGS AND LORD OF LORDS." All the birds of prey are summoned to watch the feast of victory as the Rider encounters the wild things and the kings of the whole world in a battle. *The Rider wins; the dragon loses.* The victors capture the wild thing and the false prophet, and they are "thrown alive into the fiery lake of burning sulfur" (19:20) while the remainder succumb to the Rider's sword (v. 21) and the birds devour their flesh. We encourage readers to imagine this vision as a graphic, unforgettable defeat and *not* as a literal description of hideous events. The fiery lake extinguishes the wild things and the false prophet.

At the time John writes about the Rider on the white horse —an image filled with pregnant images from the Old Testament— stories were commonly told about the triumphs of military commanders. The Romans glorified their warriors and military heroes, as did the Jews, with the Dead Sea community at Qumran drafting its own war manual. John's Revelation is sedate compared to the triumphalism of the Roman emperor Augustus, but it is especially so when compared to the graphic details of the Qumran community's "prophetic" announcements. One notable feature of the Qumran battle scenes is found in a scroll called 1QM. It is the participation of the saints in war and bloodshed, though God is the ultimate warrior (1QM 11:1–5). The Christian vision we have in Revelation ratchets up God's participation one full notch: *the Rider on the white horse alone slays his enemies.* None of the allegiant witnesses draw so much as a knife or a fist. The most graphic moment in John's vision is of birds picking at the corpses. (Rather, they "eat" them, as we see in 19:18, and then in 19:21 we read that they "gorge themselves on their flesh.") The point is clear: the battle is the Lord's, as is the victory that is won.

The words of Augustus's autobiography are dominated by the word "I" and "I" and "I." But John's depiction of the Rider on the white horse is intended to turn our minds toward God, not the success of a human conqueror.

The Last Judgment

Following the celebration over the fall of Babylon and the white horse Rider, Revelation gives us one last judgment. John splits this last judgment into *four scenes*, one in Revelation 20:1–3 (locking up Satan), followed by 20:4–6 (the millennium), then 20:7–10 (judging Satan), and finally 20:11–15 (the "great white throne" judgment).

Again, there is Old Testament imagery behind these judgment scenes. For instance, Revelation 20:4's words "I saw thrones on which were seated those who had been given authority to judge" point us to Daniel 7:9, and Revelation 20:11's words ("Then I saw a great white throne and him who was seated on it. The earth and the heavens fled from his presence, and there was no place for them.") point us to Daniel 7:10. It is worth pausing to quote Daniel and read his words so we can get a firmer grasp on what John is saying here. Notice first that the "little horn" of Daniel lines up (in some ways) with the wild thing and those allegiant to it who were defeated and cast into the fiery pit in Revelation 19:11–21. That's one clear connection, but even more connections are found with the judgment itself. Note the portions we've italicized for emphasis:

> While I was thinking about the horns, there before me was *another horn, a little one*, which came up among them; and three of the first horns were uprooted before it. *This horn had eyes like the eyes of a human being and a mouth that spoke boastfully.*
> As I looked,
>
> > *thrones were set in place,*
> > and the Ancient of Days took his seat.
> > His clothing was as white as snow;
> > the hair of his head was white like wool.

His throne was flaming with fire,
>   and its wheels were all ablaze.
A river of fire was flowing,
>   coming out from before him.
Thousands upon thousands attended him;
>   ten thousand times ten thousand stood before him.
The court was seated,
>   *and the books were opened.*

Then I continued to watch because of *the boastful words the horn was speaking. I kept looking until the beast was slain and its body destroyed and thrown into the blazing fire.* (The other beasts had been stripped of their authority but were allowed to live for a period of time.) (Dan 7:8–12)

The "Millennium"

From his Daniel-inspired sketch of judgment, John moves into another image, what today is often called the "millennium" (20:4–6). At the outset we'd like to note that almost everything said today about the millennium by those speculating about the future does not come from this text. Yet it is the *one and only* passage about a millennium in the whole Bible. Many simply fill in the blanks of Revelation 20:4–6 with visions of grandeur and peace and justice from passages found in the Old Testament prophets. What's even more irritating is that what is actually said about the millennium in this one-and-only text is almost entirely ignored! One more time it bears repeating, beware the speculators!

Symbolic Values of Numbers in Revelation

Seven: represents completeness, perfection
>   Each of the following occurs seven times or in multiples
>   of seven:

- Seven judgments
- "Every tribe, tongue, people and nation"
- Lord God Almighty
- The "One who sits on the throne"
- "Christ"
- Jesus: mentioned two times seven times

Four: represents universal, what is earthly

Six: symbolic of humanity, incompleteness, fallibility, imperfection

666: three times imperfection, ultimate imperfection

Twelve: the people of God in their fullness

Twenty-four: the fullness of the people of God times two

144,000: twelve times twelve thousand, the ultimate fullness of God's people

One thousand: a large number, an immensity

The Old Testament prophet behind Revelation 20's visions, the one who wrote Daniel 7, spoke of the defeat of a beast and the shifting of that kingdom's rule to the Son of Man and the people connected to him. John turns that defeat in Daniel into the binding of Satan and the "millennium" vision of Revelation 20. Following the victory of the previous chapter, the dragon, now called "that ancient serpent, who is the devil, or Satan," is bound up in the abyss. Defeats in Revelation are also victories, and victories are not about vengeance but about establishing the conditions for justice. This defeat leads to the victory of the martyrs and their rule.

John narrows the victors in this passage to a very small group.

What is the victory? A resurrection. For whom? *Only* for the witnesses to the Lamb who did not love their lives more than death, the martyrs. They come to life to rule with Jesus for one thousand years (another perfect number, this one suggesting immensity and long duration; see appendix 9, "The Millennium"). The wild thing loses; the people of Jesus are winners. The millennium, in this narrative context, is a *graphic symbol of the victory of those who were murdered by the wild things and Babylon*. If we didn't have chapter divisions in our Bible (which are a later addition), we would read the millennium of Revelation 20:1–6 as the consequence of the defeat of Babylon and the wild things found in chapters 18 and 19.

Because the millennium is *only for martyrs*, one must wonder if there can actually be a time in history when martyrs rule with Christ, judging the world and becoming its priests. (We think this very unlikely.) Instead, it is better to read the millennium as simply *a numerical symbol of victory and rule* for those who have suffered under the rule of the dragon. Richard Bauckham, a major advocate of this approach, concludes: "The theological point of the millennium is *solely to demonstrate the triumph of the martyrs*." And consider: nothing was more encouraging for the seven churches than to hear that their own martyrs would be vindicated. Bauckham also wonders how such an event could occur in real history. John, he says, "no doubt expected there to be judgments, but his descriptions of them are *imaginative schemes designed to depict the meaning of the judgments*."

At the end of this scene, the dragon is unbound and goes ballistic! Notice that a dragon unbound springs from Daniel 7 as well. Look at the words at the end of the passage quoted above in Daniel 7:12: "(The other beasts had been stripped of their authority but were allowed to live for a period of time.)" The dragon gathers its forces again and moves to battle with God at Jerusalem. There are several "final defeat" battles in Revelation, one of which is Armageddon (see appendix 4). Unfortunately, some interpreters choose to combine them all into a single, final battle. We're better off reading them as distinct images of final defeat and not earthly bloodbaths. With the dragon and its forces summoned to a battle, John tells us that "fire came down from heaven and devoured them" (20:9). Then the devil and its forces are tossed into the fiery lake to be "tormented forever and ever" (v. 10).

How are we to read this? Again, the same rules of reading apply. This is a picture of the elimination of evil and evil forces so the new Jerusalemites can dwell in peace.

Are You Premill, Amill, or Postmill?

We are frequently asked what our "view" of Revelation is, and the question is often framed in terms of the millennium: Are you premillennial, or amillennial, or postmillennial? We answer back: *Why is the so-called (literal, physical) millennium the interpretive framework for reading the book of Revelation?* The millennium, regardless of your view, is a sideshow in this book (at best). Three verses are the grand sum of verses about the millennium in Revelation.

The question itself builds on a premillennialist foundation. Assuming there is one, this group charges that the most common view of church history, amillennialism, *denies* the millennium (that's what the *a* in amillennialism means). Another quite popular view in the history of the church is that Christ will return *after* the millennium (a *post*millennial return). But to call one view *a*millennial is inaccurate, for the amillennialist believes in a millennium, just not a literal one, affirming that it refers instead to the church age. You could call amillennialists symbolic millennialists while the premillennialists are literal, physical millennialists. Postmillennialists tend to be literal too.

The bigger issue is that Revelation should never be read through the framework of the millennium. Doing so is a colossal example of missing the whole point of the book.

A better question is, "Ignoring the millennium entirely, what is your view of the book of Revelation?" Our answer: *It is an apocalyptic-prophetic book revealing the evils of the empire and summoning readers to a discerning, dissident discipleship as we live into the new Jerusalem.*

The Great White Throne, Death, and Hades

What John saw next is vital for comprehending the message of this book: a judgment for all the dead, a judgment based on what humans have done (20:13). Some are included in the book of life and some are not, and those who are not will join the dragon and the wild things and the false prophet and their armies in the fiery lake. But something critical now happens: "death and Hades were thrown into the lake of fire" too (20:14)! Which leads us to ask: Is "death" a person? Is "Hades" a god? What is actually being tossed here? A big furnace? A colossal casket? Again, these are all images of the dragon's aim in its work: *to kill and destroy*. If the dragon and its minions are put away in the fiery lake, then death and Hades—the gods of the dead—can be tossed into the lake of final destruction as well.

The fiery lake is the place where all evil—the dragon, the wild things, the false prophet, and their armies—is eradicated. These are eliminated so the new Jerusalem can come. How we talk about hell, if it is informed by this text, requires understanding the *divinely revealed intent of the fiery lake*. This is not a place of vindictive punishment but the place where evil is erased so the new Jerusalem can be established and God's people can enjoy life without harassment, violence, injustice, and evil. All discussions about how long hell endures, or how intense the pain, or how hot the heat, or how dark the darkness, or how conscious the participants fail to grasp John's imagination and intent.

In addition, we must also consider the use of hyperbole. For instance, Isaiah announces a judgment on Edom in chapter 34, describing it in these words (and if you don't see hyperbole here you aren't looking closely):

> Edom's streams will be turned into pitch,
>   her dust into burning sulfur;
>   her land will become blazing pitch!
> It will not be quenched night or day;
>   its smoke will rise *forever*.

> From generation to generation it will lie desolate;
> no one will ever pass through it again.
> (Isa 34:9–10, emphasis mine)

It is reasonable to ask if the endlessness of Isaiah's "its smoke will rise forever" (Hebrew, *le-olam*; LXX: *eis ton aiōna chronon*) is hyperbole. We assert it is. And one can note such language in other places in the prophets. So is this what Revelation is doing also when it says in 20:10 that the devil, the wild things, and the false prophet "will be tormented day and night for ever and ever"? John simply wants us to hear and understand that evil has written its last line, and God has penned the exclamation point.

This is John's finest hour. The day for which he longed. This is the day on which evil will be eliminated from God's creation so the people of God can live in safety and peace and justice and so they can forever bask in the light of the Lamb. And his point is that these two belong together: eliminating evil and establishing justice. Nothing would be more chest-swelling to the seven churches than to know that someday the Lamb would rule, someday they would be safe to worship God, and someday the evils of Babylon would be erased into a long-forgotten history.

CHAPTER 15

A New Jerusalem Imagination

The final, and perhaps most radical vision of all those John saw now completes his visions, and nothing stimulates our imagination more so than John's vision of new Jerusalem. His vision stands in profound dissidence with the political theories and ideal societies of his day. Dreamers dream and dissident disciples dream of the perfect city, in the perfect nation, in a perfect world. Politicians dream and may get down to the business of plotting a path from where they are to the kind of city they desire. Two of the great thinkers of John's time, Aristotle in Athens and Cicero in Rome, did some dreaming and plotting toward this end. But here we are concerned with John's vision of the new Jerusalem. He has taken images from the prophets and fashioned them into a new image, shifting the chorus into a new key, and in doing this we begin to see how his "utopian" vision contrasts with the predominant Greco-Roman visions (see appendix 10, "Utopia, Eutopia, Euchronia, and Progressivism").

The Five Foundation Stones of John's New Jerusalem

What Isaiah foretold and anticipates, the book of Revelation consummates in a first foundation stone, the *new creation*, which sets the stage for the next four foundation stones that are laid. The new Jerusalem, a city that comes into existence by a sheer act of

God, is the city called "new creation." We must remember that new Jerusalem does not complete some plan or journey, nor is it the work of a group of zealous politicians and their supporters. As Jacques Ellul says, "The city of God is not at the end of human progress, at the end of history by a sort of accumulation of the works of man; at this end there found only Babylon. Our works then are not a linear and cumulative preparation for the celestial Jerusalem." Rather, *new Jerusalem is an act of God.*

1. New Creation

At a macro-level, the book of Revelation is one more expression of the New Testament confidence that the kingdom has been inaugurated in Jesus but awaits consummation. George Ladd often says the kingdom is "present without consummation." John's new Jerusalem *is* that consummation. Inauguration without consummation sometimes uses the language of "new creation." The apostle Paul says we are "new creation" (2 Cor 5:17; see also Gal 6:15). The gospel itself—the life, death, burial, resurrection, ascension of Jesus—launches the new creation, as N. T. Wright has been saying for four decades. The old creation is marked by sin and death, and the new creation is marked by righteousness and life eternal.

A good reading of Revelation recognizes that the transition from the defeat of Babylon and the erasure of evil to the new heaven and the new earth with the glorious new Jerusalem is *new creation itself.* All the designs of God for creation and the redeemed people of the world become an embodied reality in new Jerusalem. The theme can be found in 21:5: "He who was seated on the throne said, '*I am making everything new!*'" We then watch the new Jerusalem formed in a new Eden-like, but even better, reality (21:9–22:5). In one sentence, we can define new Jerusalem as *God present among God's people in God's place.*

2. Theocracy

In comparison with Greek and Roman conceptions, Jewish sensibilities about an ideal state, about government, and about politics were very different. Jewish visions didn't embrace a monarchy, an aristocracy, or a democracy. They believed in a *theocracy*, the rule of God.

Theocracy was a covenant commonplace for Jews and formed the building blocks that construct John's ideal city, the new Jerusalem. A theocracy challenged the political thinking of the Greeks and the Romans, who had wandered in and out and between monarchies and aristocracies and democracies, yet never having a theocracy (even if the emperor thought he was a god). And while theocracy is a great idea, reality again slips out of the boot. It's one thing for the Jews to say God rules Israel, but the reality was often more like what we find in Greece and Rome. Rule, of what we call politics, was determined by those with the most power—not by a theocracy mediated by priests. Still, Jews maintained theocracy as their ideal.

Writing in Rome at nearly the same time as John's Revelation was the Jewish historian Josephus. Earlier in his writing, Josephus called the law of Moses the Jewish aristocracy. But by the time he wrote the following lines, we see the ideal of a theocracy mediated by priests on full display:

> What could be finer or more just than [a structure] that has made God governor of the universe, that commits to the priests in concert the management of the most important matters, and, in turn, has entrusted to the high priest of all the governance of the other priests? . . . So, what regime could be more holy than this? What honor could be more fitting to God, where the whole mass [of people] is equipped for piety, the priests are entrusted with special supervision, and the whole constitution is organized like some rite of consecration?

It's no wonder, then, that Josephus begins with some strong questions for those advocating another way: "What part of it [the law of Moses] would one change? What finer law could one invent? What could one bring from elsewhere as an improvement?" (Josephus, *Ag. Ap.* 2.185, 188, 184). The Romans made their own claims of ancestry, but with the Jews it was a claim to a priestly family that gave one the upper hand, and Josephus—never one to avoid a boast or two—made his own boastful claim to priesthood (*Life* 1–2, 6), which is a claim of privilege with God.

The ideal for the Jew contradicted the ideals of Greeks and Romans: *a theocracy governed in a temple by a law from God and mediated by priests*. This system can be called a theocracy or might be better described as a hierocracy (rule by priests). The center of life is a temple, the instruction for life is the God-revealed religious and civil Torah of Moses, and citizenship is shaped by living before God in obedience to the law. If one of the building blocks of the new Jerusalem for John was theocracy, the next block he adds is the temple, a key part of the ideal Jerusalem.

3. Ideal Temple

There are several points in the Old Testament where we find evidence of hope for an ideal temple in an ideal Jerusalem. Isaiah, thinking of a rebuilt temple, spoke of trees from Lebanon being used to "adorn my sanctuary" and that God would "glorify the place for my feet" (60:13). The most noteworthy description of the ideal temple is found in the prophet Ezekiel. He singularly prophesied the end of exile and a return to the land, where there would be an ideal temple in a massive (and ideal) Jerusalem of some fifty square miles. The biggest promise of all was God's visible, palpable presence with them (Ezek 40–48). On a "very high mountain" (40:2) an angelic-like figure walks Ezekiel through the new city with its new temple, and detail after detail is described in a precise way that would delight any architect. The glory of God floods the temple with God's presence, and the prophet is told of homes to be built in the ideal Jerusalem, as well as a river flowing from the temple toward the Jordan valley that will make the land fertile. Ezekiel does not see a *rebuilt* Jerusalem or a *rebuilt* temple; he sees a brand new temple where, as God tells him, "I will put my sanctuary among them forever. My dwelling place will be with them; I will be their God, and they will be my people" (37:26–27).

Another vision of New Jerusalem is found on a scroll from cave five near the Dead Sea. The scroll is now called "New Jerusalem" (5Q15), and in it we find measurements as detailed as those of the new Jerusalem in Revelation with one difference— that "all the streets are paved with white stone . . . alabaster and onyx" (5Q15, frg. 1, 2.6–7). As with John's description, there are apparently twelve huge doors/gates with towers on each side of the doors with staircases and porches (perhaps for a lookout?). Houses inside the city are all the same size with identical rooms in each. This Qumran scroll anticipates a rebuilt Jerusalem and reworks the temple of Ezekiel, who himself had reworked Isaiah!

What should we make of these idealized plans for Jerusalem and its temple? Can they be distinguished from one another? Some believe there will be a rebuilt temple during the millennium of one thousand years, a period called the "messianic kingdom," but even that millennial temple will then be eclipsed by John's new Jerusalem—a city without a temple. Again, we would suggest that such literal readings of Ezekiel or Revelation fail to enter the imaginative world of the writer. There is not a shred of evidence in *the only* passage about the millennium that there will be a temple rebuilt in Jerusalem (Rev 20:1–6). In addition, Ezekiel's architectural plans are physically impossible to build, which indicates he is operating with an ideal vision. A river of water flowing from the temple? A large temple on top of a mountain? Boundaries for the tribes that can't line up with Israel's geography? Ezekiel's vision dances in the imaginations of the exiles with possibilities of what God will do for them when they return. Each of these writers—the prophets, the visionaries at Qumran, and John—presents us with a vision of an ideal Jerusalem that stimulates their audiences to hope in God.

But what stands out in John's vision? In the next building block, we see a glimpse of the radicality of John's vision, and it's so radical we don't know what to call it. Our best attempt is "the no-temple temple."

4. No-Temple Temple

Rome was a forum. Jerusalem was a temple.

John wipes both of these significant cities off the stage of history and ushers in the most radical part of his vision of the new Jerusalem. Here, he is clearly interacting with Ezekiel, in effect saying, "Anything you can do I can do better!" In Revelation 21 John tells us (reminiscent of Ezekiel) that an angel carried him away "to a mountain great and high" (Rev 21:10). Both like and unlike Ezekiel, John sees the new Jerusalem descending "out of heaven from God" (Rev 21:10), bedazzled in jewels, with mind-numbingly high walls, twelve gates attended by twelve angels, and twelve foundations with the names of the apostles (21:11–14). Do you think Ezekiel's temple was big? This one is massive—about fifteen hundred miles—and it is a perfect cube (like the holy of holies)! Its walls are around sixty-five feet thick, made of jasper, and the entire city is of pure gold with jewels on each foundation. As incredible as that is, here is where John goes crazy, stepping over the line:

> I did not see a temple in the city, because the Lord God Almighty and the Lamb are its temple. The city does not need the sun or the moon to shine on it, for the glory of God gives it light, and the Lamb is its lamp. (21:22–23)

Jerusalem was a temple city, and Jerusalem *without* its temple is just not Jerusalem. But the new Jerusalem has no temple—and yet it does. *God and the Lamb are the temple!* This is an escalation where Jerusalem becomes something new—Jerusalem times Jerusalem. A world without a sun and moon is not our world. But the new Jerusalem needs no sun or moon because *God and the Lamb are its lights.* This calls to mind Isaiah 60:19–20, and six chapters later in Isaiah we read an explanation of why this is so, that God's immensity and sovereignty require a throne too big for a temple:

> Heaven is my throne,
> and the earth is my footstool.

> Where is the house you will build for me?
> Where will my resting place be?
> Has not my hand made all these things,
> and so they came into being? (Isa 66:1–2)

All of this sets the stage for John's vision of a no-temple temple. Israel's temple was the house where God dwells. But God had left that house with the promise that he would return. Revelation 21 announces that God has returned to the house. But not quite. Instead of dwelling in a house, *God becomes the house.* The new Jerusalem vision of John is something new, going beyond any vision in Israel's history. It is a radical vision of the new creation and forms the core of what John wants the seven churches to know in the book of Revelation.

Theocracy, ideal temple, and a no-temple kind of temple—all key concepts John is presenting to the churches. We continue this chapter with words from Revelation 21:

> And I heard a loud voice from the throne saying, "Look! God's dwelling place is now among the people, and he will dwell with them. They will be his people, and God himself will be with them and be their God. 'He will wipe every tear from their eyes. There will be no more death' or mourning or crying or pain, for the old order of things has passed away."
>
> He who was seated on the throne said, "I am making everything new! [cf. Isa. 43:19]" Then he said, "Write this down, for these words are trustworthy and true." (21:3–5)

The greatest blessing of all in the story of Israel is now a settled reality: *God with us.* The presence of God in a smoking pot between the split animals of Abraham, the presence of God in a cloud and fire as the children of Israel wandered, the presence of God's inescapable glory in the temple, the evacuation of that glory in exile, and the promised return of that glory is finally reality forever and ever.

This is what new Jerusalem means to John, the churches, and

to us today: *God's presence with God's people in unending intimacy and splendor*. God provides water and food and a city and shelter and safety, and all the jewels and materialism of Babylon are turned toward God, flooding the new Jerusalem with gifts stacked on gifts like a cosmic Christmas tree. He gives his people a perfectly constructed city where a temple is no longer needed. The temple was a place to "house" God, but God and the Lamb flood this place and are present everywhere (21:22).

Imagining all of this takes some effort, but give it a go. The inhabitants of the new Jerusalem won't even need to shut the gates at night because safety, which was a massive need in the ancient world, is no longer a concern (21:25). But open gates almost certainly communicate another idea as well. We get a hint of this from Isaiah:

> Foreigners will rebuild your walls,
>> and their kings will serve you.
> Though in anger I struck you,
>> in favor I will show you compassion.
> Your gates will always stand open,
>> they will never be shut, day or night,
> so that people may bring you the wealth of the nations—
>> their kings led in triumphal procession.
> (Isa 60:10–11)

Do you remember John speaking of worldwide evangelism and the inclusion of all tribes and languages and nations in the kingdom of God? The open gates of the new Jerusalem indicate that people are now coming into the city with gifts for the king as an act of worship and thanksgiving. The inclusion of the nations in God's redemption opens those gates. And this is even more radical: the "kings of the earth" (21:24) bringing their splendor and riches indicates the conversion of pagan, persecuting kings. Evangelism during the divine disciplines has harvested the fruit of faith, and everyone in new Jerusalem belongs there, and everyone who belongs is there. Everyone loves the Lord, and the Lord showers his endless blessings on everyone.

We would also add a brief comment to anticipate what comes later in the book: *every time we experience the presence of God in Christ through the Spirit, we glimpse the new Jerusalem.* Every time. Babylon is now and temporary; new Jerusalem is now and eternal. The seven churches at the table, the seven churches singing their redemption songs, the daily communion of the saints, and their ongoing allegiance with one another to the Lamb are all experiences of the new Jerusalem in the *here* and *now*.

5. Replacing Rome

Step back and look at what John tells us at the end of the book. Babylon, aka Rome, falls in defeat, and Jerusalem, aka new Jerusalem, replaces Rome as the world's great power. It's a bit like someone in Perth, Australia, announcing that Beijing or Washington DC is about to fall to God's powers and Perth will be the center of the world. It's a bit silly to consider, even in private (unless you are gung-ho about Perth). But John went public with this idea, and now he's on Patmos for it. Here is John's final cornerstone:

> Rome—that is, every Babylon throughout history—
> will be replaced by new Jerusalem.

In the first century no city dared rival Rome, and for good reason. But this didn't stop Jews from admiring their glorious Jerusalem. Historians like Josephus described Jerusalem as not only a rival but perhaps even greater than Rome. Herod the Great is the one responsible for Jerusalem's architectural glory, and he got his ideas from Rome, seeking to slake his ego and to construct his image as someone devoted to the Caesars. The stones of the western wall of the temple mount, stones that are impressive even by modern standards, have no rival in Rome. Herod's palace was designed to compete directly with Rome's opulence. Nothing could compete, however, with Herod's temple, a massive complex on top of a hill that gave to some the impression of an acropolis or sacred site. Jerusalem was the temple, and the temple was Jerusalem, filled with ceaseless activity.

For all Rome's undeniable splendor, it could never rival Jerusalem for those committed to the God of Israel. Jerusalem was the one and only city of God and was profoundly anti-Rome. As Wes Howard-Brook and Anthony Gwyther have said, "New Jerusalem is a territory carved out of empire that embodies an alternative social reality." Beloved by its inhabitants, the words of Psalm 122 magnify Jerusalem, calling the people to pray for it:

> Pray for the peace of Jerusalem:
>> "May those who love you be secure.
> May there be peace within your walls
>> and security within your citadels."
> For the sake of my family and friends,
>> I will say, "Peace be within you."
> For the sake of the house of the LORD our God,
>> I will seek your prosperity. (Ps 122:6–9)

In the first century BC, not long after the Romans had captured Jerusalem the first time, someone penned what is now called the *Psalms of Solomon,* and one of its psalms announces the future glory of Jerusalem. It begins: "Sound in Zion the signal trumpet of the sanctuary; announce in Jerusalem the voice of one bringing good news, for God has been merciful to Israel in watching over them" (Pss. Sol. 11:1). It announces the return from four directions of the dispersed people and how God has made their paths straight and easy to travel "so that Israel might proceed under the supervision of the glory of their God" (11:6). Rome's defeat will be overturned, and the people will dwell in Jerusalem in safety again. The final lines put all of this in perfect focus:

> Jerusalem, put on (the) clothes of your glory,
>> Prepare the robe of your holiness,
>>> for God has spoken well of Israel forevermore.
> May the Lord do what he has spoken about Israel
>> and Jerusalem;

may the Lord lift up Israel in the name of his glory.
May the mercy of the Lord be upon Israel forevermore
(Pss. Sol. 11.7–9).

John's vision of Rome's defeat and new Jerusalem fits into a Jewish belief that God will bring victory for his own people. *And that future lay on the slopes and the top of Mount Zion.* Though the Jerusalem of John's day was probably destroyed, he knew that someday, by an act of God that would defeat the very army that broke the back of Jerusalem, a new city would be established, and it would become the center of the world.

In summary, we have *five cornerstones*: new creation, theocracy, a new temple, a no-temple temple, and a city that puts Babylon into the rearview mirror. John's vision is a promise that stimulates faith and courage, shaping the message he wants to communicate to the seven churches. New Jerusalem *is* the promise given to the faithful in the seven churches.

CHAPTER 16

New Jerusalem as Promise for Victors

M any readers of Revelation miss the connections between the messages to the seven churches and the new Jerusalem, a forgivable error since they are separated by eighteen chapters! Still, it is important that we connect the seven churches and the new Jerusalem by demonstrating that the new Jerusalem is the promise given to the victors—it is the final erasure of evil and the establishment of God's ideal city. This chapter seeks to uncover the connection between the seven churches and the new Jerusalem, setting up the next section of this book, which looks at how to live faithfully as followers of the Lamb.

New Jerusalem and the Seven Churches

This next section is information heavy, so you may need to read it slowly. Here is the pattern we will follow. We will quote a promise to one of the seven churches (italics added to highlight the key phrases) and then provide references to that same promise appearing in new Jerusalem.

- John says to one of the seven churches, "To the one who is victorious, I will give the right *to eat from the tree of life,* which is in the paradise of God" (2:7), and that tree of life is in new Jerusalem (22:2, 14, 19).

- John says to one of the seven churches, "Be faithful, even to the point of death, and I will give you *life as your victor's crown*" (2:10), and we find that life in new Jerusalem (20:12, 14, 15; 21:6, 27; 22:1, 17).
- To one of the seven churches he promises this: "[To the one who is victorious,] I will also give that person *a white stone* [or voting or admission pebble] *with a new name written on it*, known only to the one who receives it" (2:17), and we see this name in new Jerusalem (22:4).
- Again, "To the one who is victorious and does my will to the end, I will give *authority* over the nations—that one 'will rule them with an iron scepter and will dash them to pieces like pottery'—just as I have received authority from my Father" (2:26–27), sounds like Revelation 19:15 (and 12:5).
- One of the most stunning promises is "[to the one who is victorious and does my will to the end] I will also give that one *the morning star*" (2:28), and in the new Jerusalem Jesus himself is the morning star (22:16).
- Another promise: "The one who is victorious will, like them, be *dressed in white*. I will *never blot out the name* of that person from the book of life but will acknowledge that name before my Father and his angels" (3:5), and we find this too in 20:12, 15; 21:27.
- One of the big ones is promised again: "Never again will they leave it. I will write on them *the name of my God and the name of the city of my God, the new Jerusalem*, which is coming down out of heaven from my God; and I will also write on them *my new name*" (3:12), and we find this in 22:4 (and we should notice also 19:12–13, 16 where the names are given).
- We finish with this promise: "To the one who is victorious, I will give *the right to sit with me on my throne*, just as I was victorious and sat down with my Father on his throne" (3:21), and we see thrones all over the place at the end (20:4, 11–12; 21:3, 5; 22:1, 3).

A fitting summary of all these promises, as diverse and varied as they are, is Revelation 21:7: "Those who are victorious *will inherit all this* [= 21:1–4], and I will be their God and they will be my children." In other words, those who conquer in the conquest of the Lamb will get it all! To summarize we can say the conquerors in Christ will inherit (1) intimate, eternal presence with God and Jesus and (2) the new Jerusalem, a flourishing, growing, and vibrant city that embodies the ever-increasing fullness of God's design for all creation.

In One Word: Blessed

Blessed is the one who reads aloud the words of this prophecy, and **blessed** are those who hear it and take to heart what is written in it, because the time is near. (1:3)

Then I heard a voice from heaven say, "Write this: **Blessed** are the dead who die in the Lord from now on." "Yes," says the Spirit, "they will rest from their labor, for their deeds will follow them." (14:13)

Look, I come like a thief! **Blessed** is the one who stays awake and remains clothed, so as not to go naked and be shamefully exposed. (16:15)

Then the angel said to me, "Write this: **Blessed** are those who are invited to the wedding supper of the Lamb!" And he added, "These are the true words of God." (19:9)

Blessed and holy are those who share in the first resurrection. The second death has no power over them, but they will be priests of God and of Christ and will reign with him for a thousand years. (20:6)

Look, I am coming soon! **Blessed** is the one who keeps the words of the prophecy written in this scroll. (22:7)

Blessed are those who wash their robes, that they may have the right to the tree of life and may go through the gates into the city. (22:14)

So, Who Are the Victors?

Life in Babylon for followers of the Lamb plays out in a battle zone between the dragon and the Lamb. The dragon will experience a few conquests, but measured against the Lamb's victories the dragon's are temporary and minor. God wins. The Lamb wins. The way of the Lamb wins. And those who walk in the way of the Lamb will also win, and this means they will enter the new Jerusalem. If you follow not the so-called arc of history but the *arc of eschatology*, you will discover new Jerusalem there at the end, an ideal city designed for the victorious followers of the Lamb.

The opening chapters in Revelation emphasize this idea of victory. Here is a sampling of texts from the NIV:

To the one who is **victorious**, I will give the right to eat from the tree of life, which is in the paradise of God. (2:7)

Be faithful, even to the point of death, and I will give you life as your **victor's** crown. (2:10)

To the one who is **victorious**, I will give some of the hidden manna. (2:17)

[To the one who is **victorious**,] I will also give that person a white stone with a new name written on it, known only to the one who receives it. (2:17)

Other mentions of victory can be found at 2:26–27, 28; 3:5, 12, 21. And we find them again in the final new Jerusalem scene:

"Those who are **victorious** will inherit all this, and I will be their God and they will be my children" (21:7). Note that every one of the Greek words behind our English translation "victorious" is a verb. Some translate this as "the one who overcomes," but we prefer "the one who conquers." The NIV's adjectival "victorious" gets it almost right. It gets right the idea that new Jerusalem is for those who conquered the dragon at work in Babylon. Grant Osborne sums up the paradoxical nature of this conquering like this:

> The image of "conquering" is one of the critical themes of the book . . . and pictures the saints as victors over temptation, the pressures of the world, and the cosmic powers of evil. Even as the beast "conquers" by killing them [refs. omitted], he is being "conquered by" the saints (12:11) and the Lamb (17:14). Their death is their final victory! As a result, the saints will rejoice in their victory (15:2–4) and inherit the new heavens and the new earth (21:7). This inheritance is especially spelled out in the seven letters.

But *how* does one conquer or overcome or become victorious in Revelation? We'll have more to say on this in the next section of the book, but for now we will summarize it this way.

> One conquers by worshiping the One on the throne
> and the Lamb, and on the basis of such worship,
> becoming an allegiant witness, even in the face
> of opposition, suffering, and martyrdom.

Brian Blount observes "that ultimately the believer will, like Christ, through the very act of witnessing, overwhelm the bestial forces of draconian Rome and obtain eschatological relationship with God." As Thomas B. Slater demonstrates, the very word John uses—"conquer"—has been transformed from being the victor of a bloody battle to being victorious as a faithful witness to the way of the Lamb, even if that means losing.

The Victors' "War Weapon"

This kind of resistant, dissident allegiant witness to the Lamb explains *how* the believers conquer and win. We italicize the critical words for you to take note of them: "They triumphed [or, conquered] over him *by the blood of the Lamb* and *by the word of their* [witness]; they did not love their lives so much as to shrink from death" (12:11). These believers do not conquer with the war weapons of Babylon, matching them or overmatching them with superior weapons of war. They do not, like the Romans who had no conscience, conquer with brutality and domination and violence and bloodshed and death. They conquer the dragon because they *stand up, speak up,* and *speak out* about the Lamb who is Lord of lords. The Logos of God, the sword from the mouth, is the "war weapon" of those following the way of the Lamb. The Lamb's word slays their opponents and eradicates evil by sending the dragon, the wild things, and the false prophets—and all those who love the way of the dragon—into the fiery pit.

We have come full circle, back to where we began: *the way of the Lamb is a form of resistance to the way of Babylon.* Those committed to the Lord of lords do not wage war as the Romans do. They do not conquer as the Romans do. And they do not worship as the Romans do. They worship the One on the throne and the Lamb, and anyone worshiping God and the Lamb is being transformed into an agent of the Lamb's peace and justice, which is the way of life in new Jerusalem.

John designs this book for the seven churches so they will enter the battle with the dragon as allegiant witnesses who live out the life of Christ in Babylon. He did not write so we would speculate on when, where, and for how long. He wrote for the seven churches, to fire their imaginations and to inspire them with courage to walk in the way of the Lamb. God will be with us eternally, and we will be with God eternally, and we will be together with Jesus—the Morning Star—eternally. We will be with one another eternally, flourishing in an eternal city.

Justice will be the way of the Lamb for all.
Peace will be the way of the Lamb for all.
Love will be the way of the Lamb for all.
Forever and ever.
Ever abounding and flourishing and increasing in glory
    and love.

My wife, Kris, and I (Scot) were in Oxford, England for a conference, and one of the options we had while there was the C. S. Lewis and J. R. R. Tolkien tour. We were excited to participate with several others at the conference. We wandered through the city, into colleges and dining rooms and libraries. But one of our aims in taking the tour was to see Magdalen College, from the green courtyard to the rooms where C. S. Lewis lived, and then walking Addison's Walk along the edge of the College. At Addison's Walk, our tour guide, who had been leading tours through Oxford for two decades, stopped us all, backed up a few paces, and then began to read the last paragraphs of *The Last Battle*. He read these words:

> And as He spoke He no longer looked to them like a lion; but the things that began to happen after that were so great and beautiful that I cannot write them. And for us this is the end of all the stories, and we can most truly say that they all lived happily ever after. But for them it was only the beginning of the real story. All their life in this world and all their adventures in Narnia had only been the cover and the title page: now at last they were beginning Chapter One of the Great Story which no one on earth has read: which goes on forever: in which every chapter is better than the one before.

Our tour guide read this to us with tears in his eyes and then added, "I can't read these after all these years without crying." Indeed.

This is the great hope John promises in Revelation. The new

Jerusalem replaces Rome as the Eternal City. This vision of New Jerusalem is a promise for those in the seven churches who want to live faithfully in Babylon; it is for the ones who *conquer*.

But what does it look like to live in Babylon in the meantime? How do we live faithfully, as John instructs the seven churches? That is what we will discuss in the next section.

PART 4

——

Living in Babylon

CHAPTER 17

Babylon in the Seven Churches

Christopher Rowland, who has plumbed apocalyptic literature as well as anyone in the modern era, counters much
of the common interpretation of Revelation when he says, "We
should not ask of apocalypses, what do they mean? Rather, we
should ask, how do the images and designs work? How do they
affect us and change our lives?" One of the recurring themes
of this book has been our desire to address that question: How
does Revelation change our lives? This is especially true for
those who use Revelation to make *predictions* and encourage
speculations.

Furthermore, for those few who do connect Revelation's
message to something about discipleship, we find that very little
attention is given to the way John's vision of discipleship is framed
as *dissidence* in the midst of Babylon. In this chapter and those
that follow, we hope to move from criticism of bad approaches to
reading Revelation to exploring the living reality of John's vision
of *discipleship*. It's here (and here most especially) that the genius
of the book of Revelation challenges us today unlike any other
book in the New Testament.

Reading Revelation means knowing for whom it was written.
We answer that by saying it was written for *dissidents*. We must

also understand how it can best impact and transform us. As we have seen, it is *through our imagination*. And we must also recognize the book's characters, beginning with Babylon, and its overarching story *from creation and covenant to Christ and the church in Babylon and finally to new Jerusalem.* The book of Revelation is written to shape a church surrounded by the swamping and creeping ways of Babylon.

So how does one live in Babylon? First, the dissident disciples of the seven churches had to learn to see how Babylon was impacting and influencing them. Like a fish in water, the way of Babylon is nearly invisible for the one swimming in it. How do you live in a world that is anti-God, devoted to opulence, consistently opposed to the way of the Lamb, full of itself and intent on being impressive, protected by a mighty military, and aiming to become *the* global superpower? How do you live in a world of constant internal betrayals, driven by economic exploitation of anyone and everyone, structured into a mysterious hierarchical system of power and honor, and driven by arrogance and ambition? How does one "escape" Babylon while living in it?

The seven churches didn't make a clean break. Babylon, like the Aegean mist in the morning, permeated everything, including those in the seven churches, at times clouding over Christ himself. To live as a follower of the Lamb in Babylon you needed to keep the face of the Lamb in view. So life as a dissident in Babylon starts by looking at Christ, as we see in Revelation 1.

The Seven Churches

If one begins in Ephesus and moves north, then east and then south, one can map the exact order of the messages to the seven churches. Some have suggested a chiastic order to the messages.

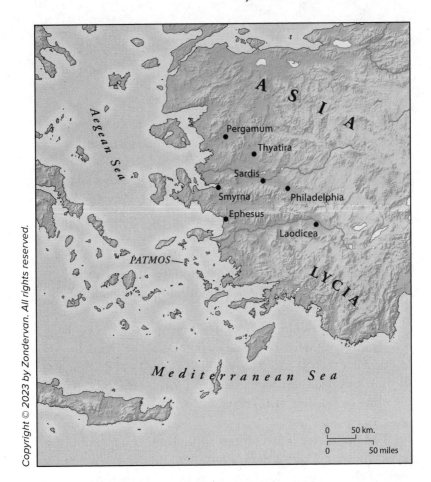

In the Harbor, the Colossus

In the harbor of the island of Rhodes, not far from Patmos, was the "Colossus," a massive, one-hundred-foot statue of Helios, the sun god. Everyone who saw it—whether a visitor or native of Rhodes—was impressed by this memorial to a military victory of the third century BC. By the time John was prophesying in western Asia Minor, however, the Colossus of Rhodes was no longer standing, having collapsed in an earthquake. But the story about it was well known, and it was counted as one of the seven wonders of the ancient world. In the "harbor" of Revelation—the first thing we see as we enter this book in chapter 1—we come face to face with nothing less than a "Colossus" of Jesus. Here is John's Scripture-soaked description of his vision:

> I turned around to see the voice that was speaking to me. And when I turned I saw seven golden lampstands, and among the lampstands was someone like a son of man, dressed in a robe reaching down to his feet and with a golden sash around his chest. The hair on his head was white like wool, as white as snow, and his eyes were like blazing fire. His feet were like bronze glowing in a furnace, and his voice was like the sound of rushing waters. In his right hand he held seven stars, and coming out of his mouth was a sharp, double-edged sword. His face was like the sun shining in all its brilliance.
>
> When I saw him, I fell at his feet as though dead. Then he placed his right hand on me and said: "Do not be afraid. I am the First and the Last. I am the Living One; I was dead, and now look, I am alive for ever and ever! And I hold the keys of death and Hades." (1:12–18)

This entire book—don't forget this please—*is for each of those seven churches.* Every vision, every interlude, every song is for each of them. The Colossus of Jesus that we meet in chapter 1 has his eyes on each church, and what he sees there is not always good, which is another reason John wrote this book. With one eye on Babylon and the other on each of those seven churches, John tells us "what Christ thinks of the church." Two of the churches, Smyrna and Philadelphia, escape the gaze of Jesus. But the other five churches are laid bare and exposed with piercing criticism.

Their sins are rooted in a struggle to walk in the way of the Lamb because Babylon was penetrating the churches and they were no longer focused on the face of the Lamb. What were some of the signs of Babylon in the church?

1. Their love had become disordered (2:4).
2. Their teachings were distorted (2:14–15, 20–23).
3. Their worship was corrupted (2:14–15, 20–23).
4. Their behaviors grew inconsistent with the way of the Lamb (3:1–2, 15–18).

Each of these problems is the manifestation of Babylon's presence in the communities of Jesus. While the fullness of the new Jerusalem is (mostly) future, the fullness of Babylon is entirely present here and now, evident in disordered love, distorted teachings, corrupted worship, and pressure on people to accommodate to ungodly practices. As Wes Howard-Brook and Anthony Gwyther have said, "It was the seduction of the Roman Empire from within a context of relative comfort, rather than terrifying persecution, that more accurately describes the situation of the original audience of the book of Revelation."

Let's take a closer look at the four problems we find in the seven churches. Then we'll turn to a positive vision for life in Babylon as an allegiant witness to the Colossus of Jesus, the one who stands in the port welcoming us to this magnificent book.

Disordered Love

The Colossus Christ looks upon the church at Ephesus, one of five greatest cities of the world at that time, and states forthrightly what he sees:

1. I know your deeds, your hard work and your perseverance.
2. I know that you cannot tolerate wicked people, that you have tested those who claim to be apostles but are not and have found them false.
3. You have persevered and have endured hardships for my name and have not grown weary.

At this point, we might think he's saying, "Well done!" But there's something more that must also be said, and it is a piercing word:

Yet I hold this against you: *You have forsaken the love you had at first.* (2:2–4)

In other words, you've got a great reputation, you're doing good, but your love is disordered. This is the anguished language of a divorcing couple: "You no longer love me. You used to love me but no longer do." It's the language of a worker saying to his coworker: "You've lost your passion, your focus, and your commitment." Jesus sees Ephesus and he knows they no longer love him the way they did at one time. This language has reverberating echoes in the prophets, especially the visual images we find in Hosea 1–3.

For John, love is the core Christian virtue. In 1 John, the word *love* occurs more than two dozen times. Love of God and love of others are so integral to one another that John says it is impossible to have one without the other. And it is essential to understand that this love *excludes* love for Babylon: "If anyone loves the world, love for the Father is not in them" (1 John 2:15). God is love, and God loves us (1 John 3:1; 4:16). The redeemed have passed from death to life, from darkness into light, and so they love one another (3:14). Jesus's own life is the measure of true love (3:16; 4:9). Love works for the good of another person (3:17–18), and love obeys God (5:3). John's message of love is summarized in 4:7–11 as reciprocation:

behold the love in God, in Christ and in the Lamb;
be loved;
become loving.

John's theology, then, is a theology of loves. The problem is that the loves in Ephesus are disordered.

We don't know specifically what was happening in Ephesus, but this disordered love could be a lack of love for God or for Jesus or even a lack of love for one another (what Weima calls "loveless orthodoxy") or what Martin Culy describes as the failure to maintain active witness to Jesus. Whatever the case, their rugged, affective commitments to God and to one another have disappeared. Saying they "lost it" or it "disappeared" isn't strong enough to capture what Jesus says to the Ephesians: "You have *forsaken* the love you had at first." The word John uses is *aphiēmi*, and it means to "release." This same word is behind the word "forgive" and refers to our sins being released from us. The Ephesians have *released* their love. It didn't escape; they *released* it.

The assemblies in Ephesus are somehow doing the right things (2:2–3) but doing the right things apart from the right context—love of God, love of others—means what they are doing is ultimately disordered. Remember that for John love of God is all or nothing, and if you don't love God, you love the world, which means you love Babylon. Babylon is forming their life because Babylon calls for allegiance, for love's devotion, and for love's commitment. While they may be doing Christian things, they are loving Babylon, and because they are loving Babylon, even their good deeds are disordered.

The three disordered loves of 1 John are ours too: "lust of the flesh, the lust of the eyes, and the pride of life" (1 John 2:16). The insatiable nature of undisciplined desire disorders the relationships of men and women in the workplace and of husbands and wives in the home. John instructs us to discern disordered love in the church and to rediscover our first love all over again.

Not only does Babylon betray its lovers, but Babylon is doomed to destruction. The false loves nurtured in Babylon become agents of death because behind the disordered loves is the dragon, whose sole aim is death. Alongside the problem of disordered love stands a problem with distorted teachings as well. Both problems, along with the two others, shape how John exhorts Christians to live in Babylon.

Distorted Teachings

From the very beginning of the church, there were problems with corrupt teachers. Think of those in Galatia imposing the law of Moses on gentile converts to Jesus. Think of the letter to the Romans with its messy situation between "the weak" and "the strong." Think of Corinth and the . . . too many to name! Think of Colossae and the strange teachings that somehow emerged among the Christians there. Think of Thessalonica and the decision to ignore work because, after all, Jesus is coming back, maybe today! Reminder: wherever the gospel goes, Babylon's false teachers arrive with fresh distortions.

The seven churches also experienced teachers with distorted teachings. Just what was being taught is not obvious to us today, but the locals all knew. Here are John's own descriptions, and they come from two different churches, the first from Pergamum and the second from Thyatira:

> Nevertheless, I have a few things against you: There are some among you who hold to the teaching of Balaam, who taught Balak to entice the Israelites to sin so that they ate food sacrificed to idols and committed sexual immorality. Likewise, you also have those who hold to the teaching of the Nicolaitans. (2:14–15)

> Nevertheless, I have this against you: You tolerate that woman Jezebel, who calls herself a prophet. By her teaching she misleads my servants into sexual immorality and the eating of food sacrificed to idols. I have given her time to repent of her immorality, but she is unwilling. So I will cast her on a bed of suffering, and I will make those who commit adultery with her suffer intensely, unless they repent of her ways. I will strike her children dead. Then all the churches will know that I am he who searches hearts and minds, and I will repay each of you according to your deeds. Now I say to the rest of you in Thyatira, to you who do not hold to her teaching and have not learned Satan's so-called deep secrets, I will not impose any other burden on you. (2:20–24)

John "names" the false teachers: Balaam, Nicolaitans, Jezebel, and Satan. Since these teachings are not easy to discern, we will keep our comments brief.

The *teachings of Balaam* and *Jezebel* appear to be worship (whole body, whole life) of false gods. In Balaam's case in the Old Testament, this involved worship of Baal accompanied by sex with Moabite women (Num 25:1–5; 31:16). The *teachings of the Nicolaitans* is even trickier because this could be a play on words: *Nikao* means victory or conquering, and *laitans* means people. Is this someone who had some secret solution for the people to find victory, or is this a specific teacher, a man named Nicolaus, who had a following? One common explanation is that the Nicolaitans thought it was entirely acceptable to eat foods offered to idols, which for John was participation in worship of false gods. In Revelation eating foods offered to false gods involved embodied participation with the dragon, the wild things, and the so-called mark of the beast in Babylon.

John's strong instructions here reveal how discernment worked in the first century and how at different times tactics varied. The apostle Paul, in both 1 Corinthians 8–10 and maybe also in Romans 14–15, states that some Christians are not bothered in their conscience about eating foods purchased in the market that had been sacrificed to pagan gods. If Romans 14–15 speaks into this issue, and we think it does, Paul advises the Romans to give freedom to persons to choose their own way on such matters. Don't forget that Paul forged many of his teachings in Ephesus, the very city where John had now centered his ministry. By the time John writes, either he had a strong disagreement with Paul, or he was facing a more dangerous form of the same practice. His instructions are quite strong: *Don't eat that stuff! It's idolatrous to do so!*

Another angle to consider is John's use of the terms "Balaam" and "the Nicolaitans." John's words in 2:14 speak of "food offered to idols," which refers to idolatries in Babylon, and then John mentions sexual sins. Since sexual immorality is a common biblical and prophetic metaphor for worshiping other gods, many think the food offered to idols and sexual immorality are synonymous. When Isaiah describes the idolatries of Israel, he connects it to sexual immorality:

As for you, draw near,
   sons of the sorcerer,
      seed of an adulterer and a whore.

Who go into heat over gods
   under every lush tree,
slaughtering children in wadis
   under crevices in the rocks.

Behind the door and the doorpost
   you have put your mark.
For away from Me you bared yourself,
   climbed up, made room on your couch.
And you sealed a pact with them,
   you loved bedding down with them,
      lust did you behold.
And you gave gifts of oil to Molech,
   and profusely put on your perfume,
and sent your envoys far off,
   as far down as Sheol. (Isa 57:3, 5, 8–9, Robert Alter)

John may be repeating Isaiah all over again when he speaks of "sexual immorality." Perhaps he means idolatries, but Balaam, it must be remembered, promoted physical sexual relations with Moabite women, so perhaps John has actual sexual immoralities in mind. John also combines food offered to idols and sexual immorality when he writes to Thyatira (2:20). These kinds of false worship and false sexual practices are integrated in the Greco-Roman world, so participation like this was participation in the ways of Babylon. And participation in the empire was the same as walking away from the Lamb.

Judaism and the Jesus movement distinguished themselves from the way of Rome in a profoundly important dimension, namely that God had revealed to his people over and over again how they should live. The gods of the Romans really had nothing to do with how to live day to day. The Jews learned morality in synagogues, and Christians were taught in their assemblies, but Rome's religious shrines and temples were not places of moral instruction. Ethics and religion were quite separate worlds in the empire. And this had big implications for converts who needed discipleship in a new way of life. These converts to Jesus would have naturally assumed that participation in a pagan temple had nothing to do with morality, that worship at a shrine was morally neutral and entirely natural. *But not so for John.* Worshiping at a shrine for him embodied surrender to the way of the dragon.

These false teachers and teachings also articulated a desire to belong by moving up the ladder of social status (called *cursus honorum*), but the eyes of the Colossus of Jesus saw corrupted worship and idolatry in these false teachings. Distorted teachings lead to corrupted worship.

Corrupted Worship

It must be said yet again: worship is more than praise choruses, though songs of praise are certainly one element of worship. Worship describes a whole life lived in devotion to the God on the throne and the Lamb who stands in the middle of that throne. If worship is one's whole life devoted to God, then any dimension of life surrendered to anything else corrupts worship. In fact, acts of eating foods offered to idols or sexual immorality—whether physical or spiritual—or exploitative economic practices all become acts of false worship for John. Either our devotion is to God or it is to the ungods, and if to the latter, then it is corrupted worship.

Babylon did not compartmentalize worship into one's private preferences. For sure, most people had shrines in their homes (*laria*), but they participated in holidays and festivals that were connected to the gods, they offered sacrifices to the gods, and they bought food taken from the altars in the open market. Art forms invoking the gods abounded in most cities and villages. People in Babylon grew into a "religion"; it was not chosen by the person but was chosen by one's parents. A "pious" (*pietas*) person was one who participated respectably in one's community in a social, religious, economic, and political manner. Piety and being a good Roman went together—in fact, Roman nationalism *was* piety.

That meant that turning from the gods of Rome (and Babylon) to the God on the throne, the Lamb, and the Seven Spirits was also turning one's back on society, family, home, and the entire fabric of Babylon. Rome was an interconnected social network—from the emperor to the local rulers to the economy and the military and the temples and gods. Nothing was more natural, less noticeable, and more tempting than for believers in the seven churches to participate in society in a way that expressed connections to these gods. Such practices were the way to "get along," the way to belong, the way to move up in society, and the way to be "*in*" for that culture and time.

It required daily exercise in resistance not to go along.

At the heart of the way of the dragon in Babylon was an anti-God (opposed to Israel, the God on the throne, and the Lamb) life of opulence, exploitation, and arrogance. And this constantly tested Christian worship by tempting believers to accommodate themselves to the Roman way of life. David Brooks, commenting on the workplace, once said, "Never underestimate the power of the environment you work in to gradually transform who you are. When you choose to work at a certain company, you are turning yourself into the sort of person who works in that company." Applying Brooks's insights to the first century, these false teachers chose to live comfortably in Babylon as ideal citizens, socially respectable leaders, and as people who belonged. But before too long they really did belong in Babylon because Babylon had formed them into good Romans.

All of this leads us to one central question for our own lives today: *How much of our faith is tied to our own nation and its power?* Forms of Christian nationalism have been infecting the church since the fourth century. It has long been a matter of Rome *plus* the church, a church ruled by the state, by the nation, or by the military. In such an idolatrous mixture, the symbols of empire morph into symbols of nationalism and religion, and religious nationalism wants to incorporate Christ into its powers. Idolatries will use religion to sanction the nation.

So how present or prominent is your nation's flag in your church? Those who have been discipled in the way of the Lamb discern the symbols of nationalism and resist them as dissidents.

And John nods his head in agreement.

Inconsistent Behaviors

Babylon and new Jerusalem have two different moralities. Any visitor to Pompeii would have been shocked by the overt sexual parading of bodies, both men and women, and so it is no surprise that a graffito in Pompeii is called the place "Sodom and Gomorrah." The behaviors of the Romans, when compared to the moral lives of Jews or Christians, made conversion to either community a moral challenge. Of course, there were some areas that overlapped. A yearning for justice topped everyone's list, and peace and love were not far behind. But what distinguished Christian converts from their neighbors was their rejection of sexual practices and idolatries. Christians must have been perceived in much the same way we think of someone as being puritanical today. Having a different moral code, however, did not mean everyone in that community lived it out.

John's world, for rhetorical purposes, is either-or: either you follow Jesus or you follow the dragon. John knew that discernment was required in particular cases, but he hasn't time for nuance. His absence of nuance derives from his purpose: *to challenge indecisive Christians to full devotion.* His language is reminiscent of Dietrich Bonhoeffer's either-or language in his book *Discipleship*: "Cheap grace is preaching forgiveness without repentance; it is baptism without the discipline of community; it is the Lord's Supper without confession of sin; it is absolution without personal confession. Cheap grace is grace without discipleship, grace without the cross, grace without the living, incarnate Jesus Christ."

This is the kind of inconsistency that we see in the seven churches. Jesus tells the church in Sardis that he knows their works and is aware of their wonderful reputation. Ah, a soft rhetorical landing. Then, he turns his piercing eyes on the church and sees not life but death in their future. He notes a good beginning but looks ahead to an incomplete, unfinished life (3:1–2). What Jesus tells Sardis is taken to the next level in what he says to Laodicea. We will quote his words in their entirety, and they are full of stingers and zingers:

> I know your deeds [works], that you are neither cold nor hot. I wish you were either one or the other! So, because you are lukewarm—neither hot nor cold—I am about to spit you out of my mouth. You say, "I am rich; I have acquired wealth and do not need a thing." But you do not realize that you are wretched, pitiful, poor, blind and naked. I counsel you to buy from me gold refined in the fire, so you can become rich; and white clothes to wear, so you can cover your shameful nakedness; and salve to put on your eyes, so you can see. (3:15–18)

Jesus uses several metaphors in his white-hot words to Laodicea as he speaks of their inconsistency, duplicity, and hypocrisy. We should also notice that Jesus's most piercing words were aimed at *frauds* (Matt 6:1–18; 23:1–39).

The word "lukewarm" has been often misunderstood, though it has been the foundation for a million effective sermons! The real problem is not being lukewarm but being neither cold nor boiling. Jesus is clear that he would prefer them to be *either* cold *or* hot. We translate his words: "I know your works that you are neither cold nor boiling," and he adds words that must be emphasized: *"wishing you were either boiling or cold."* Here it is very likely that he is riffing off their geographical location. The nearby city of Hierapolis has hot-water springs that flow onto the hillsides, leaving behind noticeable and beautiful (from a distance) white patches of minerals. (My students find it breathtaking.) Colossae, another near city sadly still not unearthed by archaeologists, sits next to the refreshing, cold streams of the Lycus River. Hierapolis has great hot springs and Colossae wonderful cold streams. But not Laodicea. The water they get from Hierapolis is no longer hot, and the water from Colossae no longer cold. Laodicean water becomes a metaphor for their works: *neither healing nor refreshing.* Jesus will "spit them out" or "vomit them out." These are words of judgment, and they reveal that Babylon is seducing the Laodiceans into lives of cheap grace.

Jesus then continues: they claim they are wealthy and in need of nothing, which is the arrogance of Babylon. Jesus tells them that in reality they are *not* wealthy and pulls out some powerful images that describe what he sees at Laodicea: "You are wretched, pitiful, poor, blind and naked" (3:17). He calls them to action: they must purchase true wealth ("gold") and true clothing and healing oils from Jesus. In other words, they stand in need of the repentance that springs from grace.

The believers of both Sardis and Laodicea were confident in their way, but Jesus says they are not following the way of the Lamb but the way of the dragon.

In summary, we find that common readings of Revelation do not connect the sins of the seven churches with Babylon, in part because too many think of Babylon as some future empire and in part because it follows some fifteen chapters after the letters to the churches. Here we have two mistakes in one: we need to bring Babylon back into the picture and recognize that the problems in the seven churches were, at the root, compromises with Babylon. John instructs these disciples in a way of life that will show them how to live in Babylon as faithful witnesses of the Lamb; but before we get there, we need a history reminder.

Disorder, Distortion, Corruption, and Inconsistency Become Destructive

Babylon is creeping into the seven churches because . . . Babylon gonna Babylon. Always. And Babylon always has one goal: *domination.* And always at the expense of faithfulness. It took three centuries for Babylon—the way of Rome—to take over the church, and in some important ways it destroyed the church. Apart from the grace of God, it would have destroyed it completely. The fallout from this has been so immense we need to slow down a bit to examine it more closely.

When Constantine became emperor of Rome and part of the church, the empire began to wind the church into a tight thread, binding it closely to itself. Church and empire, empire and church, closely knit to the point that the difference was often unnoticeable. This interwinding today is often called "Constantinianism," but more accurately it should be called "Christendom"—that is, the process whereby Christianity became an institutional political power that sought power in Europe, North Africa, and (western) Asia. Constantine, emperor of Rome from 306 to 337 AD, began this process, and it took half a century (if not more) to turn the Roman empire into Christendom. Constantine used his government powers to

establish churches,
demolish pagan temples,
restore exiled Christians to their homes and jobs,
"unify" the theology of the church,
and banish or silence threatening voices.

Constantine unquestionably operated at times with a charitable tolerance, but the dirty deed had been done: *the state became the power of the church.* States do what states do, and they do this through war and violence. An expert on Roman history, Ramsay Macmullen, states it this way, "The empire had never had on the throne a man given to such bloodthirsty violence as Constantine." Though he was a supposedly Christian emperor, he was known for violence and was a man with a sword in his fist, not the word of God. But Constantine only *began* the turn to Christendom. It was not until Theodosius I, emperor from 379 to 395 AD, that the full integration of church and state into Christendom occurs. This is perpetuated and passed on as tradition for centuries. Theodosius I

reawakened the principle of a family dynasty (as with the
earlier emperors),
"unified" the western and the eastern empires,
appropriated the powers of bishops into the empire,
and demanded confession of the Christian faith.

His theological foundation for this was simple: as there was
one God (monotheism) there should be only one emperor, and that
emperor would act as God's agent. With Theodosius I the empire
completes its "Christianization" and becomes Christendom.
A more forceful way of saying this is that when the church ties
itself to political powers, as it did from Constantine to Theodosius
I, it becomes Babylon. Christendom was the most tragic mistake
in the history of the church.

Aligning with Babylon turned the church into an agent
of empire; put differently, the church surrendered its calling
to the powers of empire. Eusebius of Caesarea (c. 260–340)
knew Constantine personally, saw some of the events of this
time firsthand, and later wrote up a fawning account called
The Life of Constantine, giving him titles like "Godbeloved" and
"Thriceblessed." Here we will drop just a few examples from
his *Life*:

> . . . putting forth this man as a lesson in the pattern of godliness
> to the human race. (1.4)

> Making him the model of his [God's] own monarchical reign,
> he appointed him victor over the whole race of tyrants and
> destroyer of God-battling giants. (1.5)

> . . . so great that all history has not reported his like. (1.10)

Perhaps the most widely known (and tragic) story about
Constantine is his claim to have a vision of the cross before a
famous battle, the one that cemented his position as the sole
ruler of the empire. The vision was written in the sky: "By this

[the cross] conquer" following which he had a vision from Christ himself (1.28–32). And here is the tragedy of tragedies: the cross became the symbol for his military might, his palace, *and* his churches. Constantine became "their redeemer, saviour and bene-factor" (1.39) even though in truth he was a brutal warmongering emperor whose goal was dominance and whose method was power through intimidation and violence. This is not to say his Christian profession was entirely fraudulent. Nor are we saying that he never acted with benevolence and tolerance. We do not deny that he built some wonderful churches (like Jerusalem's Church of the Holy Sepulchre). And we're not saying he was not a Christian or that he only "converted" for political advantage.

What is clear, however, is that the man with a cross for a ban-ner was a bloodthirsty man who defaced the way of the Lamb as he ruled in the way of the dragon. Violence, empire, and power would forever mark the churches that bound themselves to the state.

Summary

The seven churches are not as free from the stains of Babylon as readers might think. Nor have churches over the last two millennia been free of the ways of Babylon. We can become discerning, dissident disciples if we learn from John's own description of how Babylon penetrates into the churches. We need to discern signs of disordered love for God and others; distorted gospel teachings; corrupted worship of God on the throne, the Lamb, and the Spirit; and the presence of behavior that wanders from the way of the Lamb. The relationship of churches to the state can often be a first indicator or warning sign of Babylon's presence inside the church. We can preserve the way of the Lamb toward new Jerusalem if we learn from this and reassert that the first act of allegiance to the Lamb is proper worship.

CHAPTER 18

———

Worshiping in Babylon

How does one live in a world that is

anti-God,
devoted to opulence,
consistently opposed to the way of the Lamb,
full of itself and intent on being impressive,
protected with the might of its militarism,
aiming to become the international power,
living on the precipice of constant internal betrayals,
driven by economic exploitation of anyone and
    everyone,
structured into a mysterious hierarchical system of
    power and honor,
and at the bottom of it all is driven by arrogance and
    ambition?

How is one to live "*in*" Babylon and not be "*of*" Babylon when boxed in by Babylon? Empires rise and empires fall, but they're always present in some form. In this section we are sorting out how John calls his hearers to live as followers of Jesus in Babylon. Babylon's reach is deep and wide, as we saw in the previous chapter. But John offers a way for followers of the Lamb to live in Babylon, and it begins with worship.

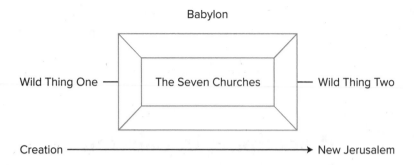

Remember how Revelation is structured, beginning with a vision of Jesus Christ followed by messages for seven specific first-century churches. John wrote up the entire Apocalypse for those seven churches. This means the book of Revelation is not a time*less* vision using the seven churches as a mask for some future world but is instead a time*ly* revelation about Jesus *for* those churches (and for churches of all times). After reading the messages to the seven churches from the Colossus of Christ, we are now at the cusp of hearing what God is about to do. But that's not what happens. Instead of a quick take-down of the enemy, we are swept up with John into the throne room of God, where twenty-four elders and four living creatures utter praise to God. Instead of judgments leading to the defeat of Babylon, we first encounter *cosmic worship*. Then we see a vision of the Lamb, who is worshiped and announced as the only one who is worthy of opening the seals. Only then do we get the seals, the trumpets, and the bowls. Even then, when we watch those three times seven disciplines unrolled, we are constantly interrupted with scenes in heaven, many of which are about worship.

> Revelation is about worship, and dissident
> disciples worship the Lamb.

How are the seven churches to live in Babylon? With worship. Too many speculators have failed to grasp the discipleship message of Revelation. Their concern is about escaping the so-called final Babylon. But what escapes their escaping mindset is the powerful message of dissident discipleship, one that begins on our knees together worshiping the Lamb as the way of God. We have read too many books about Revelation that ignore discipleship, ignore the centrality of worship, and ignore the call to a dissident way of life in this world.

Worship

Before we explain how worship is at the heart of Christian living in Babylon, we call your attention to a growing (and healthy) trend among evangelical thinkers, namely, the importance of habits in the formation of character. The proper name for this trend is "virtue ethics," and the theory is that if we practice the right habits—like worship—they will form us into the right persons, and right persons will do the right things in the context of the right story. So the body's habits lead to character formation, and good characters do good things. Here is what James K. A. Smith, a well-known advocate of this approach, says:

> In short, the way to the heart is through the body, and the way into the body is through story. And this is how worship works: Christian formation is a *conversion of the imagination* effected by the Spirit, who recruits our most fundamental desires by a kind of narrative enchantment—by inviting us narrative animals into a story that seeps into our bones and becomes the orienting background of our being-in-the-world.

Smith gets to the heart of how John is forming the seven churches: he *narrates the story of everything, encourages embodied habits, and relies on the Spirit of God.* He wants the churches to learn to worship in the context of the story of everything and to see that embodied worship works into our hearts and forms us into people who walk in the way of the Lamb. And these habits don't do their work alone; the Spirit must be given more emphasis than the habits themselves. The habits, as Dallas Willard often said, make us available to the Spirit and to God's grace, because it is the Spirit, not the habits, that ultimately forms us. If the habits did the work alone, then those who did those habits (and we shall omit names and denominations) would be the most allegiant in the way of the Lamb. But as Lauren Winner has shown, many churches throughout church history have practiced the most important habits—baptism and the Lord's supper among others—in a manner that somehow leads not to *formation* but to *deformation*! She gives the example of Christians in medieval Europe storming out of a eucharist service in Holy Week to murder Jews. So, yes, habits matter but only if drenched in the Spirit of God and only if we practice these habits as gratitude for God's redemption.

The major habit of the book of Revelation is worship.

One of the most interesting writers about Revelation in the last fifty years is Elisabeth Schüssler Fiorenza, and we believe she asks the right question for understanding this book: "What does a reading of Revelation *do* to someone who submits to its world of vision?" We can now ask this even more narrowly: What does it *do* to the person who turns constantly to God *in worship*? And the short answer is that worship changes us—worship as a whole body, whole voice, whole mind, and whole life lived in gratitude to God for redemption and a whole life surrendered to the way of the Lamb. The "interruption" of Revelation 4–5 takes us to a scene in the throne room where the activity is worship. John wants his readers to know this one thing: worship of God on the throne and the Lamb is required to comprehend all that follows in the three times seven divine disciplines in chapters 6–19.

Spirituals, Not Hymns

Yes, the book of Revelation contains visions that can make us cringe. Interrupting those visions, however, are songs that have themselves generated thousands of additional songs sung by over a billion Christians. The glorious *Messiah*, with words penned by Charles Jennings and music by Georg Friedrich Handel, lifts words right out of Revelation. Who can read this sentence and not have your mind filled with "King of kings and Lord of lords!" and perhaps resist the temptation to pull it out on your device for a quiet listen? There's something about these songs that shatters our comfort and leads us to ache for something more.

There are nine songs in the book of Revelation (4:8–11; 5:8–14; 7:9–12; 11:15–18; 12:10–12; 15:3–4; 16:5–7; 19:1–4 and 19:5–8; cited at appendix 11, "The Songs of Revelation"). They are often called "hymns," but we join others who think that term is not entirely accurate. Why? Because hymns are the music we sing in a life of comfort. These songs in Revelation were not the music of the comfortable but the cries of the oppressed. They are not the songs of simple praise for redemption but pleadings for justice. These songs interrupt scenes of persecution, battle, and judgment. They shift our focus from the conditions of earth to reveal the realities of heaven. They transform oppressed believers from fearful disciples into dissidents who challenge life in Babylon.

There is a better label for these songs. We propose calling these nine songs *spirituals*. How would it shift the way we envision the music and the tone and the body posture of worship if we called these the *nine spirituals of Revelation*? Brian Blount, an African American New Testament scholar, has shown that Negro spirituals of America's Black slaves derive from the Bible's major themes, especially the exodus liberation and the "Spiritual" (Song) of Moses in Exodus 15, sung as a response to the oppressive conditions of slavery. The Negro spirituals used the exodus theme to counter their own slavery, just as John's nine spirituals counter the way of Babylon. Think of it this way: the slaves of America heard the Scriptures in white sermons and white songs. They grabbed those sermons and Scriptures, remade them, reactualized them, and created a new reality, a new world. They forged a social imaginary that both subtly subverted a white slave system and framed a new Black order closer to the kingdom of God *by using the same words and texts*. As one of the truly great civil rights thinkers, Howard Thurman expressed the subversive ways of the slaves, "The slave undertook the redemption of a religion that the

master had profaned in his midst." The verbal subversion of the
slave spirituals was cryptic to the slaveowners, if they happened
to listen in on Black worship. We cannot now think of the nine
spirituals of John apart from this subversive tactic. One suspects
the same dynamic is at work here with John's churches.

These are nine songs for dissident disciples of the Lamb.

Blount continues, noting that the sorrowful tones of the
enslaved were shaped toward this-world transformation even
when using language of the world beyond this world. Negro
spirituals exhorted singers to "endurance, hope, and resistance."
One of the notable features of their songs was that they were
improvised: each performance could add and subtract and shift
and dance to adjusting conditions. Let's be clear. The nine spirituals of Revelation are not Negro spirituals. Our point is one
of comparison, that the songs of Revelation were to the empire
what the spirituals were to American systemic slavery. They are
not the same, but they are similar. And calling them "spirituals"
may help us today reorient how we read them and hear them.
The nine spirituals, like the later slave spirituals, do "not receive
the historical circumstance complacently; instead [they begin]
with that circumstance and [reach] beyond it for an interpretative
tool that can provide the possible parameters of hope even in the
midst of despair."

The heaven of American slaves was also coded language, at
times, for what might come tomorrow.

> I look'd over Jordan, an' what did I see
> Comin' for to carry me home,
> A band of angels comin' after me,
> Comin' for to carry me home.

One of the "angels" in that song was Harriet Tubman, and home
was north of the Ohio River. Brian Blount again comments:

The black slaves, then, in an effort to bring meaning to their tortured existence, create a unique language of song whose restricted codes are fully comprehensible only to those who are members of their oppressed community.

Pause and close your eyes for a moment, then open them as you read the next words: "This language and its context predict how they will interpret Scripture, defiantly." These songs, he tells us, gave "listeners the spiritual energy that would one day destroy" slavery. In other words, these songs are songs for dissidents.

So are John's.

Actions in the Nine Spirituals of Revelation

Worship is not passive; it is active, coming into expression. Worship is not sitting quietly with a Mona Lisa smile. Worship is *act*, and there are various acts of worship that are described in the nine spirituals of Revelation. There are several terms used, so we want to list them with corresponding verses for those who want to look them up in context:

1. Saying: 4:8, 10
2. Singing: 5:9; 15:3
3. Ode: 5:9; 14:3; 15:3
4. Crying out: 7:10
5. Uttering "Oy!" or "Woe!": 12:12
6. Splendoring the name of God: 15:4; 19:7
7. Shouting "Hallelujah!": 19:1, 3, 4, 6
8. Rejoicing exuberantly: 19:7

These eight terms are hardly all the terms that could be gathered from the Bible to express worship. But it is a good starting place. Still, worship includes the whole body. Here is yet another list, this one of various embodied actions found in the worship scenes of Revelation.

1. Bowing down: 4:10; 5:8; 7:11; 11:16; 19:4
2. Tossing their crowns to God: 4:10
3. Encircling the throne of God: 5:11; 7:11
4. Standing: 7:9, 11; 15:2
5. Holding date palm branches: 7:9
6. Using instruments to make music: 5:8; 15:2
7. Uttering "Amen!": 5:14; 7:12

These words describing activities of the voice and for the body express how God's people in God's presence respond to the glorious redemption they are experiencing in the middle of Babylon. They are both relieved and excited to be in God's presence; they find words after searching their hearts and minds; and their uniform response is to bow in praise before the God on the throne, the Lamb, and the Seven Spirits.

Here are three implications from studying this list:

> the worship of Revelation (1) is rooted in
> redemption over and over (5:9, 12; 7:10),
> (2) worship comes to expression in verbal
> praise and thanksgiving,
> and (3) worship leads to a life of allegiance
> in the way of the Lamb.

In Revelation worship is a whole body, whole voice, whole mind, and whole life lived in gratitude to God for redemption, a whole life surrendered to the Lamb. Reducing worship to Sunday at 11 a.m. violates the heart of worship. Worship is Sunday through Saturday, 24-7.

Worship Forms a New Imagination

When all of life is lived in devotion to God and when we engage in embodied acts of worship that launch us into the story of God, we are formed by God's Spirit into a completely different imagination. We call this "faith." We are formed into humans who know our redemption and who know God is on the throne and the Lamb is the victor even if we are surrounded by and assaulted by Babylon. We know that justice will be established, that peace is the final word, and that the way of the Lamb is what C. Kavin Rowe calls the "one true life." The more this story penetrates our bones, the more we are capable of living the way of the Lamb.

Those suffering injustices in a workplace, those experiencing systemic racism, those marginalized to back corner rooms whose voices are barely heard can now turn to the God on the throne and the Lamb, they can bow down, and they can toss all the glory to God. They can plead with this God of the three times seven disciplines to grant glimpses of the new Jerusalem in the here and now. Their worship develops a new imagination that can usher them into a life of faithful witness.

Worshiping this God inevitably leads to resisting Babylon's gods and converts the people of the Lamb into dissidents in the world. Those who worship the Lamb *do not* worship the emperor and his gods. The Roman historian, Tacitus, describes the emperor Nero surrounding himself with those who praised him: "Day and night they ... applied to the emperor's person and voice the epithets of deities" (*Annals* 14.15). Suetonius, another one of Rome's historians, in one of his descriptions of Nero, relates that the emperor recruited more than five thousand "sturdy young commoners" whose responsibility it was to give him rhythmic applause (*Nero* 20.3). We don't know if John knew about such things, but it is foolish to think people in the empire sensitive to worship of the one true God had not heard of the arrogance of the emperors. It's all part of the game, but Christians choose to play the game another way: worshiping God on the throne and the Lamb. Worshiping God becomes an act of dissent, and dissenters subvert the powers that be.

The Heart of Worship Is God

Remember how John presents all of this. We meet Jesus in chapter 1, the churches in chapters 2–3, and then John's intentional

decision is to "interrupt" the flow from chapters 3–6. He wanted
the seven churches to know that to live as God wants in a doomed
Babylon meant they would need to form a life of worship. The
central chorus of all their spirituals is found in Revelation 11:15:

> The kingdom of the world has become
>> the kingdom of our Lord and of his Messiah,
>> and he will reign for ever and ever.

The God of their spirituals gets all the "good" terms: worthy,
glory, honor, power, riches, wisdom, strength, blessing, salvation,
thanksgiving, the kingdom of God, the authority of Christ, great
and marvelous, just, true, and holy. These are the terms they
attribute to God, and by using them of God they can no longer
be used for the empire's rulers.

So what happens to the person who has cultivated the habit
of singing these spirituals? They create *an alternative world* to
Babylon. If in Babylon the dragon seduces the world to worship
the wild things, what the Christians need to hear is that the wild
things are not the world's true Lord. The only one true Lord is
God and the Lamb on the throne of God. A *social imaginary*, as
the philosopher Charles Taylor has said over and over, is one's
reality. The throne room interrupting the flow from chapters 3–6
gives to the Christians a new social imaginary. It becomes, like the
experience of knowing the invisible God in God's visible world,
a reality that is even more real than Babylon's reality. Instead of
creating an imaginary of escape and safety, as the speculators
would have us create, worship creates the possibility of seeing
Babylon through God's eyes and living in Babylon as a dissident.

If these nine spirituals really were akin to early Christian
spirituals, and we believe they were, we want to make one further suggestion. Words turned into music, combined with other
voices, combined with instruments, turn words into an aesthetic,
emotional experience that lifts the spirits of the believers from
their mundane reality into this wonderfully sensory alternative
world called God's throne room. In singing, the believer transcends

her reality and enters a new reality—God's reality, the kingdom of God, the new Jerusalem. Singing these spirituals is an act of resistance, dissidence, and what some call "foot-dragging" and obstructing.

One additional observation about these nine spirituals. Occasionally we observe a concentric circle of praise, a series of different voices surrounding the throne. This means the music reverberates throughout the throne room from the center to the edges of all creation. We hear the voices of the four living things, the angels, the twenty-four elders, and the martyrs. Call them the choir of heaven! To repeat, the "chorus" of this choir is found in 11:15:

> The kingdom of the world has become
> > the kingdom of our Lord and of his Messiah,
> > and he will reign for ever and ever.

That is the heart of the music around God's throne. It is the spiritual of victory, a spiritual that transcends even the wonderful spiritual of Moses.

The way of the Lamb begins in whole life worship—and it results in a *witness* to the Lamb. That's where we want to head next: looking at how whole-body *worship* must become whole-body *witness*.

CHAPTER 19

Worship as Witness

When your faith's motto is that the dragon's kingdom is destined to become the Messiah's kingdom, when you know that Jesus and not the emperor is the Lord of lords, and when you know the story of everything that leads you to worship the God on the throne and the Lamb in the center of that throne, you are summoned to walk in the way of the Lamb. As we've said before, too many readings of Revelation are shaped by predictions and speculations that turn this book into a giant puzzle to be solved. Those readings view nearly everything as an obscure future event, narrowing its impact to far-off sightings. This leads one to either miss or ignore the implications of the book for living now, for seeing Babylon as something right now.

Which leads us back to the question driving John. How does one live in a world that is anti-God, devoted to opulence, consistently opposed to the way of the Lamb, full of itself and intent on being impressive, protected with the might of its militarism, aiming to become the international power, living on the precipice of constant internal betrayals, driven by economic exploitation of anyone and everyone, structured into a mysterious hierarchical system of power and honor, and driven by arrogant ambition? His answer is worship, yes. But what kind of worship? John points us to a life of embodied worship, a worship of both *words* and *works*.

Worship as a Witness of Works

Along with "worship," another word pulls the Christian life in Babylon together: "witness." This term collects all that the Colossus of Christ (Rev 1) affirms about the seven churches (Rev 2–3). In the passages that follow, we have replaced the NIV's use of the word "deeds" with the word "works," with the principal terms in italics for ease of reference. All the italicized words add up to this one key concept: *witness*.

> I know your *works*, your *hard work* and your *perseverance*. I know that *you cannot tolerate wicked people*, that *you have tested* those who claim to be apostles but are not, and have found them false. You have *persevered* and *have endured hardships for my name*, and *have not grown weary*. (2:2–3)

> I know your *afflictions* and your *poverty*—yet you are rich! I know about the *slander* of those who say they are Jews and are not, but are a synagogue of Satan. (2:9)

> I know your *works*, your *love* and *faith*, your *service* and *perseverance*, and that you are now *doing more* [works] than you did at first. (2:19)

> I know your *works*; you have a reputation of being alive, but you are dead. (3:1)

> Yet you have a few people in Sardis *who have not soiled their clothes*. (3:4)

> I know your *works*. See, I have placed before you an open door that no one can shut. I know that you have *little strength* [or, "a little power"], yet you have *kept my word* and *have not denied my name*. (3:8)

As you can see, there are many terms here, and even these verses we have quoted don't cover the entirety of Revelation. But they are enough to show us what Jesus wants. The most oft-repeated word is "works," which emphasizes both behaviors and actions. Yes, the book of Revelation balances works with teachings and beliefs. But what Jesus likes most about these churches is their works. Their lives, or works, are a visible expression of their allegiance to the way of the Lamb. Their works *are* their worship.

> *Just as the slain Lamb has replaced the Lion of Judah, witnessing faithfully even unto death has replaced making war for the Apocalypse. . . . Revelation tells Christians to be witnesses, not warriors.*
> —Thomas B. Slater, *Revelation as Civil Disobedience*, xi, 98

We add to worship and works one additional word, "witness," and offer a crisp definition of the Christian life in Revelation:

Jesus calls the seven churches to an *allegiant witness to the lordship of Jesus Christ in their various public expressions as they encounter in Babylon a variety of stressors and oppositions to the way of the Lamb.*

To live in Babylon as a Lamb-follower challenges Babylon's dragon and the dragon's efforts to hook and drag Lamb-followers into the realm of the dead. The response to the way of the dragon is to worship God and the Lamb and to live faithfully as allegiant witnesses to the way of the Lamb.

Worship as the Words of One's Witness

Let's think more about this term "witness," which in Greek is *martus*, from which we get our English word "martyr." Some interpreters today mistakenly think this term and the verb like it (*martureō*) can be reduced to the witness of one's life. But this turns the meaning of the word upside down! "Witness" describes a person speaking up or out about one's experience. At times it refers to the language of a court witness, but more fundamentally

it is about **what one says** *about what one believes or has experienced.*
As Brian Blount puts it,

> In a time and place where Christians were not subjected to a
> programmatic plan of persecution (as they had been during the
> time of the emperor Nero), but were often economically, socially,
> and even physically abused when they took it upon themselves to
> stand out and stand apart from the expected show of deference
> to Roman lordship, John was essentially asking his people to
> pick a social and religious fight. He was asking them to witness.

Blount gets this exactly right: in a context of Babylon breathing
the dragon's breath all over the seven churches, the message of
this book is for the Christians to recognize Babylon, to speak up
and to speak out, and to stand firm in the way of the Lamb.

At times they will suffer to the point of death. John was
himself on the island of Patmos "because of the word of God and
the testimony of Jesus," or the "Jesus witness" (1:9). He's exiled,
he's imprisoned, he's suffering for speaking up for Jesus. For his
witness. Jesus speaks to the church at Pergamum about "Antipas
my faithful witness, who was put to death in your city" (2:13). In
chapter 6 we read of the "souls of those who had been slain because
of the word of God and the testimony [or "witness"] they had
maintained" (6:9). In chapter 11 we read of the two witnesses, both
of whom were put to death. Similar descriptions of martyrdom
are found in other places in the book of Revelation (12:11, 17;
20:4), and in chapter 17 we read that the woman (Babylon) was
"drunk with the blood of God's holy people, the blood of those
who bore testimony [witness] to Jesus" (17:6).

A witness **verbally** affirms the lordship of the Lamb in public,

walks daily in the way of the Lamb,

and **faces suffering** for resisting the way of Babylon.

A full witness to the Lamb is one of both words and works,
and often involves suffering.

Worship as the Witness of Works and Words

Martin Luther King Jr., closing down one of his sermons in the early days in Montgomery, speaks of what it means to be a witness:

> Honesty impels me to admit that transformed nonconformity, which is always costly and never altogether comfortable, may mean walking through the valley of the shadow of suffering, losing a job, or having a six-year-old daughter ask, "Daddy, why do you have to go to jail so much?"

Being a witness has two sides: it is public affirmation in *word and life* of the lordship of Jesus, and it is public resistance in *word and life* to the way of the dragon embodied in Babylon. Eugene Peterson observes that for the first three hundred years of the church, the most important image for a Christian was a martyr. To our shame today, the most popular and resonant images among Christians in the United States are athletes, millionaires, and movie stars. Oy!

A Witness

Dietrich Bonhoeffer grew up in a privileged home as a cultural elite. After years of studying the Bible and the history of theology, he had formed a backbone that led him to speak out with piercing discernment. As Hitler's power increased, Bonhoeffer's perception of how to be a witness did as well. He became a significant voice in the then ecumenical discussions about church unity. One of the highlights of his life was studying at Union Theological Seminary in New York City and experiencing the power of the Black gospel, its community, and its spirituals. He experienced the witness of the Black church and returned to Germany with fresh faith and a revived sense of his own witness.

When Bonhoeffer later returned to the United States from Germany in the summer of 1939, he experienced a momentous perception of his own calling. In New York City, as Hitler's power was on the rise back in Germany, Bonhoeffer began feeling conflicted about his safety in the USA and the plans church and seminary leaders had for him while he was there. As he heard the constant stream of debilitating news from Germany, he thought about his own place as a member of the Confessing Church and how best to resist German Christians' horrendous compromises with the *Führer*'s National Socialists (Nazis). His calling was clarified into a clear mission to educate seminarians in how to be an allegiant witness to the Lord Christ. He wrote a book during this time called *Discipleship*, formerly titled *The Cost of Discipleship*.

He was given a room at Union Theological Seminary in New York City and spent a month in anguishing prayer and pondering, smoking cigarettes nonstop and typing out thoughts that were later abandoned as crumpled wads all over his room. He writes, speaking of that time:

> I do not understand why I am here.
> It is almost unbearable.
> The whole burden of self-reproach because of a wrong decision comes back again and almost overwhelms me.

Despite receiving several offers for meaningful ministry in the USA, some motivated in part to protect him from the dangers of Germany, Bonhoeffer said *Nein!* to them all. The leaders had prayed for his coming, and when he came, they saw it as an answer to their prayers. After all, they needed him, and they had powerful opportunities for him in the United States. Yet Bonhoeffer found doubts and a lack of clarity as he sought the mind of God, and he wondered if those doubts were a sign *from* God. He eventually decided on June 20, 1939, to return to Germany that autumn. The ongoing catastrophe in Germany led him to the conviction that he was escaping his pastoral mission in Germany by remaining in the United States. His close friend and brilliant biographer, Eberhard Bethge, summed up his decisions with these words: "He had to relinquish the [work for one church] in order to share his nation's destiny and guilt in those evil days."

At the end of June, Bonhoeffer wrote to Reinhold Niebuhr, America's leading theologian at the time, and said,

> I have made a mistake in coming to America. I must live through this difficult period of our national history with the Christian people of Germany. I will have no right to participate in the reconstruction of Christian life in Germany after the war if I do not share the trials of this time with my people.

These are followed by some of the most momentous words he ever penned.

> Christians in Germany will face the terrible alternative of either willing the defeat of their nation in order that Christian civilization may survive, or willing the victory of their nation and thereby destroying our civilization. I know which of these alternatives I must choose; but I cannot make that choice in security.

This dramatic correspondence between two great theologians reminds us that decisions to walk in the way of the Lamb may be painful and can lead to martyrdom. Bonhoeffer chose to return to Germany and departed, not in the autumn, but much sooner, on the 7th of July. The war quickly turned the German authorities against him and he was arrested, held in prison for too long, and eventually hanged in Flossenbürg. He is an example of those whose blood witnessed to their verbal witness to Jesus as the world's one true Lord. Bonhoeffer conquered a wild thing named Hitler and a Babylon called Berlin.

Worship as Allegiance

At the time Revelation was written, there was no widespread or *official* persecution of Christians in western Asia Minor. But was there any persecution? For sure. Some Christians experienced opposition and social ostracism and suffering. Some of it was economic suffering—jobs and clients lost. Much of it was social suffering—the loss of one's status in a culture where status was everything. Some of it was familial suffering—fathers or mothers or siblings or relatives cutting off a relationship. The most common experience involved losing your social standing because to be truly Roman, a citizen of Pergamum or Ephesus, required living a life of social respectability that was inherently tied to religion and worship and sacrifice and celebration. A socially respectable life was called "piety" (*pietas*), and a disciple walking in the way of the Lamb could not participate in the expected *pietas*. Many, if not most, Christians in the seven churches had some experience of suffering because their choice to follow Jesus was not a one-and-done worship and witness. It required a daily, ongoing, fluctuating capacity to discern the presence of the dragon. Followers of the Lamb were regularly called on to express their *allegiance*.

In light of this, take note of several verses in the book of Revelation. We have altered the NIV in each instance we quote to the word "allegiance" where the word is often translated as "faithful." The Greek term *pistos* has both the sense of an act of faith *and* ongoing acts of faith. Since Jesus is the Lord of lords and the King of kings, faithfulness to Jesus is *allegiance*. And Jesus, too, was allegiant in his own witness:

> Grace and peace to you . . . from Jesus Christ, who is the *allegiant* witness, the firstborn from the dead, and the ruler of the kings of the earth. (1:4–5)

> These are the words of the Amen, the *allegiant* and true witness, the ruler of God's creation. (3:14)

> I saw heaven standing open and there before me was a white horse, whose rider is called *Allegiant* and True. With justice he judges and wages war. (19:11)

What the Colossus Christ has revealed to John and the seven churches in this book is also reliable, trustworthy, and allegiant to God's purposes (21:5; 22:6).

In Revelation believers are called to be allegiant—faithful witnesses—to Jesus as Lord in whatever situation they find themselves.

> Do not be afraid of what you are about to suffer. I tell you, the devil will put some of you in prison to test you, and you will suffer persecution for ten days. Be *allegiant*, even to the point of death, and I will give you life as your victor's crown. (2:10)

> I know where you live—where Satan has his throne. Yet you remain true to my name. You did not renounce your *allegiance* to me, not even in the days of Antipas, my *allegiant* witness, who was put to death in your city—where Satan lives. (2:13)

> I know your deeds, your love and *allegiance*, your service and perseverance, and that you are now doing more than you did at first. (2:19)

> This calls for patient endurance and *allegiance* on the part of God's people. (13:10)

> This calls for patient endurance on the part of the people of God who keep his commands and remain *allegiant* to Jesus. (14:12)

> They will wage war against the Lamb, but the Lamb will triumph over them because he is Lord of lords and King of kings—and with him will be his called, chosen and *allegiant* followers. (17:14)

The most common virtue prescribed for followers of Jesus is that they become faithful or allegiant to Jesus. If he is their Lord, they should be allegiant witnesses to his lordship in both their *word* and *works*.

Notice the stressors at work against that allegiance: persecution, imprisonment, and martyrdom (2:10, 13). Faithful allegiance involves walking in the way of the Lamb by engaging in good works with love, serving others with resilience, and by generally trying to do the right thing. In 13:10 and 14:12 we see the wild things breathing fire on the woman's children, and the call here is for allegiance to Jesus and resilience in the face of suffering and martyrdom. In the final battle, with all its buzz and fright, the Lamb goes to battle with his "chosen and allegiant followers" (17:14).

Allegiance flows directly from worship and is attached to our witness. We witness to Jesus as Lord in the daily routines of life as well as the tests and trials of life.

The Aim of All Worship: Christoformity

How shall we sum up the major themes of the Christian life as we find them in Revelation? Walking in the way of the Lamb means *worshiping* God on the throne and the Lamb in the center of that throne. It means being *an allegiant witness in word and works.* There is a term coined by one of our favorite teachers, James D. G. Dunn, that sums up what it means to worship God and the Lamb while living in Babylon as an allegiant witness: "christoformity." That is, to be formed into the image of Christ. Look once again at these three texts:

Grace and peace to you . . . from Jesus Christ, who is the *allegiant* witness. (1:4–5)

These are the words of the Amen, the *allegiant* and true witness, the ruler of God's creation. (3:14)

I saw heaven standing open and there before me was a white horse, whose rider is called *Allegiant* and True. (19:11)

Three times in Revelation Jesus is called *allegiant,* and twice this is connected to *witness.* Jesus *is* the Allegiant One and Jesus *is* the Witness. For the Christians of western Asia Minor to be allegiant witnesses it meant participating in who Jesus is and entering into the work he has given us in extending the gospel. It is to be Christ's presence in Babylon.

Especially today. In the USA.

It's time to turn the heat up and look at the relevance of Revelation for our day. It's not pretty.

PART 5

Discipleship for Dissidents Today

CHAPTER 20

Four Marks
of Babylon Today

The ways of reading Revelation that spend time speculating about the questions *When will all this happen?* and *Who is the antichrist?* fail the church in discipleship. Instead of a discipleship that teaches us to discern Babylon among us and shows us how to live in Babylon as *dissidents* instead of *conformists*, these speculative questions teach Christians how to wait for the *escape* from Babylon. They encourage questions like *Will I be left behind or raptured?* and *Am I "in" or "out"?* or *Am I saved or not?* By making future-focused judgments central to reading Revelation and treating Babylon as a world-class city of the future or giving the USA and Israel a central role in the divine plan, this speculative method teaches adherents to trust in the wrong things—especially the false safety of the all-powerful American military.

However, as we have seen, Babylon was and is a *timeless trope* for empires and nations and powers that systematize injustices, oppress the people of God, and suppress the truths of liberation. Babylon is no more a city of the future than it is a city of the here and now. If we want to live out the message of Revelation today, we need to develop eyes that discern Babylon's power, violence, and injustice in our midst today. We must recognize the Babylon all around us. *New York Times* columnist Ross Douthat once described his search for a home in a more rural setting, noting that he sometimes pictures himself "flying around to various Babylons for important meetings and interviews." Here, Douthat clearly conceives of Babylon as a trope. And in this chapter, we will do the same by clarifying four characteristics of Babylon today, the Babylon all around us here and now. And—fair warning—we will explain how America is its own kind of Babylon.

Arrogance

The heart of Babylon will always be arrogant self-sufficiency that has no need for God, no care for the people of God, and no commitment to the ways of God. The haunting words of Babylon, perhaps only muttered in the privacy of one's mind and heart, are "There is none besides me" (from Isa 47:8). John's Babylon says, "I will never mourn" (Rev 18:7). This gives us insight into how Babylon thinks: *it thinks of itself, for itself, about itself, and everything revolves around itself.* This is an empire called "narcissism." It thinks of itself in comparative terms and is always on the hunt for potential competitors. It either draws others into its circle and under its power, or it works to silence, exploit, and kill all rivals. Opposition prompts rage. Discerning eyes detect Babylon by its arrogance.

This arrogance is found—and no doubt you've been thinking along these lines already—in Babylon's political leaders. Over the past years, many Americans noted the arrogant desire expressed in the motto "make America great again." The rest of the world was gobsmacked by a mentality reeking of colonialism and global dominance. America can flourish as a nation without having to denigrate other countries, and it should rejoice in the economic growth of other nations. America can aid poorer nations without acts of paternalism and condescension. Only arrogant people refer to others as "sh-thole countries." That president's comments, in particular, were hideous, and the commentary and denunciations that followed were justified. We can confidently say that American arrogance comes not from new Jerusalem, but from Babylon, and any claim that we're on the road to new Jerusalem while living like Babylon unmasks our hypocrisy.

Arrogance is not exclusively a mark of politicians—past, present, or even presidential:

> one finds it among business owners, small or great;
> in fathers in families;
> in bullies in neighborhoods;
> in pastors and church boards;
> in megachurches and rural churches;
> in institutions, Christian or not.

Arrogance is the way of the dragon and the way of the wild things.

So, what are the marks of national arrogance that Revelation teaches dissident disciples to discern? First, there is a sense of *grandiosity*, thinking you live in the world's greatest nation. Second, there is *competition* with other nations in a vain quest to dominate. Third, there is the exercise of power by *cutting off relationships* with other nations who desire their own autonomy and sovereignty. What America wants for itself, in other words, is too often not what it wants for other nations, a denial of the principle of the Golden Rule. Fourth, there is *an irredeemable inability to empathize, sympathize, and show compassion for "less fortunate" nations*. And finally, there is *rage and retaliation when criticized*.

There's too much Babylonian arrogance in the United States of America.

Babylon is closer to home than many of us realize.

Economic Exploitation

Arrogant Babylon also economically exploits others for its own prosperity. Money and status are power and the love language of Babylon, what we might call a "meritocracy." In America's meritocracy, the wealthy are considered wealthy by virtue of their work ethic while those in poverty are poor because of their lack of a work ethic. The "virtuous wealthy" look down on the "unvirtuous poor." The wealthy lack gratitude for their achievements and grow proud and arrogant, while the poor are shamed as "deplorables" and resent the "elites." Money means power, status, and virtue in the Babylons of this world.

Economic exploitation, as we find in the mind-boggling disparity of income in the USA, is a sign of Babylon. The prophet Isaiah directly connects silver and gold to idols, saying: "For in that day every one of you will reject the idols of silver and gold your sinful hands have made" (Isa 31:7). We especially like Robert Alter's translation, finding (as he often does) a clever twist with the "ungods of silver and his ungods of gold."

There is no reason a nation with as many Christians as the USA has (or claims to have) should have such disparity in income, in housing, in wages, in healthcare, and in community social capital. We may not embrace a radical solution like equal incomes, but as Christians we ought to be firmly committed to influencing our policies in the direction of greater economic justice. Dissident disciples ask questions about free market capitalism. Benjamin Friedman, in a brilliant study of the religious nature of the rise of America's capitalism, asks a question we believe more Christians need to ask:

Is capitalism, as a free market system,
coherent with the Christian faith?

And the question behind that one is,

Do we even think morally about our economic system?

Friedman's argument is that Adam Smith and those who formed capitalism were swimming in religious waters even though they were turning away from a robust Christian faith. In rejecting Calvinism's determinism, the capitalists built a system on the following three ideas:

(1) self-interested freedom,
(2) a self-interested freedom that was to be disciplined or constrained by competition in the markets,

and (3) a belief that self-interest and competition would lead to the common good with economic benefits for the most.

But what is driven by self-interest and competition and then measured by the economy is not a *Christian* system of economics. A Christian version of common-good competition requires a people of character. That is, the citizens need to be just and generous, and they need to aim for an equitable society.

Capitalism alone has no character.

Without a virtuous character, everything is measured by markets and fueled by ambition, competition, self-determination, and self-interest. Absent character, capitalism naturally produces a culture of greed. And it gets religious icing on its cake far too often. As Wayland-Smith puts it, "Americans have always genuflected before the inscrutable power of the free market to distribute favors both earthly and heavenly. That the market is righteous," she sardonically remarks, "is a national article of faith."

But the free market does not produce disciples on the way to the new Jerusalem. It produces Babylon.

The sin that underlies economic exploitation flows from malformed character. Generations of greed do not create or guarantee a generous economy. Perhaps a new generation filled with character, with the moral tendons and ligaments of justice, equity, and generosity, might lead America away from its dragon-based Babylonian economics toward the economics of new Jerusalem. We need a moral revolution in the economic sector. Babylon has made its home in the American economy. The church can lead the way out of this by forming a culture of economic justice for the common good.

Militarism

Nothing is more overtly akin to Babylon than an addiction to militarism. At least 108 million humans were killed in wars in the twentieth century. Between 650 thousand and 1 million were killed in the American Civil War, fought between a "Christian" south and a "Christian" north. Between 500 thousand and 2 million were killed in the Mexican Revolution, between 500 thousand and 1 million in the Spanish Civil War, between 16 million and 40 million in World War I, between 5 and 9 million in the Russian Civil War, and between 8 and 12 million in the Chinese Civil War. World War II: between 56 and 85 million! We'll stop there, but the death totals mount as we add more and more wars between nations and within nations.

The numbers are atrocious.

Mind-numbing.

Beggaring beliefs.

And the USA has the largest military the world has ever known. According to one site, each year the United States spends more than 700 billion dollars on its military, while China spends 261 billion. We spend more than twice as much as India, Russia, Saudia Arabia, France, Germany, the UK, Japan, and South Korea combined.

This is a sign of Babylon. The dragon loves war because wars produce death.

I (Scot) came of age during the Vietnam "conflict" where between 2.4 and 4.3 million died and then began my career as a professor during Ronald Reagan's slogan of "peace through strength," now recognized as code language for military buildup, multiplication of nuclear strength, and development of satellite technology and spying. We had the hubris to remind the world of "our" victory in World War II. Peace through strength intimidates others with power and evokes the myths of Babylon's ungods. It is reminiscent of Rome of the first century, and if you doubt this, read Julius Caesar's *The Gallic War* or Josephus's *The Jewish War.*

The words of Revelation 18:2 eternally refute the militaristic claims of Babylon, whether it is ancient Babylon, ancient Rome, or modern Russia or the USA: "Fallen! Fallen is Babylon the Great!"

The might that made Rome an empire will bow to the might that makes God God and the Lamb the Lamb. Brian Blount sums it up best: Babylons will be "sLambed."

The power of military might is a Babylonian reality, not a new Jerusalem one. The Lamb was slaughtered because he refused to use Babylon's weapons, and the way of the Lamb is to conquer by the "sword from his mouth," not a sword drawn from a scabbard. The Word of God is the weapon of choice for those walking in the way of the Lamb. The way of the Lamb is the way of peace, through peacemaking and reconciliation. It means dropping the sword and beating that sword into a garden tool.

Blessed are the peacemakers, Jesus said, and he meant it.

Christian "realists" counter the biblical vision of peace by claiming that if we really live that way we will lose and emphasize that each country has a responsibility to defend itself. They argue that in a sinful fallen world, a military is both a necessity and a last resort. Their contention is that the way of the Lamb is for *another world*, not the *real* world in which we live. In this world militarism will always be needed.

Jesus was no realist, and neither was John.

The weapon of choice for Jesus was the cross. The Lamb of Revelation slays with the sword that proceeds from his mouth. Christian realism compromises the way of the Lamb because true realism is a deep reality that sees God on the throne and the Lamb in its center.

Peace through strength hollows out the Lamb's
gospel into a shell of fraudulent piety.

Christians in America today live under the umbrella of Babylon's arrogance, economic exploitation, and militarism.

Oppression

John writes from Patmos because he spoke up and spoke out. He was a witness. And Babylon still oppresses today. Take China. Reports are that there are around a million Muslims in prison. In North Korea, a country that tolerates less freedom than any nation in the world, some 70 thousand Christians are in prison. Six million Jews were exterminated under Hitler. Looking even further back, medieval Europe was Catholic and intolerant of reformers. The Lutheran Reformation along with the Swiss Reformed became intolerant of the more radical Anabaptist reformers. The plot to move from England to North America led to various regions tolerating only one dominant denomination—Anglicans in Virginia, Catholics in Maryland—and a country established in part for freedom of religion at times became intolerant of other Christian expressions of faith. Our First Amendment—that "Congress shall make no law respecting an establishment of religion or prohibiting the free exercise thereof"—promised toleration rooted in freedom.

> *I confess that I never intended to become adjusted to the evils of segregation and the crippling effects of discrimination, to the moral degeneracy of religious bigotry and the corroding effects of narrow sectarianism, to economic conditions that deprive men of work and food, and to the insanities of militarism and the self-defeating effects of physical violence.*
> —Martin Luther King Jr., *Strength to Love*, 18

Intolerance draws battle lines for Babylon. And even though American freedom combines that freedom with tolerance for others, Babylon responds with various forms of intolerance and oppression: silencing, obstructing, boundary marking, exploiting, manipulating, harming, causing suffering, persecuting, killing, and narrating an ungod story of everything. One of Babylon's major forms of intolerance and oppression is racism, what a recent professor called the "American blindspot" and what others have called America's "original sin." In a bold move by an even bolder writer, Isabel

Wilkerson proposed that the fundamental term we use in the USA should not be "racism" but "caste." America's treatment of non-white persons is nothing less, she contends, than a race-based system that has now become a caste system. And this American version of caste is the fruit of Babylon. It is uniquely American, propped up and created by "Christians," and it has now become systemic.

Isabel Wilkerson's Eight Pillars of the Caste System in America

1. Caste expresses God's will and the laws of nature.
2. Caste is inherited from birth.
3. Caste is controlled by restricting marriage to one's caste.
4. Caste guards the pure caste from the polluted castes.
5. Caste creates a hierarchy of occupations with lowest castes at the bottom.
6. Caste intentionally dehumanizes and stigmatizes.
7. Caste is enforced by terror and controlled by cruelty.
8. Caste segregates superior persons from inferior persons.

Isabel Wilkerson, *Caste: The Origins of Our Discontents*
(New York: Random House, 2020), 97–164.

Here are three of the statements she makes in her proposal to recognize racism in the USA as a caste system:

Caste is the infrastructure of our divisions. It is the architecture of human hierarchy, the subconscious code of instructions for maintaining, in our case, a four-hundred-year-old social order.

A caste system is an artificial construction, a fixed and embedded ranking of human value that sets the presumed supremacy of one group against the presumed inferiority of other groups on the basis of ancestry and often immutable traits, traits that would be neutral in the abstract but are ascribed life-and-death meaning in a hierarchy favoring the dominant caste whose forebears designed it. A caste system uses rigid, often arbitrary boundaries to keep the ranked groupings apart, distinct from one another and in their assigned places.

Race, in the United States, is the visible agent of the unseen force of caste. Caste is the bones, race the skin. Race is what we can see, the physical traits that have been given arbitrary meaning and become shorthand for who a person is. Caste is the powerful infrastructure that holds each group in its place.

Many will want to know how she defines caste in comparison with race. Here is a concise summary of her answer to that question:

What is the difference between racism and casteism? Because caste and race are interwoven in America, it can be hard to separate the two. Any action or institution that mocks, harms, assumes, or attaches inferiority or stereotype on the basis of the social construct of race can be considered racism. Any action or structure that seeks to limit, hold back, or put someone in a defined ranking, seeks to keep someone in their place by elevating or denigrating that person on the basis of their perceived category, can be seen as casteism.

We would say that both racism and casteism are Babylonian. The Apocalypse teaches us that the dragon loves racism because it brings death, the wild things enforce racism because it coerces into conformity, and Babylon embodies racism. In both South Africa and the United States, Christianity was welded from toe to head with racism until it became systemic in these so-called Christian countries. There's much more to say about this, as we have only begun to recognize the systemic nature of racism and its impact on our country. A conversion of imagination can bring a revolution in character formation, but until characters are transformed, racism will remain a cultural habit. Laws may restrain systemic racism and policies may prompt some conversion of the imagination. And that is what is required—a conversion of the imagination similar to what John experienced—for us to see that all nations, all tongues, all races, all tribes will bow before God. Only on our knees before God and the Lamb will we as Christians be transformed into equals.

Converts on their knees become dissidents.

How do we act as dissidents?

How do we live in our Babylon today?

CHAPTER 21

How Then Shall We
Live in Babylon?

Though we have said it before, it cannot be said often enough: too many interpretations of Revelation miss its message of discipleship because those interpretations are obsessed with speculations about *who* and *where* and *what*. They barely recognize the message of dissident discipleship, and readings of the book become an exercise in comparing newspapers to the so-called predictions of the end time. This approach fails the church, especially the evangelical church. Our goal in this book, however, is to learn to read Revelation through the lens of Babylon's timeless presence in the world to understand how Christians are to be allegiant witnesses to Jesus amid Babylons. This is a message of discipleship that turns hot lights on every Babylon in the world—including the USA and the complicity of American Christians in the ways of Babylon.

American evangelicalism has lost its way and is suffocating in its own urp. We apologize for being graphic, but we are motivated by something deep in our hearts to teach and disciple Christians to go where they may not have gone in the past. Even if you aren't sure of the connections we make, give us a couple pages to explain and set up the case we wish to make. In brief, we believe evangelicals in the USA have been seduced into partisan politics in such a way that they have effectively abandoned the way of the Lamb. In what follows, we hope to survey the results of this seduction.

In a respectable poll,

82% of Republicans think the Democrat party has been taken over by socialists.

80% of Democrats think the Republican party has been taken over by racists.

86% of Democrats think President Trump encouraged white supremacy groups, while only 17% of Republicans agree with that.

A politic of hate has overwhelmed the American public. Christians are on both sides of the divide, which means Christians are part of these numbers.

The most embarrassing moment I (Scot) have ever experienced as an American citizen was the day a group of incited insurrectionists stampeded the US Capitol Building while Congress was in session. Our president at the time had egregiously misunderstood the Constitution. He was insisting that the vice president decertify the electoral college votes and hand the election victory over to him. Even the writer of the conservative *National Review*, Andrew C. McCarthy, could point out the legal error he was making: "The context for the rioting was Trump's demagogic undermining of the Twelfth Amendment and principles of federalism. Such a betrayal of the Constitution he was sworn to preserve, protect, and defend is itself worthy of an impeachment article." A president who doesn't follow the law is an embarrassment.

But an even deeper embarrassment was seeing many of the insurrectionists carrying Christian signs and symbolically performing Christian behaviors like praying and singing. Those various displays of "Christian symbols" forced one to ponder *what kind* of Christian faith such persons had. What they were doing and saying is not recognizable as Christian faith. My sense of embarrassment was exacerbated because of a reckless claim made over and over by Eric Metaxas, a populist Christian apologist, that the election was stolen by Democrats manipulating the votes. Where, I wondered, did Metaxas lose his way? How are so many evangelical Christians deceived by such preposterous claims? Why are so many of them attending prayer rally exorcisms and hymn sings and public speeches as expressions of what they believe to be the Christian faith—all on behalf of an election they think was stolen?

Premillennialism, Politics, and "Christian" Nationalism

Though there are many historical factors at work, one touchpoint that helps us understand the larger narrative begins in the 1970s and 1980s. At that time, and in the decades that followed, the evangelical movement became politicized to the point that the very term "evangelical" began to lose its core meaning. In recent years, one thinker after another has concluded that the term "evangelical" today is largely equivalent to "Republican." And in some cases, it may even be more Republican than Christian. For decades good thinkers described evangelicalism in different terms, as Bible-centered and cross-centered and promoting born-again-ism and activism in both evangelism and worthy social concerns. Others might (correctly) add that it is ecumenical in that it cannot be narrowed down to one denomination. These five big ideas are said to form a theological definition of evangelicalism. While this may at one time have been a good set of categories for determining who was and who was not an evangelical, something began to change in the 1970s. Today, the word "evangelical" now largely overlaps with "Republican" and "anti-Democrat" and alignment with other GOP platform positions. Ryan Burge, among other astute observers of American evangelicalism, has drawn attention to this change.

Despite the claims of many in the media, evangelicalism is not fading away any time soon. In a recent article in *National Interest*, which anticipates his book *The Nones*, Burge makes the following observations:

But just because the share of Americans who identify as an evangelical has not changed in a statistically meaningful way doesn't mean that the composition of that group has not. *A crucial part of this story is that the term "evangelical" has, I believe, become somewhat detached from its theological roots and morphed into a term that seems to capture political sensibilities as well.* As political scientist John Green observes, "[Evangelicals have] become very strongly associated with Republican and conservative politics, because since the days of Ronald Reagan up until today, that group of believers have moved in that direction politically."

In other words, evangelicalism has increasingly become identified not by its theology, its mission, or its evangelism, but by its politics. And the problem is that these political motives are rooted in Babylon and not new Jerusalem. Burge also points to church attendance decreases by those claiming the label "evangelical," as evidenced in several major social science surveys:

There's evidence of this move from the theological to the political. In 2008, 59% of evangelicals said that they attended church at least once a week. Just 16% said that they attended services "seldom" or "never." By 2019, those percentages had shifted significantly. The share who were weekly attenders declined a full seven percentage points, to 52%. On the bottom end of the spectrum, nearly a quarter of self-identified evangelicals said that they attended church "seldom" or "never" (24.2%). The share who never attended nearly tripled from 2.7% in 2008 to 7.3% in 2019.

What can we draw from this decrease in church attendance among those claiming the moniker "evangelical"? Here, we believe, is the most important finding of these studies:

The implication is that for many of those who self-identified as "evangelical," it is not just about devotion to a local church, but to a general orientation to the world. *As Republicanism and the religious right have become more enmeshed, it seems logical to assume that these less religiously devout people may consider their evangelicalism to be a question of political identity, rather than religious beliefs and customs.*

Burge concludes that evangelicalism in the USA is no longer definable by its theological beliefs and has instead been captured by politics.

Kristin Kobes Du Mez, a professor of history at Calvin University, in her book *Jesus and John Wayne,* demonstrates over and over that American evangelicalism can no longer be defined by its theological convictions *but by its cultural impulses, desires, and politics.* Du Mez knots this cultural evangelicalism to power and patriarchalism exhibited in masculinity and militarism. What happened at the US Capitol then was not the work of fringe nutjobs but a movement that tapped into the hard-core cultural shifts happening among evangelicals for the last half century. Thus, Du Mez writes,

> Evangelical support for Trump was no aberration, nor was it merely a pragmatic choice. It was, rather, the culmination of evangelicals' embrace of militant masculinity, an ideology that enshrines patriarchal authority and condones the callous display of power, at home and abroad. By the time Trump arrived proclaiming himself their savior, conservative white evangelicals had already traded a faith that privileges humility and elevates "the least of these" for one that derides gentleness as the province of wusses. Rather than turning the other cheek, they'd resolved to defend their faith and their nation, secure in the knowledge that the ends justify the means. Having replaced the Jesus of the Gospels with a vengeful warrior Christ, it's no wonder many came to think of Trump in the same way. In 2016, many observers were stunned at evangelicals' apparent betrayal of their own values. *In reality, evangelicals did not cast their vote despite their beliefs, but because of them.*

We quote these words from Kristin's book with regret, though we do not regret quoting. We regret how perceptively true her book is. She's not alone in this analysis of evangelicalism, nor can this be relegated to the province of wussy progressives. I have watched this happen, not as a progressive, not as a Republican, but as an independent who loves liberty and who loves justice and peace.

This is a book about reading and understanding Revelation, not American evangelicalism. So why do we include this analysis here? Because reading Revelation gives us clues to perceive Babylon today, and we believe Babylon has infiltrated American evangelicalism. Which raises a good question: Is one's eschatology—dispensationalism in particular—at work in shaping the evangelical world toward becoming increasingly Republican? For sure. Consider this chart found in a book by Samuel Perry and Philip Gorski showing a correlation between premillennial, predictive prophecies about the rapture and the kind of "Christian" nationalism that stormed the Capitol on January 6, 2021.

Figure 21.1 Predicted adherence to Christian nationalism across belief in a literal Rapture and Armageddon.

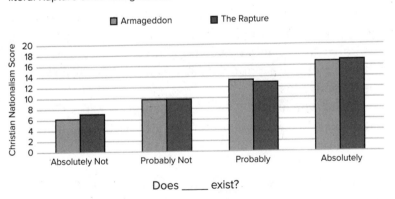

Source: 2007 Baylor Religion Survey.
Note: Ordinary least squares regression models predicting Christian nationalism scale. Controls include political party identification, political conservatism, religious tradition, religiosity, beliefs about the Bible, age, gender, educational attainment, income, and region of the country.

I (Scot) grew up immersed in this kind of eschatology, so it's easy for me to see the correlation patterns: the USA was tied at the hip to Israel, Israel was the apple of God's eye, Russia or some godless socialist or communist country or then the European Union were brewing themselves for Armageddon while we were safe because we would be raptured, and soon it would all happen. All of this was accompanied by an utter confidence that America and the red, white, and blue was on God's side and our politics were God's politics. My homegrown eschatology was as American—if not more American than it was biblical. Ask any who have read the *Left Behind* series how American, and thus how nationalistic, these books were. (Very.)

> Christian nationalism is the "perfection" of the
> right-wing politicization of evangelicalism.

In their book *Taking America Back for God*, a book about how Christian nationalism is at work among evangelicals, Andrew Whitehead and Samuel Perry make this stunning observation: "Holding to beliefs most associated with premillennial eschatology is one of the leading predictors of Americans' adhering to Christian nationalism." If you ask those most associated with premillennialism—from Billy Graham on—what their politics are, you will find a clear correlation with conservative politics that often veers into American Christian nationalism.

All of which raises the next question. What is Christian nationalism? Here is a short and helpful definition. Christian nationalism is:

> A cultural framework that blurs distinctions between Christian identity and American identity. . . . It is undergirded by identification with a conservative political orientation (though not necessarily a political party), Bible belief, premillennial visions of moral decay, and divine sanction for conquest. Finally, its

conception of morality centers *exclusively* on fidelity to religion and fidelity to the nation.

This is Christian nationalism—Christianity co-opted in the service of ethno-national power and separation.

Whitehead and Perry, and we could mention others like John Fea, have offered compelling evidence and arguments demonstrating that what is happening today among many evangelicals is a perversion of biblical Christianity. They name some of the most visible culprits: Jerry Falwell Sr., D. James Kennedy, Ralph Reed, James Dobson, Michele Bachmann, David Barton, Wayne Grudem, Robert Jeffress, and Mike Huckabee (and we would add Eric Metaxas).

Again, you may wonder what all this has to do with the book of Revelation. To quote the apostle Paul, "much in every way!" (Rom 3:2). Revelation is written to shape disciples of Jesus into dissidents who can discern the dominant influence of empire (Babylon) and who have the courage to follow the way of the Lamb in a world run by the dragon. Those who utilize Revelation to speculate about the future have turned the book into a predictive timeline for people to ask *who* and *when*, while John wrote the book for disciples of Jesus who want to faithfully follow Jesus while living within Babylon. Christian nationalism is a new iteration of wannabe Christendom, led by its own versions of Constantine and Theodosius and some of the Puritans (to get closer to our time). Those who don't recognize Babylon in Christian nationalism need a new reading of Revelation. We need the discerning eyes of people like Ryan Burge, Kristin Kobes Du Mez, Andrew Whitehead, Samuel Perry, Philip Gorski, and John Fea to help us see what is happening today, and we are grateful to God for each of them.

Another voice we are grateful for is Randall Balmer, a professional historian of American evangelicalism. After sketching the political poppycock of evangelical leaders like Metaxas calling the election fraudulent and referring to their cultural "losses" as persecution, Balmer speaks up and speaks out against this new "mutant form" of evangelicalism, challenging us all to think again. He says,

> As someone who grew up evangelical and as a historian of the movement, I want to yell: *You're better than this!* and remind evangelicals of their noble history of concern for those on the margins of society, those Jesus called "the least of these." I fear, however, that their trumped-up sense of beleaguerment, their embrace of far-right ideologues and demagogues and, yes, racists has produced a mutant form of the movement that can no longer be recognized as Christian.

There is one more point we wish to emphasize before we conclude: fear is lurking behind all of this. In his excellent review of Du Mez's *Jesus and John Wayne*, Sean Michael Lucas (in *Mere Orthodoxy*) writes,

> The other historical (and really, pastoral) contribution that Du Mez makes is the way she puts her finger right on the heart of evangelicalism's public stance. As she puts so well, "Fear had been at the heart of evangelical postwar politics—a fear of godless communism and a fear that immorality would leave Americans defenseless" (59). For those who grew up in evangelicalism, the twin evils trumpeted in the 1980s were Communism and secular humanism; fast forward past 9/11, those were exchanged for radical Islam and the militant gay agenda; today, "critical race theory" would fit somewhere in the rogues' gallery.
>
> But while the rogues change, *it is fear upon which evangelical leaders always trade.* That's how all too often they build their platforms, secure donations, justify their reasons for existence. And fear is what drove the past two national election cycles: fear of Hillary Clinton, fear of various agendas, fear of Black Lives Matter, fear of "socialism" and AOC, fear of "losing our country." Fear is what has caused evangelical

believers to fall for QAnon and will keep them from receiving the COVID vaccine.

People who are afraid often tend to embrace conspiracy theories. These alternate realities provide a form of security, allowing them to live within their self-constructed fantasies. When power is your hope and goal, if that power is not on your side, it is easier to turn to the fantasy of conspiracy.

Evangelicalism's core theological convictions have now been augmented and supplanted by politics. James Dobson, James Kennedy, Jerry Falwell Sr. and Jr. provide excellent case studies of this. For them, the world has become apocalyptic and they are on the downside of this shift, viewing the other political party as the dragon, the wild things, and Babylon. Again, their speculation fails to teach the dissident and discerning discipleship of Revelation. They have failed to understand the timelessness of Babylon, that Babylon is always with us. One careful reading of the major chapters about Babylon is all one needs to form a Babylonian hermeneutic that provides discernment of Babylon in America and in its churches. Yet repeated failed readings of Revelation have today led to a failure to discern Babylon. These leaders and those who follow them have been duped by the promise of political power as redemption. American evangelicalism is what it is today because of a tragic decision in the 1970s and 80s—a decision to become more like Babylon. We are now living with the long-term fruit of those decisions.

Nathan Hatch, one of America's finest church historians, is another who is now onto what has happened. He broadens his lens to scope out some of the challenges also to progressivism, not least that it secularizes Christian hope (see appendix 12, "The Progress of Progressivism" for a deeper discussion):

> Some thirty years ago, sociologist Robert Wuthnow said that the basic intellectual and cultural divide among Christians in America is not the fault line of their theology but the cultural divide between a conservative and progressive worldview,

a chasm deeper and more formative than any theological debate. I agreed with him in the 1980s. And I think today his point could be made with much greater emphasis. A divide has become a chasm. Dominant political and cultural values, left and right, have washed over churches and come to dominate their respective worldviews.

Here is the point we have been making in his words:

What one witnesses today, like the eighteenth century, is the politicizing of reality—for all of us, conservatives and progressives alike.

Churches clearly need to form the faithful in how to think—and sometimes act—in the arena of politics and society.

What we all need, conservative or progressive (see appendix 12, "The Progress of Progressivism"), is a lens for detecting Babylon's corruption that impacts the whole American church. And along with that, a lens for hope.

An Eschatology of Hope

It is not our aim to take sides among the two major approaches to Christian engagement in politics (conservative and progressive). Rather, we are urging Christians to comprehend what is happening in this cultural moment and find ways to discern the good and the bad on both sides. Revelation's portrait of Babylon gives us the tools we need for discernment and hope. Some who were nurtured in dispensationalism's speculations and outlandish theory of history have rejected that eschatology, but instead of opting for progressivism they have become pessimists. Brian Daly, an expert on the first few centuries of Christianity, concluded this about the hope of the early church: "One thing is clear from the beginning of Christian literature: hope for the future is an inseparable, integral dimension of Christian faith, and the implied condition of possibility for responsible Christian action in the world." To surrender hope teeters on surrendering what makes Christianity Christian, and hope is surely what makes Revelation Revelation!

Christian Eschatology's Major Themes

1. A linear view of history: beginning and goal
2. Resurrection of the body
3. A universal judgment
4. Judgment at the end of each person's life
5. Retribution or redemption
6. The dead are involved in this life

From Brian J. Daly, *The Hope of the Early Church*, 219–23

Christians differed on the time and nearness of the end of history, the nature of the resurrection body, the extent of redemption for all, the possibility of continued transformation after death, and the possibility of purgation after death.

Christian eschatology is the alternative to Babylon's eschatology. Christian eschatology formulates hope in the midst of lament, petition in the face of the dragon, and it knows from the incarnation of Christ that God is with us all the way to the hideousness of crucifixion. Christian eschatology enables us to grow through resilience and allegiant witness into the shape of the Lord who is the Lamb. Christian eschatology, contrary to Christian nationalism, progressivism, and pessimism, assumes evil, does not explain it away, and knows what lies beyond and in front of us. Christian eschatology turns us away from both progressivism and pessimism, not by denying progress or working to improve life, and not by pretending harsh realities don't exist, but by trusting the God of promise who broke the power of death in the resurrection of the Lamb and who also promises that someday new Jerusalem will descend, and justice will finally arrive on the earth.

The church has lost its voice because it has lost its eschatology. If we were preaching or lecturing right now, we'd slow down the pace, pausing to grab your attention.

And we'd say this to you:

> We need discipleship, that's what we need.
> We need political discipleship, that's what we need.

Now a third sentence, a little slower and a little lower:

> What we need is a manifesto for dissident discipleship.

CHAPTER 22

A Manifesto for
Dissident Disciples

The book of Revelation requires us to take a stand for the Lamb in this world. To read it well we must learn to think "theo-politically," or to say this another way, the entire book of Revelation is about *public discipleship*. Revelation "reveals" God's perspective on God's world, and it does this by showing us how to discern the dragon, the dragon's wild things, and the dragon's Babylon. When we opt for social engagement but leave God behind the walls of our private life, we fail to put the book of Revelation into practice. For this book, God's politics is the only politics. Revelation, as Elisabeth Schüssler Fiorenza reminds us over and over, "will elicit a fitting theo-ethical response *only in those socio-political situations that cry out for justice.*"

Churches and pastors, professors and authors, and citizens and children are looking for a leader who will demonstrate a different Christian posture toward politics, asking for discipleship that challenges politicization in all its forms. They want pastors to preach a gospel that subverts Babylon. They ache for a clear, courageous voice of conviction. They believe in a gospel that forms dissidents who follow the Lamb and who have the courage to speak up and out about partisanism as capitulation to Babylon.

We have not been discipled to think like this. We have not learned to think Christianly about government and political powers.

So, we have flattened the world into a game of human power, and we are "in" the game itself. Our cosmology, unlike Revelation's cosmology with angels and the dragon and wild things, is secular. We pretend it is about voting and parties when there is a deeper and oft-ignored reality. As a result, many have fallen for the dragon's ways and are party to the wild things as they seek to make Babylon a more Christian place. But the only way to make Babylon a Christian place is to do what John says—"Come out!" We must come out from Babylon and live in new Jerusalem by witnessing to the truth of the Lamb. This does not mean we abandon work in the public sector or cease advocating for the common good. This would be irresponsible. Instead, we do these things with our eyes open, discerning the ways of the dragon. Babylon will never be the new Jerusalem; it cannot be Christianized.

Beginning to Worship a False God

What, then, can we offer as a final encouragement about a Revelation-shaped discipleship? Without dramatizing our country's deep divisions, we find it helpful to take our cues from the Barmen Declaration, drafted by Karl Barth in May 1934. The Barmen Declaration discerned what was at stake in the populist movements of Germany that Hitler coagulated into National Socialism. The German Lutheran Church became a hideous display of the (non)Christian faith and fell for the way of the dragon with its singular Wild Thing, Adolf Hitler, and sycophants Hermann Göring, Heinrich Himmler, and Rudolf Hess. Church members aligned with Hitler were called "German Christians" or *Die Deutsche Christen*. Barth discerned the depth of error in Hitler's *Deutsche Christen* movement, and through the tragic events leading up to and including World War II, Barth relentlessly and courageously opposed National Socialism. After he had been pushed out of Germany, Barth's courageous outspokenness was denounced by many, even in his native Switzerland, where he was banned from all political speech in 1941. The Swiss authorities considered locking him up to silence him, reminiscent of what ancient political leaders did to Israel's prophets or what the Roman emperor did in exiling John.

Barth's biographer, Eberhard Busch, relates how Hitler seized power in January 1933 and how quickly and discerningly Barth took a stand against him, saying "I saw my dear German people beginning to worship a false God." He knew instinctively that National Socialism would destroy the Christian faith unless it was resisted. Busch's own comments speak prophetically to us today, as the church of that day was not equipped to handle the power of the wild thing, nor did it have the eyes to discern it for what it really was. Why? *Because for years and decades it had accommodated itself to the ways of the dragon without even knowing it.* The National Socialists were onto the agenda of professors and pastors like Barth. On July 1, 1933 Barth sent a letter along with a copy of a published essay he had written in *Theologische Existenz heute* (Theological Existence Today) to Hitler. The publisher immediately reprinted it a week later. But by July 28, 1934, with 37,000 copies already in print, Hitler had banned it.

Hitler quickly seized control of the German Christian church, appointing compromised Babylonian leaders as its leaders. Before long the theology of the church was corrupted with devotion to the wild thing and other idolatries. When Barth refused to give the required Hitler salute in his classes, he was pulled into court for his dissidence. His response? He expounded the First Commandment before the three judges.

> I am the LORD your God, who brought you out of Egypt, out of the land of slavery.
> You shall have no other gods before me. (Exod 20:1–3)

Barth lost his case and was forced into retirement in Germany—along with nearly 1,700 others!—but was offered a teaching position at Basel in his home country of Switzerland, where he remained the rest of his life, eventually becoming the most famous theologian of the twentieth century. Barth's theology was not only for the lecture halls; he had a heart for the common worker and kept his piercing eyes on the powers of this world.

Today, some American Christians are worshiping false gods and their politics have replaced their faith. After forty years of partisanism, their knees have grown accustomed to bowing before the dragon and his wild things as they walk arm in arm—both unconsciously and consciously—into Babylon. There is much we, as American Christians, can learn from Barmen and Barth.

Barmen

The Barmen Declaration was written by Karl Barth and ratified on May 31, 1934. It was a statement by the only resisting branch of the German Church in response to the growing encroachment of Germany's radical nationalism, its National Socialism, in the church. The government and its megalomaniac dictator wanted control of the church of Germany, and the Barmen Declaration built a wall that said, "Beyond these the government must not go!" German pastors and parishioners who signed onto the Barmen Declaration were given red membership cards. Barth drafted the statement, but he and the declaration itself were accused of being too strong, too resistant, and too combative. Today, however, the Barmen Declaration is a paradigm for dissident disciples in how we can speak up and speak out whenever politics or government begin to encroach on our Christian faith.

We encourage any who read this to take what follows as a *manifesto for dissident disciples,* a manifesto that riffs off Barmen's paradigmatic declarations.

First the Word of God

God has spoken.

God's speech is the Logos, Word.

That Word is Jesus, and in Jesus we see the essence of God. John's Gospel puts it this way:

In the beginning was the Word, and the Word was with God, and the Word was God. He was with God in the beginning. Through him all things were made; without him nothing was made that has been made. In him was life, and that life was the light of all mankind. The light shines in the darkness, and the darkness has not overcome it . . .

The Word became flesh and made his dwelling among us. We have seen his glory, the glory of the one and only Son, who came from the Father, full of grace and truth. (John 1:1–5, 14)

In the book of Revelation this Word become flesh is the Lord of lords, the Lion, the Lamb of God who was slaughtered and gains victory over the dragon, the wild things, and Babylon by the sword that proceeds from his mouth. Christian dissident discipleship begins right here: *with a commitment to the Word of God in Scripture as the revelation of God for God's people.* Take and read. Eat this scroll, John was told. That is, look at it, hold it in our hands, embrace it, listen to it, chew on it, digest it, and let it do the work it alone can do. Those who surrender to the Word of God become disciples who are dissidents in Babylon.

Too many today have surrendered their minds to political ideology and colonized the Word of God to their ideology. They cease being prophets and instead become ideologues and demagogues. Such persons cannot disciple people in the book of Revelation but instead they disciple people into partisan politics. Jesus ceases being their Lord and instead becomes their ideological tool who is summoned into the room to sanctify their ideology.

Jesus Is the One True Lord

The dragon seduces humans to worship the wild things and thereby to reject worship of the Lamb and the God on the throne. The Lamb is the Lord and Savior. His redemption, by God's grace and through the power of the Spirit, transforms us as we gaze into the face of our Lord. As Paul puts this in memorable lines, "And we all, who with unveiled faces contemplate the Lord's glory, are being transformed into his image with ever-increasing glory, which comes from the Lord, who is the Spirit" (2 Cor 3:18). The Lord is also our Light: "For God, who said, '*Let light shine out of darkness*,' made his light shine in our hearts to give us the light of the knowledge of God's glory displayed in the face of Christ" (2 Cor 4:6).

We are to walk in this Light that liberates us from the way of the dragon and empowers us to be faithful witnesses to the Lamb. Too many settle for the way of the dragon, justifying it as the "way the world works," and others hide behind the difference between our public and our spiritual/private life. There is no division for dissident disciples. Jesus—Lord, Lamb, Logos, and Light—is over all, all the time.

American Christians, made stunningly clear in the trajectory of the last forty years, have compromised the lordship of the one true Lord by diminishing their first love and allegiance. Instead of a deep and rich dissident discipleship, we have a split discipleship. We have surrendered some parts of life to Babylon and other parts to New Jerusalem. Here we follow Jesus, there we follow the US Constitution. Here we are generous, there we pay what's due. Here we live in love, there we live in vindictive judgment. Here we are at peace, there we wage war. Christian leaders have sometimes failed us, contending that there is both a kingdom of this world and a kingdom of God, and we are to dwell in each. One is Babylon, and the other is new Jerusalem. We can't dwell in both. We call for a forthright dissident discipleship of allegiant witness.

We have not sufficiently taught, preached, lived, and required the lordship of the Lamb over all. Instead, we have bowed down before the powers of Babylon, and the sycophantic preachers and pastors are leading the way. Fawning over an opportunity to be in the limelight, stirred by closeness to power, and excited about making America more Christian, these sycophantic leaders have led a nation away from the gospel. Thinking proximity to power will make the church more influential is as likely as the corner shop thinking Amazon will be the source of that business's flourishing again. Babylon tolerates no rivals.

Dissidents Discern

For some this may sound too suspicious. No government is entirely toxic, but no government is entirely good either. The US government does enough good to stir admiration and gratitude, yet corruptions infiltrate every department every day. No government is the new Jerusalem. Babylon extends its reach into every legislature, every justice system, and every executive branch. We do not live in new Jerusalem, and that means we must have the *suspicion of a discerning dissident.*

One can trust that God empowers government, one can love one's country, one can be patriotic, one can vote and engage in the political process, and one can even serve in office, but that does not mean we bend the knee, casting our crowns before the government or declaring our allegiance. Every government combines Babylon with doing what is right, and it is the dissident's responsibility to detect the difference, to speak up and speak out, and embody the kingdom as it heads for new Jerusalem. Dissident disciples have a healthy dose of discernment and suspicion.

The Church Transcends

Fawning over Babylon's leaders divides the church. Nearly half of the American church votes one way as one half votes the other. If one's allegiance is to a party, if one thinks one's party is truly Christian, one has cut off one's sisters and brothers. Each group, because political alliance forms so much of their convictions, divides the church by appealing to Caesar. This violates our confession: the church transcends party and politics because, as the book of Revelation says often, those who worship God and the Lamb are from *every tribe, nation, and tongue.* The church is universal— politics and parties are local and national. Any allegiance to Caesar is nothing more than idolatrous worship of the wild things that will create division.

The dragon loves division, and the church divided loses its witness. Nothing is more obvious to America's commentators, columnists, and editors than the church's limpid presence in culture. No longer does our society wait for a word from the church. Our society no longer cares because the church no longer has a clarion witness. It directs the fight at its own ranks and considers Christians of a different political commitment to be unworthy, undeserving, corrupted, and deplorable. Babylon forms allegiances to candidates as if he or she is a messiah, and anchors hope deserving only of the kingdom of God in that candidate. When the candidate wins, celebration ensues; when the candidate loses, depression envelops. Celebrations and depressions indicate the directions of trust, hope, and allegiance. The church is called to follow the Lord of lords, the Lion who is the Lamb.

Dissident disciples of the Lamb join hands with *all* followers of Jesus, but we call *all* followers of Jesus to embody the church transcendent.

Dissident Disciples Proclaim the Gospel

Babylon has seized the church's heart. Its grip is so tight many can no longer distinguish their politics from the gospel. The church must return to the gospel and make the gospel the message of the church—the one heard each Sunday, the one heard in each Bible class, the one heard on the Christian's podcast, the one heard through the Christian's social media. For years social media has gained a bigger and bigger foothold on public discourse, and it has become our (un)spiritual formation's biggest influence. Daily outrage and daily defense, from both sides, have become the diet of American Christians and our "conversation" so politicized we have nothing left in our energy sources for the good news about Jesus.

It is time, then, to return to the gospel. The gospel, as sketched by the apostle Paul as he passes on the apostles' gospel, is found in 1 Corinthians 15:1–8. Paul begins by telling us that this gospel is the gospel of the whole church:

> Now, brothers and sisters, I want to remind you of the gospel I preached to you, which you received and on which you have taken your stand. By this gospel you are saved, if you hold firmly to the word I preached to you. Otherwise, you have believed in vain.

He then confesses he is but a transmitter of that gospel:

> For what I received I passed on to you as of first importance:

Here then is that gospel:

> that Christ died for our sins according to the Scriptures, that he was buried, that he was raised on the third day according to the Scriptures, and that he appeared to Cephas, and then to the Twelve. After that, he appeared to more than five hundred of the brothers and sisters at the same time, most of whom are still living, though some have fallen asleep. Then he appeared to James, then to all the apostles, and last of all he appeared to me also, as to one abnormally born.

Dissident disciples tell people about Jesus, about his life, about his death and resurrection and ascension, and the redemption he has accomplished. This text in 1 Corinthians reminds us of Revelation: *the Lamb who died for us becomes the Lord who wields the sword of the Logos that slays the dragon, whips the wild things, and beats Babylon.* This is not about speculation or winning but about the victory of God and the Lamb over the dragon so we can live in justice and peace in the new Jerusalem. That is our gospel message.

Babylon despises the gospel.

A dissident disciple discerns the dragon's gospel, which is (1) worship the wild thing, and (2) be loyal to Babylon. The disciple perceives this because the disciple is trained to see the dragon behind Babylon.

Dissidents of Babylon understand the power of the powers.

A Christoform Power

Power, one might think, is a neutral energy. In some world it might be, but in our world, power is not neutral. Power in our culture exerts power *over* for the sake of power *for* one's agenda. Jesus taught his disciples a potent lesson about power when they were clamoring for it:

> Jesus called them together and said, "You know that those who are regarded as rulers of the Gentiles lord it over them, and their high officials exercise authority over them."

Instead, Jesus said,

> Not so with you. Instead, whoever wants to become great among you must be your servant, and whoever wants to be first must be slave of all. For even the Son of Man did not come to be served, but to serve, and to give his life as a ransom for many. (Mark 10:42–45)

Dissidents pause with these words as a motto: *"Not so with you!"* Power for Jesus was power *for* the other and not power *over* the other. The way of the dragon aches for power *over,* and the wild things wield the dragon's power over and climb their way into high places where they exert power over others. A dissident disciple does not grasp for power over others. Instead, the dissident disciple, following the way of the Lamb, serves the other. Their politics is a politics *for others.*

Our churches have not discipled people in the last forty years in Christoform power but have instead discipled them into playing Babylon's power games. They have decided who might be their next king, only to realize that kings become wild things.

Instead of giving more and more power to presidents, to senators, to representatives, to Washington DC and states and cities and villages and towns, we need to search again for Christoform power. A dissident disciple does not trust in politics but in the Lamb who is the Lord. A disciple walks in the way of the Lamb, not in the way of the wild things.

The church is neither a democracy where each person votes, nor is it a monarchy with changing human leaders. The church is a mutual indwelling body of different persons living together under Christ, the Lord, Lamb, Logos and Light. In our local context, the pastors and elders and deacons are disciples of Jesus, called to submit first to him and to nurture others into serving one another as Jesus himself served his disciples. The strangest words in the church ought to be the words "authority" and "power." Heresy lurks when the pastor appeals to and exerts power and authority, when the pastor sees leadership as imposing his will on the congregation. There is but one Lord and one authority: Jesus, the Lamb, the Lord. Climbing "up" the church's hierarchy as a quest for power subverts the Christoform shape of (un)power in the church. One does not climb up because there is no hierarchy; one does not accumulate more and more authority. The true up is down, and the true down is up. Those who are attempting to climb up into authority are destroying the church and making themselves lords over the church instead of using the power of Christ for others. As Barmen taught, the church is a "Christocracy of siblings," not a hierarchy of powers.

We Live in a World of Government

We are not only the church. We are also citizens in a country. Jesus, Peter, and Paul each recognized the government, and not always in affirming ways! Yet, as Paul taught the Romans to use their freedom with wisdom and not reckless rebellion (Rom 13:1–7), and as Peter instructed empire Christians in Asia Minor to respect the emperor and to do good for the sake of others because such goodness would reap benefits for the church (1 Pet 2:11–17), so we are called to do our part, to be good citizens, and to become public Christians in a way that brings good reputation to our Lord—without fawning over the wild things or trying to make Babylon the new Jerusalem. In the last forty years the church has done irreparable harm by insinuating itself into government. Instead of doing good as witnesses, we grabbed for power. Instead of witnessing to Jesus, we have become known for political allegiances, so much so that our politics are reshaping our witness into a corrupted witness.

The book of Revelation reveals to us that the way to counter the government's overreach is to begin with worship of the One on the throne, the Lamb in the middle of the throne, and the Seven Spirits around the throne. Dissidents see their preeminent act as worship. As Walter Brueggemann says,

> Is liturgy a world-creating act? Does worship make a world? . . . The action of worship is indeed unavoidably constructive. It is constitutive sociologically, engaged in Peter Berger's 'social construction of reality.' It is constitutive literarily as Amos Wilder understood, for imaginative literature does generate worlds in which we can live. It is constitutive of Psychology, as Robert Kegan, Roy Shafer, and Paul Prusyer have understood, for in such moments we are being formed, and formed again, and re-formed as persons. It is constitutive theologically, as Gordon Kaufman proposes, for we are engaged in the articulation of God who is not known or available in this particular way until the speech of the gospel makes God available in a distinctive rendering of concrete speech. . . .
>
> Israel's praise is a dangerous, joyous witness of a different world, a world 'this age' does not suspect, permit, or credit. No wonder the rulers of this age want to stop the singing, or pollute it with ideology and managed slogans! But Israel has not stopped singing and Yahweh has not stopped governing enthroned on the praises of Israel (Psalm 22.3). Against the deathliness of idolatry and the falsehood of ideology, Israel sings another world into reality. The subject of Israel's songs is Yahweh who works

wonders in the earth, wonders marked by justice, equity, and righteousness. The outcome of Israel's praise is another world marked by justice, mercy, and peace. . . . Such a praise is indeed our duty and our delight, the ultimate vocation of the human community, indeed of all creation.

Each act of worship, which leads as we have said to a whole life of allegiance, is an act of dissidence and subversion of the way of the dragon, who desires the worship of the wild things and loyalty to Babylon. Dissident disciples live with government but do not surrender the lordship of Jesus to any part of it. Disciples reject the lordship of the president and of Washington DC and call government to be a servant for the people in a way that mimics the service churches provide in their communities. Disciples reject the state's powers to control the church and dissident disciples shaped by Christ refuse to let the way of the dragon's power take hold in the churches. Disciples reject becoming an agent of government and discern when political leaders want to use the church as a tool for their own power.

The Church's Mission Is Gospel Mission

Babylon wants us because the dragon wants us. If Babylon gets us, it knows we are no longer the Lord's. Our mission is to declare the glories of Christ, to preach the gospel, to teach the Word, to administer the sacraments, and to live in fellowship with one another as a *signpost* of the new Jerusalem. This fellowship turns us into dissidents who live in Babylon as allegiant witnesses of the throne-God and the Lamb.

This mission is by all and for all. A fundamental response to Barmen was that many in Germany criticized its lack of orientation to the German nation. The mission of the church is not nation-centric, but *cosmic*. Jesus, the book of Revelation clearly reveals, rules all because he conquered the dragon, the wild things, and every iteration of Babylon by his death, resurrection, and Logos-sword. A noticeable theme in Revelation, already shown in this book, is that the worship of God is from all *nations and tribes and tongues*. Our mission then is not an American thing. No, it is an international gospel mission.

As such we don't make mission stations in the world outposts of colonialism, nor do we attempt to colonize other countries. Instead, we preach the gospel about Jesus and call those peoples to follow Jesus in their country in their way. Mission is organic and not colonial. Missionaries are not agents of a country but agents of Jesus. That mission, then, ties us back to the gospel and to the lordship of Jesus. In our partisan nation the gospel, the lordship of Jesus, and the mission have become so entwined with politics that one's party has become the kingdom! This is something to repent for, not something to tolerate.

Above All, Confess and Pray

As we worship, we need daily to confess our faith. Over and over disciples of Jesus need to recite, alone and in assembly, what it is that we believe and where our allegiances lie. We need to recite texts like 1 Corinthians 15:3–5 and Romans 10:9–10 and 1 Timothy 3:16:

> For what I received I passed on to you as of first importance: that Christ died for our sins according to the Scriptures, that he was buried, that he was raised on the third day according to the Scriptures, and that he appeared to Cephas, and then to the Twelve.

> If you declare with your mouth, "Jesus is Lord," and believe in your heart that God raised him from the dead, you will be saved. For it is with your heart that you believe and are justified, and it is with your mouth that you profess your faith and are saved.

> He appeared in the flesh,
>   was vindicated by the Spirit,
> was seen by angels,
>   was preached among the nations,

was believed on in the world,
was taken up in glory.

This is what we believe. Better yet, this is *in whom* we put our trust and *to whom* we are allegiant. We need to confess as an act of subversion and as expressions of the way of the Lamb.

With confession comes prayer. Engaged disciples pray for their political leaders. In an era of emperors, none unwilling to use brutal force and none with the slightest care for the gospel, the apostle Paul urged the Christians in Ephesus to pray for "kings and all those in authority," and here are his words:

> I urge, then, first of all, that petitions, prayers, intercession and thanksgiving be made for all people—for kings and all those in authority, that we may live peaceful and quiet lives in all godliness and holiness. This is good, and pleases God our Savior, who wants all people to be saved and to come to a knowledge of the truth. (1 Tim 2:1–4)

Some of our prayers will be petitions and intercessions, some thanksgiving, and at times they will become imprecations and pleadings for justice.

Routine prayer for the president of the USA should be made each Sunday in every church in the USA, and we particularly like the wording of *the Book of Common Prayer,* and we believe we should mention the president's (first) name.

> For our President [Joseph], for the leaders of the nations, and for all in authority, let us pray to the Lord.
> *Lord, have mercy.* (BCP, 384)

Yes, Lord, have mercy on us today. May God unleash the kind of mercy that awakens us unto a discipleship that discerns the dragon, weeps over the wild things, and believes that Babylon will never go away until You, Lord of lords and King of kings, give to us the new Jerusalem.

Appendices

APPENDIX 1

Dispensationalism's Seven Dispensations

Criticized and at times labeled a heresy because it was not fully formulated until the nineteenth century, dispensationalism is a method of reading the Bible (a hermeneutic) as well as a system of theology. It has often sorted the Bible into dispensations in which God administers redemption in (usually seven different) stages, or economies, that entail a stage-based response on the part of humans. A classic seven dispensations approach includes the following stages:

> innocence (pre-fall)
> conscience (to flood)
> civil government (after flood)
> patriarchs
> law
> grace
> millennium kingdom

Dispensationalism has been popularized into the following major ideas, and these have shaped the American church's perceptions of eschatology. This can be called populist dispensationalism:

creation

time of Israel, beginning with the covenant with Abraham

Moses with the law

Jesus and his life and crucifixion

church age until rapture

rapture leading to work with Israel again in tribulation
(rebuilt temple for some)

tribulation ends at battle of Armageddon

second coming with launch of millennium

release of Satan and final defeat

great judgment

eternity as new Jerusalem

Many dispensationalists do not believe all or even most of these ideas, though their disagreements with the classical viewpoint have not filtered down into a better populist presentation. The most common populist dispensational approach today is the *Left Behind* series.

Dispensationalism's Approach to Theology

There are three vital convictions in classical dispensationalism, which is a version of premillennialism (that there will be a millennium preceded by the second coming):

(1) Israel is radically distinct from the church. Israel is about the earthly plan of God (sometimes "kingdom of heaven" in the millennium), and the church about the heavenly plan (sometimes kingdom "of God"). Hence, central to this view is a belief in a future for national/ethnic Israel, among whom God will establish an earthly kingdom to bless all the nations. It does not believe the church is the fulfillment of Israel, replaces Israel, or that Israel symbolizes the future church.

(2) A distinct hermeneutic. Though often referred to as the literal, normal, plain meaning of language, the hermeneutic

is more about how the Old relates to the New Testament, with the Old being read on its own, literal terms. The New thus fulfills what was literally stated in the Old.
(3) A philosophy of history that anticipates completion of both God's physical as well as spiritual promises.

The first distinction (between Israel and the church) is the engine of dispensationalism, and hence the church is a parenthesis (or intercalation) in God's dealings with Israel (from Pentecost to the Tribulation). God deals with Israel, not the church (which has been raptured), during the great tribulation period (Rev 6–19). For some older approaches, the Sermon on the Mount was a message of repentance and designed for Israel in the millennium.

Revelation's various visions depict literal fulfillments of Old Testament prophecies, especially about the Davidic kingdom. From chapter 4 on, Revelation is about the future. Some root a futuristic reading of Revelation to 1:19's statements about the past, present, and what is to come. Israel and the church are consistently distinct in God's plans, and thus there is a rapture of the church prior to chapters 4–19's tribulation (sometimes mistakenly seen in 3:10–11), often called the "pre-trib rapture." Its central premillennial conviction includes that Jesus will return before the one-thousand-year reign of Christ on earth.

Dispensationalism, especially of the populist (*Left Behind*) sort, cannot be equated with premillennialism.

Major proponents: John Nelson Darby, C. I. Scofield, *The Scofield* [and *New Scofield*] *Bible*, Lewis Sperry Chafer, Dwight D. Pentecost, John Walvoord, Hal Lindsey, Salem Kirban, Charles C. Ryrie, John MacArthur, Tim LaHaye, Jerry Jenkins.

For Further Reading

Paul Boyer. *When Time Shall Be No More: Prophecy Belief in Modern American Culture*. Cambridge, MA: Harvard Belknap, 1992.
John S. Feinberg. "Systems of Discontinuity." Pages 67–85 in *Continuity and Discontinuity: Perspectives on the Relationship between the Old*

and the New Testaments. Edited by J. S. Feinberg. Wheaton, IL: Crossway, 1988.

Charles C. Ryrie. *Dispensationalism.* Rev. ed. Chicago: Moody, 2007.

Matthew Avery Sutton. *American Apocalypse: A History of Modern Evangelicalism.* Cambridge, MA: Harvard Belknap, 2014.

Robert L. Thomas. "A Classic Dispensationalist View of Revelation." Pages 177–229 in *Four Views on the Book of Revelation.* Edited by C. Marvin Pate. Grand Rapids: Zondervan, 1998.

Michael J. Vlach. *Dispensationalism: Essential Beliefs and Common Myths.* Rev. ed. Los Angeles: Theological Studies, 2017.

For Criticism of Dispensationalism

Clarence Bass. *Backgrounds to Dispensationalism.* Grand Rapids: Eerdmans, 1960.

Craig A. Blaising and Darrell L. Bock. *Progressive Dispensationalism.* Grand Rapids: Baker, 1993.

Robert Jewett. *Jesus against the Rapture: Seven Unexpected Prophecies.* Philadelphia: Westminster, 1979. This book is valuable because it engaged the dispensationalists in the heat of their popularity.

APPENDIX 2

What's an Apocalypse?

Too many writers reduce apocalyptic literature to simplicities or to fanaticisms. Reduction is fine as long as it is accurate, but most reductions we have seen and heard are not accurate. Instead of reduction, the best thing to do is rely on experts. In the 1970–1980s an academic group in the Society of Biblical Literature led by John J. Collins composed a complex set of characteristics of apocalyptic literature. We have reformatted and numbered those characteristics into a teaching outline:

An apocalypse is
   a [1] genre of revelatory literature
   [2] with a narrative framework
   [3] in which a revelation is mediated by an otherworldly
      being to a human recipient,
   [4] disclosing a transcendent reality that is
   [5] both temporal, insofar as it envisages eschatological
      salvation,
   and [6] spatial, insofar as it involves another, supernatural
      world.
         —Collins, "Apocalyptic Eschatology," in *Oxford
         Handbook of Eschatology*, 46; numbers added.

To this definition was later added this: apocalyptic literature

is intended [7] for a group in crisis

[8] with the purpose of exhortation and/or consolation
[9] by means of divine authority.
—J. J. Collins, *The Apocalyptic Imagination*, 5, 51; slight
variations from J. J. Collins, *Apocalypse, Prophecy, and
Pseudepigraphy*, 13–14; numbers added.

Read each of these characteristics again and place checkmarks next to those that fit John's Apocalypse. (We check all eight.)

John created a vision-based narrative that exposes the present in light of a heavenly, supernatural, transcendent reality and wants to reorient the life of Christians in the seven churches in light of that vision. In so doing he appeals to all the senses of the readers or listeners. He wants them to see what he saw, to feel what he felt, to hear what he heard, to touch what he touched, and because of these sensations to imagine an alternative world and *to live in that alternative world now.*

It takes an apocalyptic imagination to write and to read the book of Revelation.

Sorting out what an apocalypse is, then synthesizing apocalypse and applying the synthesis to Revelation is simplistic and unhelpful. Revelation does what it does not because that's how apocalypses work but because that's how Revelation works. In fact, Revelation is the first book in history to call itself an "apocalypse" (Rev 1:1).

For Further Reading

Greg Carey. *Ultimate Things: An Introduction to Jewish and Christian Apocalyptic Literature.* St. Louis: Chalice, 2005. Carey composes a comprehensive approach in proposing "apocalyptic discourse" as one mode of probing ultimate things.

John J. Collins. *The Apocalyptic Imagination: An Introduction to Jewish Apocalyptic Literature.* 3rd ed. Grand Rapids: Eerdmans, 2016.

Klaus Koch. *The Rediscovery of Apocalyptic.* Studies in Biblical Theology 2.22. London: SCM, 1972.

Christopher Rowland. *The Open Heaven: A Study of Apocalyptic in Judaism and Early Christianity.* New York: Crossroad, 1982.

The Antichrist

The word "antichrist" (*antichristos* in Greek) is a compound word comprised of the words "anointed one" (*Christos*) and "instead of" (*anti*). It appears only *five times* in the New Testament (1 John 2:18, 22; 4:2–3; 2 John 7) and *once* in the Apostolic Fathers (Polycarp's *Letter to the Philippians*). Several images, however, have been conflated with the idea of the antichrist throughout the centuries: the Gospels refer to "pseudo-Christs" who will appear and produce signs and omens to lead the people astray (Matt 24:24 and Mark 13:22). Second Thessalonians speaks of "the lawless one" who epitomizes evil and leads a deception campaign against the people of God (2:3, 8, 9). Finally, Revelation refers to the wild things that will rise from the sea and the land (13:1–18). None of these images, however, need to refer only to one future figure who will rise and draw all peoples together against God. Rather, "antichrist" refers to a class of people (comprised of individuals) who oppose the work of God in Christ.

In other words, since "antichrist" functions as a representative symbol for anyone opposed to Christ, anyone who does not follow the slaughtered but standing Lamb (Jesus) is antichrist.

Two important points remain: (1) The term "antichrist" does not appear anywhere in the book of Revelation. (2) References to the "antichrist" in the letters of John do not speak of a singular individual, but all those who oppose Christ. Thus, "Many deceivers have gone out into the world, those who do not confess that Jesus

Christ has come in the flesh; any such person is the deceiver and the antichrist!" (2 John 7 NRSVUE).

We are better *not* assigning the word "antichrist" exclusively to one specific person who will rise into world leadership in the future, but rather we should see in the term, and terms connected to it like "wild things" and "Belial" and "the little horn" of Daniel 7, those who oppose God. Rather than looking for one antichrist, we should discern the presence of antichrists among us.

For Further Reading

D. A. Hubbard. "Antichrist." Pages 60–61 in *The Evangelical Dictionary of Theology*. Edited by D. J. Treier and W. Elwell. 3rd ed. Grand Rapids: Baker Academic, 2017.

Craig R. Koester, *Revelation: A New Translation with Introduction and Commentary*. Anchor Bible 38A. New Haven: Yale University Press, 2014. Pages 530–40.

Mitchell G. Reddish, *Revelation*. Smyth & Helwys Bible Commentary. Macon, GA: Smyth & Helwys, 2018. Page 268.

Paul Trebilco. *The Early Christians in Ephesus from Paul to Ignatius*. Grand Rapids: Eerdmans, 2004. Page 268.

APPENDIX 4

Armageddon (Har-Magedon)

H*ar-Magedon* is a Hebrew term combining the prefix *har* ("mountain") with the name *Megiddo* (a place in northern Israel), which combined means Mount Megiddo. There is no mountain at Megiddo. But Meggido is often combined with the words of Revelation 14:20, where blood flowed "as high as the horses' bridles for a distance of 1,600 stadia." Hence, Armageddon often refers to the world's final battle, the bloodiest of all. Not all is well with reading Armageddon as the geographical location of the world's last battle.

The name is borrowed from various places in the Hebrew Bible:

- Zechariah references profound grief "as great as the mourning for Hadad-rimmon in the plain of Megiddo" that the ethnic groups will experience on account of future defeat (Zech 12:10–11 NRSVUE; cf. Rev 1:7; 19:11–21).
- The book of Judges speaks of Deborah's victory over Israel's enemies by the waters of Megiddo (Judg 5:19–20).
- King Ahaziah, ally of Ahab and Jezebel, is destroyed at Megiddo (2 Kgs 9:27).
- King Josiah is killed because he refuses to "listen to the words of Neco from the mouth of God" (2 Chr 35:22 NRSVUE), and the reference to mountains (*har*) recalls the visions of God defeating his enemies on the mountains of Israel (Ezek 38:8–21; 39:2, 4, 17).

Combined, the name *Har-Magedon* symbolically functions as a composite image to describe (perhaps the location of) the final destruction of all that stands in opposition to God. John was not expecting a future battle to take place at a nonexistent mountain north of Palestine; rather, he was expecting the defeat of God's adversaries represented by Rome (Babylon). Thus, the name *Har-Magedon* is an image for assembling, resisting, and ultimately defeating the antichrist forces that stand in opposition to the Lamb.

Those familiar with Revelation, however, will know that the battle of *Har-Magedon* never actually takes place—all may assemble, but resistance ends at the parousia of Jesus Christ.

For Further Reading

G. B. Caird. *The Revelation of St. John*. Black's New Testament Commentaries. Peabody, MA: Hendrickson, 1966. Pages 206–7.

Darrell W. Johnson. *Discipleship on the Edge: An Expository Journey through Revelation*. Vancouver: Canadian Church Leaders Network, 2004. Page 290.

Craig R. Koester. *Revelation: A New Translation with Introduction and Commentary*. AB 38A. New Haven: Yale University Press, 2014. Pages 667–68.

APPENDIX 5

Ancient Mythologies

It may surprise some readers, but John uses images from ancient mythologies in chapter 12 too. That is, John recasts characters in the various playbills of Greco-Roman mythology. That basic mythology was this: *the birth of a divine child to a cosmic mother and the threat posed by the chaos monster.*

Greco-Roman Mythology: The great dragon, Python, learned through an oracle that he would one day be killed by one of the children of Leto. Following the impregnation of the goddess Leto by Jupiter, Python tried to hunt down the goddess to kill her before she could bear the child, but she was preserved and protected by the North Wind. She bore twins, Apollo and Artemis, upon the isle of Delos, forty miles west of Patmos. After the birth (at four days old), Apollo hunted down Python, initially wounding and finally killing the monster at Delphi with his bow (Apollo and Artemis were archers). In the Greco-Roman context, this story was used as imperial propaganda to celebrate the emperor as Apollo, the son of the gods who has defeated the chaos monster (Virgil *Ecl.* 4.10; Dio Cassius, *Hist. Rom.* 62.20.5).

The Book of Revelation: Here's how some of the hearers of this book would have understood the images. John portrays the cosmic woman about to give birth, while the chaos monster, the dragon, seeks to devour the child. The woman is preserved with the wings of the great eagle and saved by the land, while her male son was seized up to the throne of God as emperor of emperors, son of the living God who has dealt the initial death blow (in his death and resurrection), which sealed the ultimate defeat of the chaos monster (Gen 3:15; 37:9–11; Exod 19:4–6; Ps 2:9; Isa 27:17–18; cf. Rev 1:4–5; 5:6; 12:7–12; 20:11–15).

Thus, John parodies and subverts the divine claims and arrogant presumptions of Rome by recasting the characters in their ancient mythology: the divine Son, the One who will shepherd the ethnic groups, conquers the forces of darkness and chaos, displacing Rome's powers from "the role of Apollo by the Davidic Messiah, and instead associating [Rome] with the chaos monster, the Dragon" (Paul, 214–215). In other words, John pulls back the curtain on the way of Rome: the Roman systems and rulers should not be hailed or celebrated, because they are nothing more than a tool of the dragon used to propagate destruction and chaos. The male Son (Ps 2:9; Isa 7:14; 66:7–8), however, has conquered the forces of chaos and should be hailed, celebrated, and followed (Rev 1:17–18; 4–5; 14:4–5).

For Further Reading

Adela Yarbro Collins. *The Combat Myth in the Book of Revelation*. Eugene, OR: Wipf & Stock, 2001. Pages 65–71.

David A. deSilva. *Discovering Revelation: Content, Interpretation, Reception*. Grand Rapids: Eerdmans, 2021. Pages 126–29.

Ian Paul, *Revelation: An Introduction and Commentary*. Downers Grove, IL: IVP Academic, 2018. Pages 214–15.

Mitchell G. Reddish. *Revelation*. Smyth & Helwys Bible Commentary. Macon, GA: Smyth & Helwys, 2018. Pages 232–33.

APPENDIX 6

The Rapture
(A Very Brief History)

The idea of *the rapture* first emerged, as we know it today, in the early nineteenth century from the spiritual vision of a teenage girl at a small revival in Glasgow, Scotland. The woman claimed to have had a vision of a *'pre-tribulation rapture'* at which time the church would be taken out of this world and swept up into heaven. British minister John Nelson Darby, having been present for the sharing of the vision, became convinced of its validity, and began sharing the vision as truth. Darby brought his rapture gospel to America, where he quickly encountered Dwight L. Moody, who soon became the worldwide disseminator of a *'pre-tribulation rapture.'*

In the early part of the twentieth century, the rapture gospel movement gained ground with the publication of the *Scofield Reference Bible*, which was not simply a study Bible with references in the margins, but one that inserted guiding headings and study notes into the biblical text (e.g., the heading for Matthew 24 is "Jesus Predicts the Rapture"). In adding these headings and study notes, readers of the *Scofield Reference Bible* became convinced that their Bible made specific references to the rapture. The rise and widespread acceptance of this lay theological movement was further solidified by the emergence of schools, publishing companies, and the (in)famous *Left Behind* series.

In other words, the rapture-gospel movement is a modern phenomenon that was nonexistent for eighteen hundred years of church history, before becoming a cultural touchstone and a central tenet of dispensationalist theology in the last two centuries.

For Further Reading

Ben Witherington III. "Where Did Rapture Theology Come From? Ben Witherington III." Seedbed. October 8, 2014. YouTube video, 5:55. www.youtube.com/watch?v=d_cVXdr8mVs.

N.T. Wright. "Farewell to the Rapture." *N. T. Wright Page* (blog). August 2001. https://ntwrightpage.com/2016/07/12/farewell-to -the-rapture/.

APPENDIX 7

Rapture or Resurrection?

In his book *The Indelible Image*, New Testament scholar Ben Witherington III reiterates a common piece of interpretive wisdom: "A text without a *context* is just a *pretext* for what we want it to mean." In other words, when we isolate and divorce particular sections of any text from the surrounding *literary, historical,* and *theological* contexts, we cultivate the conditions for importing our own meaning. In considering key passages that surround the rapture, it seems that many have isolated and divorced passages from their contexts in attempts to create biblical support. Two key passages have been stripped of their *literary, historical,* and *theological* contexts.

In Matthew 24, Jesus compares the future return of the Son of Man to the days of Noah, because before the flood "people were eating and drinking, marrying and giving in marriage, up to the day Noah entered the ark; and they knew nothing about what would happen until the flood came and took them all away" (Matt 24:37–39; cf. Gen 6–9). Jesus uses the flood as an image for future judgment: *when the flood comes one will be taken and the other left behind* (v. 40). While many have removed the passage from the context to suggest that some will be left behind to endure the tribulation, in the story of Noah, only the righteous are preserved and left behind. In other words, within the imagery, the righteous are left behind, while all others are swept away in the flood of judgment.

There is but one "clear" text about the rapture in the entire New Testament. All others are used for rapture thinking but are not clear. That text is 1 Thessalonians 4:15–17.

> For this we declare to you by the word of the Lord, that we who are alive, who are left until the coming of the Lord, will by no means precede those who have died. For the Lord himself, with a cry of command, with the archangel's call and with the sound of God's trumpet, will descend from heaven, and the dead in Christ will rise first. Then we who are alive, who are left, will be caught up in the clouds together with them to meet the Lord in the air, and so we will be with the Lord forever. (NRSVUE)

This text is clear to many even though a rapture of humans into the sky is not found anywhere else in the New Testament. It is certainly not in Revelation, a text that one would think would have had it. Many today, therefore, see Paul using imagery from the city leaders going out to meet an emperor or some dignitary before he enters the city. The crucial term ("to meet") is often used of a group of people exiting a city to have an official meet and greet to prepare for a proper welcome in the city itself.

In 1 Thessalonians, Paul writes to those in Thessaloniki about the final return of Jesus Christ, when the "Lord himself will come down from heaven, with a loud command, with the voice of the archangel and with the trumpet call of God," and the dead in Christ will rise and they will meet the Lord in the air (4:16–18). Paul uses technical language to describe *welcoming* and *celebrating* the royal king as he returns to his city (similar to the entrance liturgy of Ps 24:7–10). The language describes the royal entourage who will ascend to welcome the King of Glory in the air (air does not mean heaven), in order to usher him back to earth in royal celebration. In other words, the language signals a common image: when the watchmen of a walled city heard the trumpet sound, signaling the proximity of their royal king, they would send out an entourage and create a royal procession as the victorious king returned. Similarly, the trumpet will sound, and we will depart to greet our royal King, not so that we might be raptured to heaven, but so that we can welcome and celebrate the return of the royal King to earth.

J. Nelson Kraybill therefore contends that the "rapture" more accurately describes not being whisked away into heaven but our going out to meet Jesus to welcome him back to earth!

When taken within their own *literary, historical,* and *theological* contexts, neither of these passages speak of a rapture but offer potent images of judgment and celebratory welcome. The *absence* of rapture texts anywhere else in the New Testament, especially in Revelation, tells against its clarity.

For Further Reading

R. T. France. *Matthew.* Tyndale New Testament Commentary. Downers Grove, IL: InterVarsity Press, 1985.

Nijay K. Gupta. *1–2 Thessalonians.* New Covenant Commentary Series. Eugene, OR: Cascade, 2016.

J. Nelson Kraybill. *Apocalypse and Allegiance: Worship, Politics, and Devotion in the Book of Revelation.* Grand Rapids: Baker, 2010. Pages 174–75.

Ben Witherington III. *The Indelible Image: The Theological and Ethical Thought World of the New Testament, Volume 1: The Individual Witnesses.* Downers Grove, IL: IVP Academic, 2009. Page 41.

———. "Is the Rapture Doctrine Biblical? (Ben Witherington)." Seedbed. October 15, 2014. YouTube video, 5:14. www.youtube.com/watch?v=cg8lRGqtMHc.

APPENDIX 8

———————

Is Revelation Fantasy?

A question some scholars of Revelation ask: "Is Revelation a type of literature commonly called 'fantasy'?" Fantasy, which departs from reality and creates a world of its own, permits the hearer to imagine a different world than one's own and challenge the hearer to hope and action. Revelation believes God is in control, the people of the seven churches are those destined for new Jerusalem, and the powers of Rome are destined for destruction. Call it what you want, a few hundred kind folks meeting privately somehow knowing they will rule and Rome will fall partakes in imagination or fantasy. Some of my younger students think of this book as mythic or mythical, not in the sense of "that's nothing but a myth" but in the sense of Marvel movies and Harry Potter stories.

One of the world's leading scholars of apocalyptic literature, John J. Collins, is fond of calling this literature "fantastical" or "fantasy" and refers to some of the visions in this literature as "fantasies of violence" (311). Bauckham and Hart define fantasy as "wanton transgression of the rules which, in our familiar world, define the boundaries of the permissible and impermissible" (89), and they state that "fantasy is what could not have happened" (311), even what is "outrageous, non-sensical, impossible" (311). They, too, know that Revelation leads "us to the very brink of the unimaginable, peering into the brilliant darkness beyond" (100).

We are inclined to think that viewing Revelation as fantastical can be helpful to modern readers—not by assigning the book to the bookshelf marked "Fantasy Literature" but seeing that fantasy overlaps with the imaginative, fictive literature we call "apocalyptic." As Elisabeth Schüssler Fiorenza says, Revelation is not "predictive-descriptive language but . . . mythological-imaginative language." That is, it "is mythological-fantastic language—stars fall from heaven . . . animals speak, dragons spit fire, a lion is a lamb, and angels or demons engage in warfare" (*Revelation: Vision of a Just World*, 25).

But notice this: apocalyptic, fantasy, and imaginative literature like this is profoundly *cathartic* and *therapeutic* for the oppressed people of western Asia Minor and for all readers since. Adela Yarbro Collins describes the process of release and catharsis that happens for the hearer of this text being read when fear and resentment-shaped feelings are projected onto the screen with images of defeat and triumph. John J. Collins puts it like this: "By enabling people to let off steam by fantasizing divine vengeance, it relieves the pressure toward action in the present and enables people to accommodate themselves to the status quo for the present" (321). Pippin, who also believes the Apocalypse takes part in the fantastic, adds to this sense of catharsis as healing the conclusion that catharsis also involves the community's scapegoating of Babylon.

To hear in whatever form, especially in the evocative set of images we find in Revelation 12–13 or 18–19, that injustice and evil will be defeated by the good victories of God offers a hope-filled life and a healing orientation toward life's rugged realities.

For Further Reading

Richard Bauckham and Trevor Hart. *Hope against Hope: Christian Eschatology at the Turn of the Millennium*. Grand Rapids: Eerdmans, 1999. Pages 72–108.

Adela Yarbro Collins. *Crisis and Catharsis: The Power of the Apocalypse*. Philadelphia: Westminster, 1984. Pages 152–60.

John J. Collins. *Apocalypse, Prophecy, and Pseudepigraphy: On Jewish Apocalyptic Literature*. Grand Rapids: Eerdmans, 2015. Pages 308–25, 326–42.

Tina Pippin. *Death and Desire: The Rhetoric of Gender in the Apocalypse of John*. Eugene, OR: Wipf & Stock, 2021. Pages 17–21.

APPENDIX 9

———

The Millennium

The idea of the millennium (*mille* [one thousand] and *annus* [years]) comes from the thousand-year reign of Christ and his allegiant martyr witnesses in Revelation 20:1–6. Despite the varying theological systems that have been constructed to try to explain the thousand-year reign (*premillennial, postmillennial, amillennial*), which deserve respect even when we completely disagree, the millennium, like all other numbers in the book of Revelation, functions not as statistic but as potent symbol. For some the millennium is the current reign of believers in heaven with Christ (see Hill).

John has taken the Jewish apocalyptic symbol of a temporary messianic reign on earth before the final judgment and new creation (2 Baruch 40:3; 4 Ezra 7:28–9; b.Sanh. 99a), and has used it as a symbol of *assurance* and *encouragement* for the martyr witnesses. John offers assurance that those who have been judged and condemned to death by the dragon and the wild things will be vindicated and rewarded with the kingdom (13.1–10; 20.4–6). In the end, when the heavenly perspective is finally revealed and the truth becomes evident, not only will all enemies be defeated and judged, but the martyr witnesses will conquer and be granted *life* and *rule*. The millennium symbolically demonstrates the triumph of the allegiant witnesses: those who have suffered on account of the Jesus Christ witness will in the end rule universally and receive the special rewards promised to those who have paid the highest price (first resurrection, reign, escape from second death). John uses the symbol of the millennium to depict "the meaning, rather than predicting the manner of their vindication."

Judith Kovacs, after sketching some major theologians' discussion of the millennium, maps various proposed purposes of the millennium: (1) it prepares the righteous for immortality and participation in the divine nature; (2) with the martyrs vindicated, John encourages radical faithfulness; (3) it affirms the goodness of creation and God as creator; (4) it exemplifies the importance of human history in God's salvific plan; (5) it motivates and directs human action in the present.

For Further Reading

Richard J. Bauckham. *The Theology of the Book of Revelation.* Cambridge: Cambridge University Press, 2015. Pages 106–8.

Charles E. Hill. *Regnum Caelorum: Patterns of Millennial Thought in Early Christianity.* Grand Rapids: Eerdmans, 2001. Hill contends convincingly that there was more "amillennialism" in the early church than has been argued by most.

Craig R. Koester. *Revelation: A New Translation with Introduction and Commentary.* AB 38A. New Haven: Yale University Press, 2014. Pages 741–52.

Judith Kovacs. "The Purpose of the Millennium." Pages 353–75 in *New Perspectives on the Book of Revelation.* Edited by Adela Yarbro Collins. BETL. Leuven: Peeters, 2017.

Mitchell G. Reddish. *Revelation.* Smyth & Helwys Bible Commentary. Macon, GA: Smyth & Helwys, 2018. Pages 391, 394–95.

APPENDIX 10

Utopia, Eutopia, Euchronia, and Progressivism

M uch later than John's new Jerusalem vision of an ideal society, and worthy of nothing other than a mention here, is the idea of "utopia," which turns our eyes toward Thomas More's book *Utopia* or even Jonathan Swift's satirical exposé of such thinking in *Gulliver's Travels*. John's new Jerusalem forms into various visions of a utopia—and it's true, new Jerusalem is idealistic, utopian, and unachievable by humans. More himself was playing with terms: "u" comes from "not" (in Greek *ou/ouk*) and "topia" from "place" (Greek *topos*). So, his *utopia* was not a place on earth, yet his famous book finishes with a poem that tells us his *utopia* is not a part of the known world, it greatly surpasses even Plato's ideal city, and its city and laws are so wonderful the place should be called *Eutopia*, which means "the good place."

Euchronia is a time of near perfection on earth, the good place of the future. Propelled, even compelled, by optimism in reason's and science's capacities to make the world better and better, euchronia succeeds the utopian visions. Social evolution then aims at euchronia. Instead of being a "no place" on some remote island one could visit by a journey, which is what a utopia is, the euchronia led humans to think they could achieve such a society and world, sometimes called the "Golden Era." In general, then, one finds here Thomas Paine and Jean Jacques Rousseau, the Pilgrims if not also the Puritans of colonial America, as well as the more radical socialist-communist utopians like Friedrich Engels and Karl Marx, and one must not ignore their totalitarian manifestations. In euchronia humans believed they could bring about an ideal society.

Much of contemporary *progressivism* conceives of humans as capable, through the enactment of better laws and promotion of better people, step by step, of achieving a better city, country, and world, and is thus a kind of euchronia. In the history of Christian eschatology, progressivism is often associated with postmillennialism, not always fairly.

New Jerusalem, even though it is beyond life and death into the next life, is the climactic fulfillment of God's design for humans in God's world. John's new Jerusalem is not in another world but is this world housing the kingdom of God. Some then use "utopia" or "eutopia" or "euchronia" for the new Jerusalem; for the Romans the book of Revelation becomes dystopian. These various utopias and euchronias and progressivist idealism have been challenged by dystopian novels like George Orwell's *Animal Farm* and *1984* or Ralph Ellison's *The Invisible Man*.

For Further Reading

Fátima Vieira. "The Concept of Utopia." Pages 3–27 in *The Cambridge Companion to Utopian Literature*. Edited by Gregory Claeys. Cambridge Companions to Literature. Cambridge: Cambridge University Press, 2010. Pages 4–5.

The Songs of Revelation

4:8–11: Antiphonal

Rev 4:8 Each of the four living creatures had six wings and was covered with eyes all around, even under its wings. Day and night they never stop saying:

> "'Holy, holy, holy
> is the Lord God Almighty,'
> who was, and is, and is to come."

Rev 4:9–11 Whenever the living creatures give glory, honor and thanks to him who sits on the throne and who lives for ever and ever, the twenty-four elders fall down before him who sits on the throne and worship him who lives for ever and ever. They lay their crowns before the throne and say:

> "You are worthy, our Lord and God,
> to receive glory and honor and power,
> for you created all things,
> and by your will they were created
> and have their being."

5:8–14: Antiphonal

Rev 5:8–10 And when he had taken it, the four living creatures and the twenty-four elders fell down before the Lamb. Each one had a harp and they were holding golden bowls full of incense, which are the prayers of God's people. And they sang a new song, saying: .

> "You are worthy to take the scroll
>   and to open its seals,
> because you were slain,
>   and with your blood you purchased for God
>   persons from every tribe and language and
>   people and nation.
> You have made them to be a kingdom and priests to
>   serve our God,
>   and they will reign on the earth."

Rev 5:11–12 Then I looked and heard the voice of many angels, numbering thousands upon thousands, and ten thousand times ten thousand. They encircled the throne and the living creatures and the elders. In a loud voice they were saying:

> "Worthy is the Lamb, who was slain,
>   to receive power and wealth and wisdom
>   and strength
>   and honor and glory and praise!"

Rev 5:13 Then I heard every creature in heaven and on earth and under the earth and on the sea, and all that is in them, saying:

> "To him who sits on the throne and to the Lamb
>   be praise and honor and glory and power,
> for ever and ever!"

Rev 5:14 The four living creatures said, "Amen," and the elders fell down and worshiped.

7:9–12: Antiphonal

Rev 7:9–10 After this I looked, and there before me was a great multitude that no one could count, from every nation, tribe, people and language, standing before the throne and before the Lamb. They were wearing white robes and were holding palm branches in their hands. And they cried out in a loud voice:

> "Salvation belongs to our God,
> who sits on the throne,
> and to the Lamb."

Rev 7:11–12 All the angels were standing around the throne and around the elders and the four living creatures. They fell down on their faces before the throne and worshiped God, saying:

> "Amen!
> Praise and glory
> and wisdom and thanks and honor
> and power and strength
> be to our God for ever and ever.
> Amen!"

11:15–18: Antiphonal

Rev 11:15 The seventh angel sounded his trumpet, and there were loud voices in heaven, which said:

> "The kingdom of the world has become
> the kingdom of our Lord and of his Messiah,
> and he will reign for ever and ever."

Rev 11:16–18 And the twenty-four elders, who were seated on their thrones before God, fell on their faces and worshiped God, saying:

> "We give thanks to you, Lord God Almighty,
>> the One who is and who was,
> because you have taken your great power
>> and have begun to reign.
> The nations were angry,
>> and your wrath has come.
> The time has come for judging the dead,
>> and for rewarding your servants the prophets
> and your people who revere your name,
>> both great and small—
> and for destroying those who destroy the earth."

12:10–12

Rev 12:10–12 Then I heard a loud voice in heaven say:

> "Now have come the salvation and the power
>> and the kingdom of our God,
>> and the authority of his Messiah.
> For the accuser of our brothers and sisters,
>> who accuses them before our God day and night,
>> has been hurled down.
> They triumphed over him
>> by the blood of the Lamb
>> and by the word of their testimony;
> they did not love their lives so much
>> as to shrink from death.
> Therefore rejoice, you heavens
>> and you who dwell in them!
> But woe to the earth and the sea,
>> because the devil has gone down to you!

He is filled with fury,
> because he knows that his time is short."

15:2-4

Rev 15:2-4 Those who had been victorious . . . sang the song of God's servant Moses and of the Lamb:

> "Great and marvelous are your deeds,
>> Lord God Almighty.
> Just and true are your ways,
>> King of the nations.
> Who will not fear you, Lord,
>> and bring glory to your name?
> For you alone are holy.
> All nations will come
>> and worship before you,
> for your righteous acts have been revealed."

16:5-7: Antiphonal

Rev 16:5-6 Then I heard the angel in charge of the waters say:

> "You are just in these judgments, O Holy One,
> you who are and who were;
>> for they have shed the blood of your holy people
>>> and your prophets,
> and you have given them blood to drink as they
>> deserve."

Rev 16:7 And I heard the altar respond:

> "Yes, Lord God Almighty,
> true and just are your judgments."

19:1–4: Antiphonal

Rev 19:1–2 After this I heard what sounded like the roar of a great multitude in heaven shouting:

> "Hallelujah!
> Salvation and glory and power belong to our God,
>   for true and just are his judgments.
> He has condemned the great prostitute
>   who corrupted the earth by her adulteries.
> He has avenged on her the blood of his servants."

Rev 19:3 And again they shouted:

> "Hallelujah!
> The smoke from her goes up for ever and ever."

Rev 19:4 The twenty-four elders and the four living creatures fell down and worshiped God, who was seated on the throne. And they cried:

> "Amen, Hallelujah!"

19:5–8: Antiphonal

Rev 19:5 Then a voice came from the throne, saying:

> "Praise our God,
>   all you his servants,
> you who fear him,
>   both great and small!"

Rev 19:6–8 Then I heard what sounded like a great multitude, like the roar of rushing waters and like loud peals of thunder, shouting:

"Hallelujah!
  For our Lord God Almighty reigns.
Let us rejoice and be glad
  and give him glory!
For the wedding of the Lamb has come,
  and his bride has made herself ready.
Fine linen, bright and clean,
  was given her to wear."

(Fine linen stands for the righteous acts of God's holy people.)

APPENDIX 12

The Progress of
Progressivism

Right-wing Christians have politicized the gospel into Christian nationalism in the Republican party, while progressive evangelicals lean Democrat or social Democrat, and at times themselves wander into thinking political power is itself redemption. Some evangelicals have shifted from traditional church-based Christianity into full-on Progressivism, that is, social justice activism that has walked away from their former faith. Yet one can't punch progressives for abandoning faith because, as Jack Jenkins more than establishes in his romp through the religious Left's impact on the last few elections in *American Prophets*, many are progressives *because of their faith*. Early in his book Jenkins makes what many would perceive to be an arresting claim since many have argued there is no coherent religion in the Left and, even more, that the Left is little more than secularization on display. But Jenkins notes with justification that "the Religious Left is the beating heart of modern progressivism." He's right.

But imbalancing faith and politics bedragons Christian progressives too. Since Revelation is for dissident disciples who are called to discern the presence of Babylon, any study of the book must deal with politics, which means both Christian nationalism and progressivism. Both have the capacity to capture and occupy, both are on display in the USA today, and both need to be understood to comprehend the potency for Revelation today. But what is progressivism? There are four major dimensions of progressivism, one leading in some ways to the others: historical, economic, social reform, and prophetic.

The standard study of the history of progress, though now more than four decades old, remains Robert Nisbet's *History of the Idea of Progress*, and here's his definition: "Simply stated, *the idea of progress holds that mankind has advanced in the past—from some aboriginal condition of primitiveness, barbarism, or even nullity—is now advancing, and will continue to advance through the foreseeable future*." Progress is the "dogma" that assumes "the slow, gradual, inexorable progress of mankind to higher status in knowledge, culture, and moral estate." Progress as a theory for history is at work in modern progressivism. Historical progressivism, when tied to capitalism and economic growth, became a kind of ever-expanding production and consumption of goods. We can call this economic progressivism, something resisted by one major thinker, Christopher Lasch, in his book *The True and Only Heaven*, and by all progressivists today. Instead of locking progress into economic growth, which leads to greater and greater inequities, many want to connect a theory of progress to social reform through voting and governmental regulations. About 20% of American evangelicals today are what came to be known at the turn of the twentieth century as "classic progressivists"; a good exposition of this system can be found in Walter Nugent's *Progressivism*.

Progressivists cannot be equated with either the social gospelers of that era or even with liberation theology. Rather, they are Christians committed to a kind of civic republicanism that focuses on urging the government to enact laws and realities that approximate justice. Today's progressivists then have taken progressivism's central impulses into new places, but they still churn their energies from the same four chambers of the heart: social justice ideals, federal government's power to get things done, centralization of power, and the agitation of the electorate. With a big chunk of verses taken from the prophets and Jesus.

Progress's essence is about the arc of history, with many

more optimistic sorts thinking it's all moving toward justice. One must, however, ask *for whom* that arc bends. The answer is utterly undeniable: *for those in power and those favored by those in power.* Prophetic progressivism, building as it does on social reform progressivism, wants progress *for all,* so the focus becomes justice and equity. While the speculators and pessimists spend their time trying to convince others that the world is falling apart, anyone willing to look at the evidence knows that in many dimensions of life the world is progressing and getting better. There is no reason to deny this will not continue. Progress can be seen in our knowledge of and the quality of food, in global sanitation, in life expectancy, in global decreases in poverty, in the reduction of violence (though many of us know increases in some areas of crime), in our knowledge of and commitment to our environment, in the expansion of literacy, and yet also in both greater expressions of freedom and equality. No one says we have arrived, but knowledge of the last century's changes establishes a belief that we are making the world a better place.

Progressivism is on the left side of the political spectrum. As something political, as is the case with right-wing Christian nationalism, it too comes under the scope of Revelation's vision for dissident disciples discerning the progress of Babylon's powers. A standard story is that 'right-wingers are religious' and 'left-wingers are secularists,' but this has been dealt a fatal blow.

As the editors of the volume *Religion and Progressive Activism* summarize the movement, "Progressive religious groups have long promoted a morally grounded view of progressive politics, used faith-infused languages and symbolism to express their political commitments, and lent moral authority to progressive movements' claims." By progress they are speaking of social reform: "advancing a more just, more loving, and more God-like society." I will call this prophetic progressivism because they themselves use this term for themselves. What the editors of *Religion and Progressive Activism* discover is four nodes of religious progressivism: progressive actions focusing on equality, progressive values that are shaped by social justice, progressive identities in that they identify with other progressives outside their own religion, and progressive theology that seeks to reform current Christian theology toward justice for all. As such, these are not secular progressives, and the jibe by conservatives that it is secularism seeking to sheer religion from society does not describe their movement. A major spokesperson for progressives is Philip Gorski, who argues for the revival of the American civil religious tradition. He calls his version of political engagement "prophetic republicanism." It emphasizes a virtuous citizenry and the social responsibility and obligation of citizens but views history less in linear and more in circular terms, which means it must routinely return to its foundations. But his themes remain progressive when it comes to equality, progress, and education. He criticizes religious nationalism as "national self-worship disguised as American patriotism" while doing the same for radical secularism as "cultural condescension disguised as radical egalitarianism." Finally, though Gorski cannot represent all prophetic progressivism, his contention is that this form of progressivism has greater capacity to check radical liberalism as well as having the capacity to open spaces for greater justice and community.

Prophetic progressivism presses hard against free market capitalism while it anchors its views in the prophetic writings of Scripture. As a theory of history, it suggests often enough an eschatology shaped by human activism more than divine intervention, and its sense of redemption at times borders more on systemic sins than personal sins. For those conversant with the study of eschatology, progressivism at times echoes postmillennialism without a millennium! In the history of Christian eschatology, many have opted for the view that the mission of the church was to evangelize the world, eventually the world would welcome the gospel, and thus the millennium would be ushered in—following which (the "post") Christ would come after the millennium ("millennialism").

Having said that, I do want to register a final observation: both Christian nationalism and progressivism are species, some more secular than others, of Christian eschatology, and both tend to lack the discerning dissidence of the book of Revelation.

For Further Reading

Ruth Braunstein and Todd Nicholas Fuist, eds. *Religion and Progressive Activism: New Stories about Faith and Politics.* Religion and Social Transformation 6. New York: New York University Press, 2017. See pp. 6, 7.

Joshua Foa Dienstag. *Pessimism: Philosophy, Ethic, Spirit.* Princeton: Princeton University Press, 2009.

Philip Gorski. "Reviving the Civil Religious Tradition." Pages 271–88 in *Religious and Progressive Activism: New Stories about Faith and Politics.* Edited by Ruth Braunstein and Todd Nicholas Fuist. Religion and Social Transformation 6. New York: New York University Press, 2017. Pages 279, 281.

Jack Jenkins. *American Prophets: The Religious Roots of Progressive Politics and the Ongoing Fight for the Soul of the Country.* New York: HarperOne, 2020. See page 3.

Christopher Lasch. *The True and Only Heaven: Progress and Its Critics.* New York: W. W. Norton, 1991.

Robert Nisbet. *History of the Idea of Progress.* 2nd ed. London: Routledge, 1994. See pages 4–5 (his italics), 9.

Walter Nugent. *Progressivism: A Very Short Introduction.* New York: Oxford, 2010.

Recommended Commentaries

R*evelation for the Rest of Us* is not a commentary, but we have made use of commentaries throughout. The best commentaries, which often include histories of interpretation and a sketch of interpretive options for significant issues, are by David Aune, Brian Blount, and Craig Koester. They can be read with great profit.

Aune, David E. *Revelation*. Word Biblical Commentary. 3 vols. Dallas: Word, 1997; Nashville: Thomas Nelson, 1998.

Beale, Gregory K. *The Book of Revelation: A Commentary on the Greek Text*. New International Greek Testament Commentary. Grand Rapids: Eerdmans, 1999.

Beasley-Murray, G. R. *The Book of Revelation*. New Century Bible. Grand Rapids: Eerdmans, 1974.

Blount, Brian K. *Revelation*. Nashville: Westminster John Knox, 2013.

Boring, M. Eugene. *Revelation: Interpretation; A Bible Commentary for Teaching and Preaching*. Nashville: Westminster John Knox, 2011.

Caird, G. B. *A Commentary on the Revelation of St. John the Divine*. New York: Harper & Row, 1966.

Fanning, Buist M. *Revelation*. Zondervan Exegetical Commentary on the New Testament. Grand Rapids: Zondervan Academic, 2020.

Fee, Gordon D. *Revelation: A New Covenant Commentary*. Eugene, OR: Cascade, 2011.

Keener, Craig S. *Revelation*. Grand Rapids: Zondervan Academic, 1999.

Koester, Craig R. *Revelation: A New Translation with Introduction and Commentary*. Anchor Bible 38A. New Haven: Yale University Press, 2014.

Kovacs, Judith, and Christopher Rowland. *Revelation*. Blackwell Bible Commentaries. Oxford: Blackwell, 2004.

Mounce, Robert H. *The Book of Revelation*. New International Commentary on the New Testament. Grand Rapids: Eerdmans, 1977.

Osborne, Grant R. *Revelation*. Baker Exegetical Commentary on the New Testament. Grand Rapids: Baker Academic, 2002.

Paul, Ian. *Revelation*. Tyndale New Testament Commentaries 20. Downers Grove, IL: IVP Academic, 2018.

Reddish, Mitchell G. *Revelation*. Smyth & Helwys Bible Commentary Series. Macon, GA: Smyth & Helwys, 2018.

Tonstad, Sigve K. *Revelation*. Grand Rapids: Baker Academic, 2019.

Weima, Jeffrey A. D. *Sermons to the Seven Churches of Revelation*. Grand Rapids: Baker Academic, 2021.

Witherington, Ben, III. *Revelation*. Cambridge: Cambridge University Press, 2003.

Recommended Studies

Studies on the book of Revelation are, like most books of the New Testament, a bit of a cottage industry with lots of insider talk. This book is designed for church folks and pastors and not specialists, so we have shuttled all technical notes to the back of the book and avoided getting into the weeds of academic discussion. We have benefited the most from the following studies, but five deserve top mentions: Richard Bauckham, Michael Gorman, J. Nelson Kraybill, Brian Blount, and David deSilva.

Barr, David L., ed. *Reading the Book of Revelation: A Resource for Students*. Atlanta: SBL Press, 2003.

Bauckham, Richard. *The Climax of Prophecy: Studies on the Book of Revelation*. Edinburgh: T&T Clark, 1993.

———. *The Theology of the Book of Revelation*. Cambridge: Cambridge University Press, 1993.

Blackwell, Ben C., John K. Goodrich, and Jason Maston, eds. *Reading Revelation in Context: John's Apocalypse and Second Temple Judaism*. Grand Rapids: Zondervan Academic, 2019.

Blount, Brian K. *Can I Get a Witness?* Louisville: Westminster John Knox, 2005.

Collins, Adela Yarbro. *The Combat Myth in the Book of Revelation*. Eugene, OR: Wipf & Stock, 2001.

Collins, John J. *The Apocalyptic Imagination: An Introduction to Jewish Apocalyptic Literature*. New York: Crossroad, 1982.

Culy, Martin M. *The Book of Revelation: The Rest of the Story*. Eugene, OR: Pickwick, 2017.

Daniels, C. Wess, Wes Howard-Brook, and Darryl Aaron. *Resisting Empire: The Book of Revelation as Resistance*. Newberg, OR: Barclay, 2019.

deSilva, David A. *Discovering Revelation: Content, Interpretation, Reception*. Grand Rapids: Eerdmans, 2021.

———. *Seeing Things John's Way: The Rhetoric of the Book of Revelation*. Louisville: Westminster John Knox, 2009.

Goldingay, John E. *Daniel*. Word Biblical Commentary 30. Dallas: Word, 1989.

Gorman, Michael. *Reading Revelation Responsibly: Uncivil Worship and Witness; Following the Lamb into the New Creation*. Eugene, OR: Cascade, 2011.

Hays, Richard B., and Stefan Alkier, eds. *Revelation and the Politics of Apocalyptic Interpretation*. Waco, TX: Baylor University Press, 2015.

Johnson, Darrell W. *Discipleship on the Edge: An Expository Journey through the Book of Revelation*. Vancouver: Canadian Church Leaders Network, 2004.

Koester, Craig. *Revelation and the End of All Things*. Grand Rapids: Eerdmans, 2018.

Kraybill, J. Nelson. *Apocalypse and Allegiance*. Grand Rapids: Brazos, 2010.

Mathewson, David L. *A Companion to the Book of Revelation*. Eugene, OR: Cascade, 2020.

Moloney, Francis J. *The Apocalypse of John*. Grand Rapids: Baker Academic, 2020.

Pagels, Elaine. *Revelations: Visions, Prophecy, and Politics in the Book of Revelation*. New York: Viking, 2012.

Peterson, Eugene H. *Reversed Thunder: The Revelation of John and the Praying Imagination*. San Francisco: HarperOne, 1991.

Pippin, Tina. *Death and Desire: The Rhetoric of Gender in the Apocalypse of John*. Eugene, OR: Wipf & Stock, 2021.

Schüssler Fiorenza, Elisabeth. *Revelation: Vision of a Just World*. Minneapolis: Fortress, 1992.

Stevenson, Gregory. *A Slaughtered Lamb: Revelation and the Apocalyptic Response to Evil and Suffering*. Abilene, TX: Abilene Christian University Press, 2013.

After Words

After teaching this wonderful book of Revelation for nearly four decades, sometimes only in one lecture and other times more spread out, I (Scot) chose to teach a full course at Northern Seminary on the book. At the time, Cody Matchett was my graduate assistant and was keen on doing research for the class and this book. His keenness became scholarly acumen of the sort that he and I were communicating with one another often, and I was learning from him as much as he was from me. So, it was not right for him to be anything less than a coauthor. As I write these words, he's about to graduate to pursue a PhD in New Testament studies.

As this book was being written, both of us were teaching Revelation to different audiences, he in Calgary at First Assembly Church (Tehillah Ministry School), and I at Northern Seminary. Those classes gave feedback that found their way into nuances and answers to questions students were asking. Our students have made this book better on every page. In addition to thanking them, we thank President Bill Shiell for his fine leadership at Northern; my dean and friend Lynn Cohick, who read an earlier version of this book and offered encouragement and feedback; Nijay Gupta, both my colleague and for whom Cody has also provided assistance; and Justin Gill, another graduate assistant who has been our librarian for a year and helped in too many ways to name.

This is not a commentary on Revelation. It is rather a theology of political discipleship rooted in Revelation and how best to read it.

Notes

Introduction

p. xiii   Matthew Avery Sutton, *American Apocalypse: A History of Modern Evangelicalism* (Cambridge, MA: Belknap, 2014), ix–x.

Chapter 1: Revelation for Too Many

p. 3   Christopher Rowland, *Revelation* (London: Epworth, 1993), 543.

p. 4   For a splendid new study on the churches of Revelation, see Weima, *Sermons to the Seven Churches of Revelation*. A distinctive emphasis for Weima is that these are not technically "letters" but more like sermons, and the reason for this conclusion is that these messages lack key elements of a letter. So also Aune, *Revelation*, 1:125; Beale, *Revelation*, 224. The "these are the words," say of 2:1, sound like prophetic oracles, which Weima translates into modern discourse into "sermon." See Weima, 3–5.

p. 5   Caird, *Commentary on the Revelation of St. John the Divine*, 2.

p. 5   Sutton, *American Apocalypse*, 326, 329.

p. 6   Amy Johnson Frykholm, *The Rapture Culture:* Left Behind *in Evangelical America* (New York: Oxford University Press, 2004), 105–29, quoting from p. 106.

p. 7   Timothy Beal, *The Book of Revelation: A Biography*. Lives of Great Religious Books 49 (Princeton: Princeton University Press, 2018), 202.

p. 7   Paul Boyer, *When Time Shall Be No More: Prophecy Belief in Modern American Culture* (Cambridge: Harvard University Press, 1992), 142.

p. 7   Gorman, *Reading Revelation Responsibly*, 70–73.

p. 8   Philip Gorski, *American Covenant: A History of Civil Religion from the Puritans to the Present* (Cambridge, MA: Princeton University Press, 2017), 22.

p. 8   Gorski, *American Covenant*, 22.

p. 9   Gorman, *Reading Revelation Responsibly*, 72.

p. 9   Rowland, *Revelation*, 544.

p. 9   Kraybill, *Apocalypse and Allegiance*, 24.

p. 9   Frykholm, *Rapture Culture*, 21.

p. 10   For a complementary sketch of populist eschatology in the UK, see Stephen Holmes and Russell Rook, eds., *What Are We Waiting For? Christian Hope and Contemporary Culture* (Milton Keynes: Paternoster, 2008), 1–10.

p. 10   On the history of evangelicals and eschatology, showing a connection between social conditions and one's preferences in eschatology, see D. Bebbington, "Eschatology in Evangelical History," in Holmes and Rook, *What Are We Waiting For?*, 75–86.

p. 10   Thomas B. Slater, *Revelation as Civil Disobedience: Witnesses Not Warriors in John's Apocalypse* (Nashville: Abingdon, 2019), 98.

p. 11   Peterson, *Reversed Thunder*, x.

p. 12   Greg Carey, *Ultimate Things: An Introduction to Jewish and Christian Apocalyptic Literature* (Saint Louis: Chalice, 2014), 228.

p. 12   Kraybill, *Apocalypse and Allegiance*, 15.

p. 13   On the expression "uncivil worship," Gorman, *Reading Revelation Responsibly*, 176–180.

p. 13   Beale, *Revelation*, 171.

p. 13   Wes Howard-Brook and Anthony Gwyther, *Unveiling Empire: Reading Revelation Then and Now*, The Bible & Liberation (Maryknoll, NY: Orbis Books), 2; see also Harry O. Maier, *Apocalypse Recalled* (Minneapolis: Fortress, 2002).

p. 14   On this chapter's general themes, see Gorman, *Reading Revelation Responsibly*, which is a model of reading Revelation well. See also Kraybill, *Apocalypse and Allegiance*, as well as Peterson, *Reversed Thunder*. A theopolitical reading is ignored by many, including Brian J. Tabb, *All Things New: Revelation as Canonical Capstone*, New Studies in Biblical Theology (Downers Grove, IL: InterVarsity Press, 2019). In preparing for this book, I read several major studies by proponents of classical dispensationalism, and there is virtually nothing in their studies about discipleship, about dissidence, or about the divine politics revealed in this book. All that matters is what is to come.

Chapter 2: For Whom Was the Book of Revelation Written?

p. 15   On the genre of Revelation, see Bauckham, *Theology of Revelation,* 1–23; Beale, *Revelation,* 37–43; Gorman, *Reading Revelation Responsibly,* 10–27; Aune, *Revelation,* 1:lxx.

p. 16   Martin Goodman, *Rome and Jerusalem: The Clash of Ancient Civilizations* (New York: Vintage Books, 2008), 3.

p. 17   Any discussion of "empire" evokes both the Roman empire, which is the culmination of a history of violent empires in the ancient world, as well as modern theories of empire. This study concentrates on the specific manifestations of Babylon, or Roman empire, and not so much on theories of empire. By focusing on the characteristics of Babylon, we move away from potential partisan politics and closer to systemic injustices and idolatries. For one sketch, with a view toward dissidence, see Howard-Brook and Gwyther, *Unveiling Empire,* 87–119, 223–35. They sketch economics, culture and cult, and the imperial myth (or story), as well as how Christians countered the myths of Rome.

p. 17   Gorman, *Reading Revelation Responsibly,* xv.

p. 17   For a proposal for Christian dissidence, we recommend Lee C. Camp, *Scandalous Witness: A Little Political Manifesto for Christians* (Grand Rapids: Eerdmans, 2020).

p. 17   For the best study of Jewish attitudes to Hellenistic rulers, see Tessa Rajak et al., eds., *Jewish Perspectives on Hellenistic Rulers* (Berkeley: University of California Press, 2007).

p. 19   Martin Luther King, Jr., *Strength to Love* (Minneapolis: Fortress, 2010), 11–20.

p. 19   On the history of interpreting details about Patmos, much of which was speculation to fill in the absence of information in Revelation itself, see Ian Boxall, *Patmos in the Reception History of the Apocalypse,* Oxford Theology and Religion Monographs (Oxford: Oxford University Press, 2013). That history reveals that some considered Patmos a symbol for the solitary location where revelation occurs—that is, a thin place. Patmos was not perceived as a prison location.

p. 20   Malcom Guite, "A Villanelle for National Poetry Day," *Malcom Guite* (blog), October 6, 2011, https://malcolmguite.wordpress.com/2011/10/06/a-villanelle-for-national-poetry-day/. Thanks to my colleague, Lynn Cohick, for pointing me to this poem.

Chapter 3: Revelation and Imagination

p. 24   On the meaning of "saw" and "heard," see Gorman, *Reading Revelation Responsibly*, 39–40; Johnson, *Discipleship on the Edge*, 27–32; Paul and Perrin, *Revelation*, 22–25; G. K. Beale, *The Use of Daniel in Jewish Apocalyptic Literature and in the Revelation of St. John* (Eugene, OR: Wipf & Stock, 2010). On Daniel's approach to writing, see John Goldingay, *Daniel*, Word Biblical Commentary 30 (Dallas: Word, 1989), 154.

p. 25   John's so-called use of the Old Testament has been subjected to intense scrutiny, with many concluding that John, in typical Jewish fashion, reused or "re-actualized" or "re-appropriated" or created a "pastiche" of the prophets Isaiah, Ezekiel, Zechariah, or Daniel. An innovative synthetic expression for understanding how John put this text together is the word "pastiche," explored by Michelle Fletcher, *Reading Revelation as Pastiche: Imitating the Past*, Library of New Testament Studies 571 (London: Bloomsbury T&T Clark, 2017). For a technical discussion, see Garrick V. Allen, *The Book of Revelation and Early Jewish Textual Culture*, Society for New Testament Studies Monograph Series 168 (Cambridge: Cambridge University Press, 2017), who concludes that John must be read in the context of various versions of Old Testament texts.

p. 26   Bruce Metzger, *Breaking the Code: Understanding the Book of Revelation* (Nashville: Abingdon, 2019), 11.

p. 26   Gorman, *Reading Revelation Responsibly*, 8.

p. 26   Richard Hays, *The Conversion of the Imagination: Paul as Interpreter of Israel's Scripture* (Grand Rapids: Eerdmans, 2005).

p. 26   Rowland, *Revelation*, 506.

p. 27   Adela Yarbro Collins, *Crisis and Catharsis: The Power of the Apocalypse* (Philadelphia: Westminster, 1984), 141.

p. 27   Richard Bauckham, "Eschatology in the Book of Revelation," in Holmes-Rook, *What Are We Waiting For?*, 48–59, here pp. 48–49.

p. 28   Trevor Hart, "Eschatology and Imagination," in Holmes and Rook, *What Are We Waiting For?*, 127–37, quoting p. 129.

p. 28   On various approaches to imagination, see Peterson, *Reversed Thunder*; Clyde S. Kilby, William A. Dyrness, and Keith Call, *The Arts and the Christian Imagination: Essays on Art, Literature, and Aesthetics* (Brewster, MA: Paraclete, 2016); Richard Bauckham and Trevor Hart, *Hope against Hope: Christian Eschatology in Contemporary Context* (London: Darton, Longman & Todd, 1999);

Ruth M. J. Byrne, *The Rational Imagination: How People Create Alternatives to Reality* (Cambridge: MIT Press, 2005); Carey, *Ultimate Things*.

p. 28   For Revelation's connection to modern fiction, see Frykholm, *Rapture Culture*, 131–51.

p. 29   Gregory Stevenson, *A Slaughtered Lamb: Revelation and the Apocalyptic Response to Evil and Suffering* (Abilene: Abilene Christian University Press, 2014), 96, 101.

p. 29   Adela Yarbro Collins, "'What the Spirit Says to the Churches': Preaching the Apocalypse," *Quarterly Review* 4/3 (Fall 1984): 79.

p. 30   On oral performance of Revelation, see Harry O. Maier, *Apocalypse Recalled: The Book of Revelation after Christendom* (Minneapolis: Fortress, 2003), 91–122; and especially Lourdes García Ureña, *Narrative and Drama in the Book of Revelation*, Society for New Testament Studies Monograph Series 175 (Cambridge: Cambridge University Press, 2019).

p. 30   On the rhetorical aspects of Revelation, no one has done more than David A. deSilva, *Seeing Things John's Way: The Rhetoric of the Book of Revelation* (Louisville: Westminster John Knox, 2009), and he makes summary comments throughout *Discovering Revelation*. The potent predictions of Babylon's fall and its destruction is "a device intended to heighten indignation against Rome" (*Discovering Revelation*, 162). For a brief discussion, see Koester, *Revelation*, 132–144; On interpretation of symbolism, see Beale, *Revelation*, 50–69; Aune, *Revelation*, 1:xc.

p. 31   J. R. R. Tolkien, *Leaf by Niggle* (London: HarperCollins: 2016).

Chapter 4: Babylon's Identity

p. 37   On the cast of characters in Revelation, see Gorman, *Reading Revelation Responsibly*, 116–36.

p. 40   Paul Minear, *I Saw a New Earth: An Introduction to the Visions of the Apocalypse* (Washington: Corpus Books, 1968), 228.

p. 40   David Mathewson, *A Companion to the Book of Revelation* (Eugene, OR: Cascade, 2020), 58.

p. 40   On the importance of the throne-room scene, see Reddish, *Revelation*, 92; Elisabeth Schüssler Fiorenza, *Invitation to the Book of Revelation: A Commentary on the Apocalypse with Complete Text from the Jerusalem Bible* (Garden City, NY: Image Books, 1981), 27.

p. 41   On women in Revelation, see Schüssler Fiorenza, *Revelation:*

Vision of a Just World; Tina Pippin, *Death and Desire: The Rhetoric of Gender in the Apocalypse of John* (Eugene, OR: Wipf & Stock, 2021); deSilva, *Discovering Revelation,* 146–66; Lynn R. Huber, *Thinking and Seeing with Women in Revelation,* Library of New Testament Studies 475 (London: Bloomsbury T&T Clark, 2013). For a fresh undertaking, see Eliza Rosenberg, "'As She Herself Has Rendered': Resituating Gender Perspectives on Revelation's 'Babylon,'" in *New Perspectives on the Book of Revelation,* ed. Adela Yarbro Collins, Bibliotheca Ephemeridum Theologicarum Lovaniensium 291 (Leuven: Peeters, 2017), 545–60, who concludes that John connects Jezebel and Babylon with evil, exploitative, and enslaving women of the Old Testament.

p. 43   On Babylon and how Jews and Christians wrote about foreign domination, see Tessa Rajak, "The Angry Tyrant," in *Jewish Perspectives on Hellenistic Rulers,* ed. Tessa Rajak et al., Hellenistic Culture and Society 50 (Berkeley: University of California Press, 2007), 110–27.

p. 43   On Babylon in the history of the church's interpretation, see Koester, *Revelation,* 637–41.

p. 45   On Babylon being identified with the city of Jerusalem, see Moloney, *Apocalypse of John,* 260; deSilva, *Discovering Revelation,* 146–66.

p. 48   William Stringfellow, *An Ethic for Christians and Other Aliens in a Strange Land* (Eugene, OR: Wipf & Stock, 2004) 51, emphasis added.

p. 49   Howard-Brook and Gwyther, *Unveiling Empire,* 157–158, all italics in original.

p. 49   Bauckham, *The Theology of the Book of Revelation,* 43.

p. 49   On Hitler learning racial profiling from the USA, see Isabel Wilkerson, *Caste: The Lies that Divide Us* (London: Allen Lane, 2020), 78–88.

p. 50   For "Gorman, deepening his accusations . . . ," see Gorman, *Reading Revelation Responsibly,* 45–56.

Chapter 5: Babylon's Characteristics

p. 52   Bauckham, *Theology of Revelation,* 43.

p. 52   For a good sketch of civil religion, see Gorman, *Reading Revelation Responsibly,* 40–45. For another list, see Howard-Brook and Gwyther, *Unveiling Empire,* 179–83: murder, whoring, illusion, sorcery, and worship of idols. See also Collins, *Crisis and Catharsis*, 121–24: idolatries, violence, self-glorification, wealth. An alternative version of the seven marks of Babylon: leaving out the living God, sensuality, injustice, worship of products, violence, deception and counterfeit, idolatry. See for this last list Johnson, *Discipleship on the Edge*, 302–3.

p. 53   On idolatries, see Moshe Halbertal and Avishai Margalit, *Idolatry* (Cambridge, MA: Harvard University Press, 1992).

p. 53   On opulence and exploitation, see Goodman, *Rome and Jerusalem*, 38, 87–88.

p. 55   Adrian Goldsworthy, *Pax Romana: War, Peace and Conquest in the Roman World* (New Haven: Yale University Press, 2017), 11; see also Mary Beard, *S.P.Q.R.: A History of Ancient Rome* (New York: Liveright, 2016).

p. 57   For the mosaics in Pompei, see Jo-Ann Shelton, *As the Romans Did: A Sourcebook in Roman Social History*, 2nd ed. (Oxford: Oxford University Press, 1998), #170; also Collins, *Crisis and Catharsis*, 88–97.

p. 57   On economic exploitation, gentile kings were at times comprehended in Jewish literature as "bandits"; see Richard Fowler, "Kingship and Banditry: The Parthian Empire and Its Western Subjects," in Rajak, *Jewish Perspectives on Hellenistic Rulers*, 147–62.

p. 58   Shelton, *As the Romans Did*, #172.

Chapter 6: The Dragon and Its Wild Things

p. 65   On the central importance of Genesis 3 for Revelation, see Tonstad, *Revelation*, 176–79.

p. 66   On comparing the "beast" language of chapter 13 with Daniel, see Keener, *Revelation*, 336–37.

p. 66   On 666, see Gorman, *Reading Revelation Responsibly*, 126–28. For an adventurous sketch of the history of interpretation, see Koester, *Revelation*, 538–40. For two longer sketches, see Rowland, *Revelation*, 528–57; Russell Morton, *Recent Research on Revelation* (Sheffield: Sheffield Phoenix, 2014); Michael C. Thompson, "The Book of Revelation," in *The State of New Testament Studies: A Survey of Recent Research*, ed. S. McKnight and N. K. Gupta (Grand Rapids: Baker Academic, 2019), 459–75.

p. 67   On Nero and the beast, see Bauckham, *Climax of Prophecy*, 384–452.

302   Revelation for the Rest of Us# 302   Revelation for the Rest of Us

p. 67 On the rejection of identifying 666 with only one historical figure, see Beale, *Revelation*, 1130–31.

p. 67 On the web of cult and commerce in the Roman world, see J. Nelson Kraybill, *Imperial Cult and Commerce in John's Apocalypse* (London: Bloomsbury, 1996).

p. 68 deSilva, *Discovering Revelation*, 135.

Chapter 7: The Lamb

p. 69 Slater, *Revelation as Civil Disobedience*, xi.

p. 70 For reading "testimony about Jesus" as the message of the book of Revelation, see Sarah S. U. Dixon, *The Testimony of the Exalted Jesus in the Book of Revelation*, Library of New Testament Studies 570 (London: Bloomsbury T&T Clark, 2017).

p. 73 Paul, *Revelation*, 71.

p. 77 Caird, *Revelation*, 73 (italics added).

p. 77 On Christology in Revelation, see Slater, *Revelation as Civil Disobedience*, 37–66. The most thorough study on the lamb in the background and world of Revelation is Loren L. Johns, *The Lamb Christology of the Apocalypse of John: An Investigation into Its Origins and Rhetorical Force*, WUNT 2.167 (Tübingen: Mohr Siebeck, 2003). A conviction of John's is that, in tension with the world around Revelation, the Lamb is a victorious lamb who conquers, paradoxically, by suffering. The image, then, is not one of force or violence but one of a vulnerable victor. See the discussion by Jan Willem van Henten, "Violence in Revelation," in *New Perspectives on Revelation*, ed. Adela Yarbro Collins, BETL (Leuven: Peeters, 2017), 49–77, who is unconvinced Revelation can be read nonviolently.

p. 77 Metzger, *Breaking the Code*, 77.

p. 79 On the "biggest copycat" see Eugene Boring, *Revelation: Interpretation: A Bible Commentary for Teaching and Preaching* (Nashville: Westminster John Knox, 2011), 157.

p. 80 On the lion, the lamb, and the dragon, see Bauckham, *Climax of Prophecy*, 174–98; idem, *Theology of the Book of Revelation*, 54–65.

Chapter 8: The Faithful Witnesses

p. 84 Richard Lischer, *Just Tell the Truth* (Grand Rapids: Eerdmans, 2021), 39.

p. 85 I will avoid naming the many Protestant authors who never even entertain the possibility that this woman may be Mary. One who does see some imagery for Mary is Johnson, *Discipleship on the Edge*, 219–220.

p. 85   On the woman of chapter twelve, see Koester, *Revelation*, 542–43; Tonstad, *Revelation*, 177; Beale, *Revelation*, 625–29; Osborne, *Revelation*, 457–58; Boring, *Revelation*, 152.

p. 87   On the possibility of the woman Babylon being the same as the woman from chapter twelve, see Tonstad, *Revelation*, 240–45.

p. 87   For a brief sketch of the history of how the seven churches have been interpreted, see Koester, *Revelation*, 231–34. For a brief refutation of the chronological, predictive reading, see Weima, *Sermons to the Seven Churches*, 19–21. For a similar approach that sees the churches as segments of Israel's history, see Moloney, *Apocalypse of John*.

p. 87   For an exceptional study of the early history of the church at Ephesus, see Paul Trebilco, *The Early Christians in Ephesus from Paul to Ignatius* (Grand Rapids: Eerdmans, 2004).

p. 89   Many make much of precise details in each city of the seven churches, and such details supposedly correlate with what John writes, sometimes with illumination and other times without credibility. Caution must be used (Weima, *Sermons to the Seven Churches*, 22–25). For details on each city, besides the commentaries (Aune, Koester, Blount), see especially Colin J. Hemer, *The Letters to the Seven Churches of Asia in Their Local Setting* (Grand Rapids: Eerdmans; Livonia, MI: Dove Booksellers, 2001; repr., Sheffield: JSOT Press, 1986).

Chapter 9: The Drama of Revelation

p. 93   On the structure and plan of John's Apocalypse, see Beale, *Revelation*, 108–51; Bauckham, *Climax of Prophecy*, 1–37. A brief bibliography of rhetorical studies can be found in Ben Witherington III, *Revelation* (Cambridge: Cambridge University Press, 2003), 53–54.

p. 95   On chronological readings in the dispensational and progressive dispensational approaches, the "major proponent" is Robert L. Thomas, *Revelation Exegetical Commentary* (Chicago: Moody, 2016), 180.

p. 96   C. Kavin Rowe, *Christianity's Surprise: A Sure and Certain Hope* (Nashville: Abingdon, 2020), 11.

p. 96   Keener, *Revelation*, 21.

p. 97   On the backstory of Revelation, see esp. N. T. Wright, *The New Testament and The People of God: Christian Origins and the Question of God* (Minneapolis: Fortress, 1992); Abraham Joshua Heschel, *The Prophets* (Peabody, MA: Hendrickson, 2007).

p. 99   On the story so far, see G. E. Ladd, *A Theology of the New Testament* (Grand Rapids: Eerdmans, 2002); Hans Schwarz, *Eschatology* (Grand Rapids: Eerdmans, 2000), 61–103.

p. 104   Gorski, *American Covenant*, esp. 13–36.

Chapter 10: An Interlude about the Interludes

p. 106   Blount, *Revelation*, 145.

p. 106   Bauckham, *Climax of Prophecy*, 233.

Chapter 11: Three Times Seven = Completion

p. 110   On the themes, see deSilva, *Discovering Revelation*, 106–24; Gorman, *Reading Revelation Responsibly*, 138–59; Koester, *Revelation*, 356–57. See also Peterson, *Reversed Thunder*, 87–101.

p. 111   On "They are imminent" and the general theme of next event as last event, see G. B. Caird, *The Language and Imagery of the Bible* (Philadelphia: Westminster, 1980), 243–271; Edward Adams, *The Stars Will Fall from Heaven: Cosmic Catastrophe in the New Testament and its World*, LNTS 347 (London: T&T Clark, 2007).

p. 111   For a more "hopeful" approach about the foreign nations in Revelation, Allan J. McNicol, drawing on the prophetic expectation of the pilgrimage and streaming of the nations to Mount Zion, contends that at the return of Christ the nations will all convert. See *The Conversion of the Nations in Revelation*, Library of New Testament Studies 438 (London: T&T Clark, 2011). Also see Bauckham, *Climax of Prophecy*, 238–337.

p. 112   For an excellent manifestation of how John re-actualizes the language of Israel's prophets, see David Mathewson, *A New Heaven and a New Earth: The Meaning and Function of the Old Testament in Revelation 21.1–22.5* (Sheffield: Sheffield Academic, 2003); deSilva, *Discovering Revelation*, 57–59.

p. 113   For a succinct and challenging account of seeing the violence of Rome flipped onto John's own violent language, see Greg Carey, "The Book of Revelation as Counter-Imperial Script," in *In the Shadow of the Empire: Reclaiming the Bible as a History of Faithful Resistance* (Louisville: Westminster John Knox, 2008), 157–76.

Carey connects this all, as well, to how John creates a voice of authority and leads modern readers of various sorts to the claims of authority. See *Elusive Apocalypse: Reading Authority in the Revelation to John*, Studies in American Biblical Hermeneutics 15 (Macon, GA: Mercer University Press, 1999). Carey, matching John's own irony, thinks John reinscribes the violence he opposes.

p. 115 Slater, *Revelation as Civil Disobedience*, 99, italics his.

Chapter 12: A Prophet Spinning Plates

p. 121 On the theme of this chapter, see Beale, *John's Use of the Old Testament in Revelation*, 60–128; Koester, *Revelation*, 123–25; deSilva, *Discovering Revelation*, 106–8.

p. 123 David Mathewson, *New Heaven and a New Earth*, 234–35.

Chapter 13: Divine Judgments or Disciplines?

p. 128 This chapter is indebted to the work of Bauckham, *Theology of the Book of Revelation*, 98–104.

p. 129 See also Eusebius, *Ecclesiastical History*, and the discussion of mission in the early centuries. Also, see the still valuable Ramsay Macmullen, *Christianizing the Roman Empire, AD 100–400* (New Haven: Yale University Press, 1984) as well as Carter, *Roman Empire*, 124–28; Gorman, *Reading Revelation Responsibly*, 150–55.

p. 132 For "sLambed," used many times by Blount in *Can I Get a Witness?* and *Revelation*.

p. 132 Bauckham, *Theology of the Book of Revelation*, 101 (italics added).

Chapter 14: Visions of Final Justice

p. 137 On reading Revelation 19–21 as nonsequential, see Paul, *Revelation*, 313–71.

p. 138 Some have compared Revelation to the War Scroll of Qumran; see Bauckham, *Climax of Prophecy*, 210–37.

p. 142 Bauckham, *Theology*, 107, 108 (italics ours).

Chapter 15: A New Jerusalem Imagination

p. 146 For major themes in this chapter, see Alan Ryan, *On Politics* (New York: Liveright, 2020), 1.71–148; for a full study of the vision here in comparison with utopianism in the ancient world, see Eric J. Gilchrest, *Revelation 21–22 in Light of Jewish and Greco-Roman Utopianism*, Biblical Interpretation Series 118 (Leiden: Brill, 2013).

p. 147   Jacques Ellul, *Apocalypse: The Book of Revelation*, trans. George W. Schreiner (Eugene, OR: Wipf & Stock, 2019 [1977]), 208–209; see also Mathewson, *New Heaven and a New Earth*; William J. Dumbrell, *The End of the Beginning* (Eugene, OR: Wipf & Stock, 2001).

p. 147   On George Ladd's "present without consummation," see his *The Presence of the Future: The Eschatology of Biblical Realism*, rev. ed. (Grand Rapids: Eerdmans, 1996).

p. 147   See N. T. Wright's many writings, including his recent *Paul and the Faithfulness of God*, 2 vols. (Minneapolis: Fortress, 2013); see also G. K. Beale, "The Eschatological Conception of New Testament Theology," in *Eschatology in the Bible and Theology: Evangelical Essays at the Dawn of a New Millennium*, ed. Kent Brower and Mark Elliott (Downers Gove, IL: InterVarsity Press, 1999), 11–52.

p. 147   On new Jerusalem in the church's interpretation, see Koester, *Revelation*, 741–50; on new Jerusalem as fulfilling scriptural themes, see Mathias Rissi, *The Future of the World: An Exegetical Study of Revelation 19.11–22.15*, Studies in Biblical Theology 2.23 (Naperville, IL: Alec R. Allenson, 1972).

p. 148   On theocracy, see Eugene Peterson, *This Hallelujah Banquet* (New York: Crown, 2021); Justin Thacker, "Heaven," in Holmes and Rook, *What Are We Waiting For?*, 112–23: feasting, fellowship, facing God—and it begins now; Drew Strait, *Hidden Criticism of the Angry Tyrant in Early Judaism and the Acts of the Apostles*, (Lanham, MD: Lexington Books; Minneapolis: Fortress Academic, 2019); on the ideal temple, see Andrea L. Robinson, *Temple of Presence: The Christological Fulfillment of Ezekiel 40–48 in Revelation 21:1–22:5* (Eugene, OR: Wipf & Stock, 2019); G. K. Beale, *The Temple and the Church's Mission: A Biblical Theology of the Dwelling Place of God*, New Studies in Biblical Theology (Downers Grove, IL: IVP Academic; Nottingham: Apollos, 2004).

p. 149   On a rebuilt temple in the millennium and beyond, see Fanning, *Revelation*, 544.

p. 155   Howard-Brook and Gwyther, *Unveiling Empire*, 129.

p. 156   R. B. Wright, "Psalms of Solomon," in *The Old Testament Pseudepigrapha*, ed. James H. Charlesworth, 2 vols., Anchor Bible Reference Library (New York: Doubleday, 1985), 2:662.

Chapter 16: New Jerusalem as Promise for Victors

p. 161   Osborne, *Revelation*, 562–63.

p. 161 Blount, *Revelation*, 52.

p. 161 Slater, *Revelation as Civil Disobedience*, 67–80.

p. 163 C. S. Lewis, *The Last Battle* (London: HarperCollins, 2014), 210–11.

Chapter 17: Babylon in the Seven Churches

p. 167 Rowland, *Revelation*, 523.

p. 168 *Sermons to the Seven Churches*, 10–11.

p. 170 For "what Christ thinks of the church," see John R. W. Stott, *What Christ Thinks of the Church: An Exposition of Revelation 1–3* (Grand Rapids: Eerdmans, 1972; repr., Grand Rapids: Baker, 2003).

p. 171 On the problems in the seven churches, see Koester, *Revelation and the End of All Things*, 60–74, who frames three problems: assimilation, complacency, persecution. DeSilva, *Discovering Revelation*, 78–87, finds three as well: tensions with synagogue, hostility from Greco-Roman neighbors, and accommodation.

p. 171 Howard-Brook and Gwyther, *Unveiling Empire*, xxii.

p. 172 Weima, *Sermons to the Seven Churches*, 41, italics in original.

p. 172 Martin M. Culy, *The Book of Revelation: The Rest of the Story* (Eugene, OR: Pickwick, 2017), 30.

p. 173 On disordered love, see Scot McKnight, *The Jesus Creed: Loving God, Loving Others* (Brewster, MA: Paraclete, 2014); Patrick Mitchel, *The Message of Love: The Only Thing That Counts* (Downers Grove, IL: InterVarsity Press, 2019).

p. 178 David Brooks, *The Second Mountain: The Quest for a Moral Life* (New York: Random House, 2019), 22.

p. 179 Dietrich Bonhoeffer, *Discipleship*, Dietrich Bonhoeffer Works 4 (Minneapolis: Fortress, 2001), 44.

p. 182 On "Constantinianism," I am grateful to George Kalantzis for suggestions that found their way into this discussion. See Macmullen, *Christianizing the Roman Empire, A.D. 100–400*; Timothy D. Barnes, *Constantine and Eusebius* (Cambridge, MA: Harvard University Press, 1981); Elizabeth DePalma Digeser, *The Making of a Christian Empire: Lactantius and Rome* (Ithaca, NY: Cornell University Press, 2000); Mark Hebblewhite, *Theodosius and the Limits of Empire* (London: Routledge, 2020). For a view opposite Eusebius hagiography, see Paul Stephenson, *Constantine: Roman Emperor, Christian Victor* (New York: Overlook, 2009).

p. 182 Macmullen, *Christianizing the Roman Empire, A.D. 100–400*, 50.

Chapter 18: Worshiping in Babylon

p. 187 On the themes of this chapter, see Gorman, *Reading Revelation Responsibly*, 176–87, who sees seven themes of discipleship: (1) worship; (2) discernment, vision, and imagination; (3) faithfulness and prophetic resistance; (4) self-criticism; (5) cruciform, courageous, nonviolent warfare; (6) embodied communal witness and mission, including evangelization; and (7) hope.

p. 187 James K. A. Smith, *Imagining the Kingdom: How Worship Works*, Cultural Liturgies 2 (Grand Rapids: Baker Academic, 2013), 14–15.

p. 187 On worship, see David Peterson, *Engaging with God: A Biblical Theology of Worship* (Downers Grove, IL: InterVarsity Press, 2002).

p. 188 Dallas Willard, *The Spirit of the Disciplines: Understanding How God Changes Lives* (New York: HarperOne, 1999).

p. 188 Lauren Winner, *The Dangers of Christian Practice: On Wayward Gifts, Characteristic Damage, and Sin* (New Haven: Yale University Press, 2018).

p. 188 Schüssler Fiorenza, *Revelation*, 4, her italics.

p. 189 For a good discussion of the impact of John's songs, see Gorman, *Reading Revelation Responsibly*, 4–8.

p. 189 On reading the songs as spirituals, see Brian Blount, "The Negro Spiritual," in *Cultural Interpretation: Reorienting New Testament Criticism* (Minneapolis: Fortress, 1995), 55–69; Howard Thurman, *Deep River* and *The Negro Spiritual Speaks of Life and Death* (Richmond, IN: Friends United, 1975); Daniel Seeger, "Revelation and Revolution," *Friends Journal*, June 1, 2015, www.friendsjournal.org/revelation-and-revolution-the-apocalypse-of-john-in-the-quaker-and-african-american-spiritual-traditions/.

p. 190 Thurman, *Deep River* and *The Negro Spiritual*, 36.

p. 190 For "endurance, hope, and resistance," Blount, *Can I Get a Witness?*, 95.

p. 190 For the following from Blount, see his "The Negro Spiritual," in *Cultural Interpretation: Reorienting New Testament Criticism* (Minneapolis: Fortress, 1995), 55–70. For "do not receive . . . ," see Blount, "Negro Spiritual," 56.

p. 190 For "I look'd over Jordan" and "the black slaves" and "this language," see Blount, "Negro Spiritual," 68.

p. 190 For "one of the angels," see Blount, "Negro Spiritual," 68.

p. 191 "The black slaves" see Blount, "Negro Spiritual," 68.

p. 191 "This language," see Blount, "Negro Spiritual," 68.

p. 191 For "listeners the spiritual energy," see Blount, "Negro Spiritual," 69.

p. 193 C. Kavin Rowe, *One True Life: The Stoics and Christians as Rival Traditions* (New Haven: Yale University Press, 2016).

p. 194 Charles Taylor, *A Secular Age* (Boston: Belknap, 2007).

p. 195 On "foot-dragging" and resistance, see Drew Strait, *Hidden Criticism of the Angry Tyrant in Early Judaism and the Acts of the Apostles* (Minneapolis: Fortress, 2019), 121–162.

Chapter 19: Worship as Witness

p. 197 On the term "witness," I am especially fond of the work of Blount, *Can I Get a Witness?* and his articulation throughout his wonderful commentary, *Revelation*.

p. 199 Blount, *Can I Get a Witness?*, ix–x.

p. 200 King Jr., *Strength to Love*, 19.

p. 200 Peterson, *Hallelujah Banquet*, 54–55.

p. 200 Eberhard Bethge, *Dietrich Bonhoeffer: A Biography* (Minneapolis: Fortress, 2000), 654–655.

p. 201 Dietrich Bonhoeffer, *Theological Education Underground: 1937–1940*, Dietrich Bonhoeffer Works 15 (Minneapolis: Fortress, 2012), 210.

p. 201 Bethge, *Dietrich Bonhoeffer*, 886.

p. 202 Bethge, *Dietrich Bonhoeffer*, 655.

p. 202 Bethge, *Dietrich Bonhoeffer*, 655.

p. 203 On worship as allegiance, see Leonard L. Thompson, *The Book of Revelation: Apocalypse and Empire* (Oxford: Oxford University Press, 1990); Sigve K. Tonstad, *Saving God's Reputation: The Theological Function of Pistis Iesou in the Cosmic Narratives of Revelation* (London: Bloomsbury T&T Clark, 2013).

Chapter 20: Four Marks of Babylon Today

p. 210 Ross Douthat, *The Deep Places: A Memoir of Illness and Discovery* (New York: Convergent, 2021), 5.

p. 210 Eli Watkins and Abby Phillip, "Trump Decries Immigrants from 'Shithole Countries' Coming to US," *CNN*, January 12, 2018, www.cnn.com/2018/01/11/politics/immigrants-shithole-countries -trump/index.html. See also Laignee Barron, "'A New Low.' The World Is Furious at Trump for His Remark about 'Shithole Countries,'" *TIME*, January 12, 2018, https://time.com/5100328 /shithole-countries-trump-reactions/.

p. 212   On economic exploitation and meritocracy, see Michael Sandel, *The Tyranny of Merit: What's Become of the Common Good?* (New York: Farrar, Straus & Giroux, 2020).

p. 212   Benjamin M. Friedman, *Religion and the Rise of Capitalism* (New York: Alfred A. Knopf, 2021); see too the changed perception of raw capitalism's ads in the life of Jean Wade Rindlaub, along with the routine accommodation of the gospel to the market in Ellen Wayland-Smith, *The Angel in the Marketplace: Adwoman Jean Wade Rindlaub and the Selling of America* (Chicago: University of Chicago Press, 2020).

p. 213   Wayland-Smith, *Angel in the Marketplace*, 6.

p. 214   On militarism, see "Military Budget of the United States," *Wikipedia*, https://en.wikipedia.org/wiki/Military_budget_of _the_United_States. And see M. Szmigiera, "Countries with the Highest Military Spending 2021," Statista, April 29, 2022, www.statista.com/statistics/262742/countries-with-the-highest -military-spending/#:~:text=The%20United%20States%20lead%20 the,year%2C%201.92%20trillion%20US%20dollars. Also, see Jacques Ellul, *The Apocalypse: The Book of Revelation* (Eugene, OR: Wipf & Stock, 2020); Scot McKnight, *The Audacity of Peace*, My Theology Book 9 (Minneapolis: Fortress, 2022).

p. 215   For "sLambed," Blount, *Can I Get a Witness?*, throughout.

p. 216   On oppression and intolerance and freedom, see Robert Louis Wilken, *Liberty in the Things of God: The Christian Origins of Religious Freedom* (New Haven: Yale University Press, 2019).

p. 216   For "American blindspot," see Gerardo Marti, *American Blindspot: Race, Class, Religion, and the Trump Presidency* (Lanham, MD: Rowman & Littlefield, 2020).

p. 216   For America's "original sin," see Jim Wallis, *America's Original Sin: Racism, White Privilege, and the Bridge to a New America* (Grand Rapids: Brazos, 2016).

p. 218   For "Here are three of her statements . . . ," see Isabel Wilkerson, *Caste*, 17–19.

p. 218   For "What is the difference . . . ," *Caste*, 70.

Chapter 21: How Then Shall We Live in Babylon?

p. 221   For the statistics in the opening paragraph: "Fractured Nation: Widening Partisan Polarization and Key Issues in 2020 Presidential Elections," PRRI, October 20 2019, https://www.prri.org/research

/fractured-nation-widening-partisan-polarization-and-key
-issues-in-2020-presidential-elections/.

p. 221 Andrew C. McCarthy, "The Impeachment Trump Deserved,"
National Review, January 21, 2021, https://www.nationalreview
.com/magazine/2021/02/08/the-impeachment-trump-deserved/.

p. 223 Ryan Burge, "Is American Evangelicalism on the Decline?," *The
National Interest*, January 28, 2021, https://nationalinterest.org
/blog/reboot/american-evangelicalism-decline-177138. Emphasis
added.

p. 224 Kristin Kobes Du Mez, *Jesus and John Wayne: How White
Evangelicals Corrupted a Faith and Fractured a Nation* (New York:
Liveright, 2020), 3. Emphasis added.

p. 225 Philip S. Gorski and Samuel L. Perry, *The Flag and the Cross:
White Christian Nationalism and the Threat to American Democracy*
(Oxford: Oxford University Press, 2022), 70.

p. 227 Andrew Whitehead and Samuel L. Perry, *Taking America Back
for God: Christian Nationalism in the United States* (New York:
Oxford University Press, 2020), quotations in order of appearance
from pp. 222n19, 15, 145.

p. 228 Randall Balmer, "Randall Balmer: Something's Wrong When
Devout Christians Praise Proud Boys as 'God's warriors," *St. Louis
Post-Dispatch*, January 25, 2021, https://www.stltoday.com/opinion
/columnists/randall-balmer-somethings-wrong-when-devout-chri
stians-praise-proud-boys-as-gods-warriors/article_d85282c8-ef0a
-5cba-9f51-d9cc3278e7d5.html.

p. 229 Sean Michael Lucas, "Jesus Plus Masculinity for America's Sake:
Replying to *Jesus and John Wayne*," *Mere Orthodoxy*, January 25,
2021, https://mereorthodoxy.com/jesus-masculinity-america/.
Emphasis added.

p. 229 On progress in the world today, see Johan Norberg, *Progress:
Ten Reasons to Look Forward to the Future* (London: OneWorld,
2017); Hans Rosling, *Factfulness: Ten Reasons We're Wrong about
the World—And Why Things Are Better Than You Think* (New York:
Flatiron, 2018).

p. 230 Nathan Hatch, "The Political Captivity of the Faithful," *Comment*,
February 13, 2020, https://www.cardus.ca/comment/article/the
-political-captivity-of-the-faithful/.

p. 230 On the civil religious tradition and prophetic progressivism,
see Philip Gorski, "Reviving the Civil Religious Tradition," in

Braunstein et al., *Religion and Progressive Activism*, 271–88; idem, *American Covenant: A History of Civil Religion from the Puritans to the Present*, 2nd ed. (Princeton: Princeton University Press, 2019); idem, *American Babylon: Christianity and Democracy before and after Trump*, Routledge Focus on Religion (London: Routledge, 2020); Bruce Ellis Benson, Malinda Elizabeth Berry, and Peter Goodwin Heltzel, *Prophetic Evangelicals: Envisioning a Just and Peaceable Kingdom*, Prophetic Christianity (Grand Rapids: Eerdmans, 2012).

p. 231 Brian Daly, *The Hope of the Early Church: A Handbook of Patristic Eschatology* (Peabody, MA: Hendrickson, 2003), 217.

p. 231 On hope, see J. Christiaan Beker, *Suffering and Hope: The Biblical Vision and the Human Predicament* (Grand Rapids: Eerdmans, 1994).

Chapter 22: A Manifesto for Dissident Disciples

p. 233 Schüssler Fiorenza, *Revelation*, 139 (italics added).

p. 234 The Barmen Declaration: https://www.pcusa.org/site_media/media/uploads/oga/pdf/boc2016.pdf.

p. 235 Eberhard Busch, *Karl Barth: His Life from Letters and Autobiographical Texts* (London: SCM, 1976), 223.

p. 236 For what is found in the Barmen paragraph, see Matthew Hokenos, *Then They Came for Me: Niemöller, the Pastor Who Defied the Nazis* (New York: Basic Books, 2018), 110.

p. 243 For "Christocracy of siblings," see Busch, *The Barmen Theses Then and Now*, The 2004 Warfield Lectures (Grand Rapids: Eerdmans, 2010), 65.

p. 244 Walter Brueggemann, *Israel's Praise: Doxology against Idolatry and Ideology* (Minneapolis: Fortress, 1988), 157–160.